SPIRITUAL
ECOLOGY

This Book Belongs To
Linda Layne

In keeping with this book's message about our individual responsibility to co-exist with nature, *Spiritual Ecology* is printed on recycled paper.

Bantam Books of related interest

THE NEXT ONE HUNDRED YEARS by Jonathan Weiner

THE AGES OF GAIA by James Lovelock

OUR EARTH, OURSELVES by Ruth Caplan and the staff of the Environmental Action Foundation

DOLPHIN DREAMTIME by Jim Nollman

ECOTOPIA by Ernest Callenbach

SPIRITUAL ECOLOGY

A Guide For Reconnecting With Nature

JIM NOLLMAN

BANTAM BOOKS

NEW YORK • TORONTO • LONDON • SYDNEY • AUCKLAND

SPIRITUAL ECOLOGY

A Bantam Book / March 1990

*Bantam New Age and the accompanying figure design as well as the statement
"the search for meaning, growth and change" are trademarks of Bantam Books,
a division of Bantam Doubleday Dell Publishing Group, Inc.*

Library of Congress Cataloging-in-Publication Data

Nollman, Jim.
   Spiritual ecology : a guide for reconnecting with nature / Jim
Nollman.
     p.   cm.
  Includes bibliographical references.
         ISBN 0-553-34823-X
  1. Ecology—Philosophy.   I. Title.
QH540.5.N65 1990   89-38257
                                                CIP

Published simultaneously in the United States and Canada

---

*Bantam Books are published by Bantam Books, a division of Bantam Doubleday
Dell Publishing Group, Inc. Its trademark, consisting of the words "Bantam
Books" and the portrayal of a rooster, is Registered in U.S. Patent and Trademark
Office and in other countries. Marca Registrada. Bantam Books, 666 Fifth Avenue,
New York, New York 10103.*

PRINTED IN THE UNITED STATES OF AMERICA

OPM   0 9 8 7 6 5 4 3 2 1

To the seventh generation

Acknowledgments

First things first. Permit me to acknowledge the incredible events that continue to unfold every day in my own front yard: that mysterious domain of deer and wasps and ants and little girls growing up.

I also acknowledge the inspiration I found within the published works of all the authors I have cited. To that list, I would like to add the contributions of a few other friends. Although they are not directly quoted, each of them continues to offer a means of support to help me distinguish between what is important and what is merely clever. Among many others, I choose to single out Mickey Remann, Gigi Coyle, Linda Tellington-Jones, Richard Osborne, Wade Doak, Bill Rossiter, Jonathan Churcher, Nancy Rumbel, Alan Slifka, Kit Tremaine, Brad Stanback, Nina Utne, and Chip Porter. I also thank Joan Halifax, for first bringing the term *Spiritual Ecology* to my attention.

I would also like to thank my agent, Felicia Eth, who has done more than anyone else to instill in me a sense that I am a professional author with more writing inside of me that needs to see the light of day. And thanks to my editor, Leslie Meredith, at Bantam, for first suggesting that this book be written.

Thank you, my wife Katy, for winning me the private space needed to write this book. She accomplished that, despite the fact that I write in the same house shared by two little children and their friends running about. And I thank Claire and Sasha for running about with such exuberance.

TABLE OF CONTENTS

Prelude

Late one summer I planted three oriental poppy plants in three different locations. The first of them grew under the sparse shade of a young plum tree, in rocky soil amid close plantings of sweet William, Canterbury bells, and montbretias. It seemed fairly happy in its well-drained location through the mild winter that followed. By mid-spring, however, it appeared to shrink as its neighbors suddenly shot up to four feet tall.

The second poppy grew just fifty feet away on the other side of the flat, mossy-covered bedrock that constitutes my front yard. Here, the conditions were quite a bit different. This one spent the winter planted in a rich compost raised eight inches above the bare rock. It was my own neophyte attempt to create a perennial garden where a standing puddle of water stood each winter. Unfortunately, this master plan worked only to a point because all the plantings spent most of that mild but wet winter standing in mud puddles. Naturally, the moisture-loving irises planted all around that poppy flourished, while several other species, including scabiosas and columbines, suffered or even died. This second of the three poppies also seemed to flourish.

The third poppy was planted well out of sight of the other two—down a hill, at the edge of a fir forest, and in rusty-colored soil composed of a thousand years of partially decomposed conifer wood. To this soil I added several helpings of wood ashes and a goodly portion of peat, and then interplanted tree peonies, geums, and foxgloves around the single poppy. By the time of the first frost of late October, this poppy had easily doubled in size. But while the other two poppies continued to grow slightly throughout the entire winter, this one seemed to stop growing.

By May first, plants one and three seemed about the same size. Plant number two, growing in its composted puddle, was by now twice as big as the other two, and displayed double the number of flower buds. Then, on May 20, between ten A.M. and noon, the first papery-textured flowers on plants one and two opened as if they had chosen one another as partners in a magnificently scheduled botanical samba. They bloomed as mirror images of one another. Each flower was eight inches across!

It is the day of blooming, and I am seated halfway between these two performers, turning first left, then right to admire their debut.

Finally I rise and walk down the hill to stare soberly at the remaining member of the poppy triumvirate. It stands reaching toward the sun, a virtual triplet to the others, but at least an entire week away from joining them in the dance.

Explanations? We humans love them, build our civilizations upon them. Without them I would never be permitted to stand here in my Pacific Northwest microclimate and gaze down upon these exquisitely silken, apricot-colored imports from Asia. Each poppy has been growing in different conditions, but two are performing in unison. I feel safe in discounting the soil, the water, and the light as explanatory factors. Actually, the only unique difference that I discern between poppies one and two on the one hand and poppy three on the other, is the fact that the first two have been in *view* of one another every single day of their lives.

The poetry of this observation implants itself deeply in my consciousness, undulating gracefully within the breeze of its own plausibility until finally it blossoms forth with the stature of personal acceptance. Do plants *see* one another? Probably not, although in this case the poppies do seem to be utilizing some kind of subtle perception of *proximity* as a means to blossom in such perfect synchronism. After all, how do any of us come to dance with one another, until first we place ourselves in an appropriate position (sometimes like a flower) or state of mind (sometimes like a human being) to share all of those overwhelming sensations that spring from the wellspring of intimacy? Is that it?

Actually, I'm starting to feel as if I have already lost my way. What else to do but try to get my bearings by returning to my original seat directly between the poppies. I drop down on the moss and gaze at first one and then the other. Both are leaning into the southern sun, while slowly surging east and west in the slight breeze. The larger of the two looks like it does not want to open any more flowers for at least a few more days, while the smaller plant should be opening another flower by early tomorrow. I look back and forth from one and then over to the other. But wait; something is amiss. Now it's my turn to join the dance. I stand, take two steps backward, sit down on the rock again, and finally swing my head toward one poppy and then toward the other. I had been sitting directly in their line of sight.

I sit on the Earth, a captive audience to the dance, and sanction an entire brass band of large intellectual concepts to parade through my mind in an attempt to explain the riddle of the synchronized poppies. Yet the longer I sit, only one idea seems to make any sense to me. It speaks more to my own role as audience than to the poppies' role as synchronized dancers. It is perhaps best expressed through a quote from a long-dead Lakota Indian chief, Luther Standing Bear:

> That is why the old Indian sits upon the Earth instead of propping himself up and away from its life-giving forces. For him to sit or lie upon the ground is to be able to think more clearly and feel more keenly. . . . The old Lakota knew that man's heart away from nature becomes hard; he knew that lack of respect for growing living things soon led to lack of respect for humans too.[1]

Spiritual ecology starts from the premise that animals and plants (who knows where the line is drawn?) possess unique awareness, intuition, perception—probably love and wisdom as well. It is a view that permits poppies to dance with each other as well as with any human willing to sit on the ground long enough to learn the proper undulation. Not such a strange view if you happen to be, for instance, a Lakota chief. However, no Lakota chief was ever accused of aiding or abetting a clear-cut through a rain forest, or running an oil tanker aground in Prince William Sound. Any person who perceives nature as primarily a source of wisdom and health is not likely to lend a hand in its destruction.

For Luther Standing Bear, nature existed as the recipient of his unconditional love. Yet take care, he murmurs from the grave; each time we harm nature we cut a little piece out of our own flesh. When we drive such creatures as sea turtles, condors, and elephants to the brink of extinction, we inevitably brutalize ourselves in the process. The connections interpenetrate.

However, many of us still subscribe to the contemporary schism that discriminates between human social relations and relations to nature as the only practical way to progress in this crazy world of ours. I imagine the old chief throwing some dirt up into the air before commenting that we are only deceiving ourselves. This schizophrenic relationship with nature is a trick of perception because, in fact, it is quite impossible to live outside of nature. Furthermore, we have accomplished all of this self-deception by first voiding our relationship to nature of its unifying spiritual principle.

Luther and I both agree that there is another view of nature that defines an essentially spiritual link to the ecology of our own surroundings. It is perhaps best explained by living within nature, best understood through the myths that guide our responsibility to it. This *spiritual ecology* is an ancient path. It is very creative and communal in its perceptions, and starts from the premise that, first of all, we simply have to accept our own fundamental interconnectedness with all of nature.

Likewise, this book about spiritual ecology offers many anecdotes about learning how to connect with nature. It suggests, for example, that we start granting sea turtles due process under our laws, grant property rights to deer and ants, treat sharks and yellow jackets and yes, even oriental poppies, as cocreators and teachers.

Yet if this spiritual ecology is already starting to sound so unmistakably positive, then why is it also considered so hopelessly unattainable (or just plain naive) in terms of the current worldview that drives our own culture? How has it come to pass that we perceive spirituality and nature as mutually exclusive realms?

The word *spirit* is especially problematic. *Spirit* is like the word *whale*: so many contradictory behaviors, varied metabolic rates, modes of consciousness, so much sheer size differential tangled up in one unassuming term. Our culture has stuck a perfectly good word full of harpoons; transmuted what is rightfully a dynamic process of living into a dead or captured object. We have pushed that object to the verge of extinction, while still encountering profound wonder at the insistent way the process pushes itself up to the surface to draw mortal breath.

But *spirit* is also very different from *whale*, because, unlike those playful creatures of the ocean, it has lost its sense of humor. It has snarled itself up with too much lifeless posturing when it should be downright sensual; too much airy solemnity about infinity when it should also be down-to-earth lighthearted. Perhaps worst of all, the word insists upon chaining itself to that secular demon of our civilization, the clock. Just as we capture whales and put them on display in oceanariums, so we also capture our own spirituality and put it on display by relegating it to Sunday mornings and uncomfortable benches.

On a personal level, why do I scowl to learn that some of the politicians deciding the final destiny of this or that ecosystem actually generate far more enthusiasm insuring that schoolchildren devote precisely two minutes each morning to saying their prayers? Why does my face sag in discouragement whenever I hear that the Pope, the spiritual father of a significant proportion of the human destitute, condemns to Hell all Catholic mothers who beg for contraception just so they won't have to watch another child grow up malnourished?

What is going on here? As I write, I am receiving mail from spiritualists who purport to channel dolphins in squeaky, sixteenth century, Biblical accents. Or for that matter, why do I feel bothered to hear someone talk about *their unique* spiritual connection to last summer's backpacking adventure, or even to their pets? I glower at what I see as the misguided elitism of it all, ready to assault them with stories about my own connection to mundane yellow jackets, whooping cough germs, vultures. I fight against these feelings, wonder if it's even possible for someone so abrasive as myself to presume to write about the spiritual connection to nature.

Nevertheless, I remain quite unwilling to give up on this word *spiritual*, which may be the single most critical concept underlying the present and future well-being of our selves and our planet. I remain deeply committed to a vision of nature that, in fact, cannot be rightly explained by any other word but *spiritual*. Here is the fiber that holds all our souls together.

I am reminded of a discussion with an Australian aboriginal elder about communicating with wild bottlenose dolphins. I was describing my own fifteen years of interspecies communication research when he startled me by offering this declaration about the outer reaches of remembering: "If I watch you do it, then I'll probably start to recall the way my own ancestors did it hundreds of years ago. At that point, you can bet I'll be able to offer you some tips you never even dreamed about." He realized that the link already existed within himself.

Current trends in environmental degradation are likewise telling you and me that now is the time to regain whatever ability we once possessed to live at peace within the larger ecological community. But just to begin this task, we first have to follow the lead offered by my Australian friend, the elder. We need to remember our own forgotten perceptions about connectedness. Consider this book, *Spiritual Ecology*, to be a course and a guidebook in remembering.

The noun of this book's title, *ecology*, is also problematic. It was originally coined from Greek roots to identify one of half a hundred earth sciences. Ostensibly, this particular discipline was set up to study the connections that tie organisms and their environments together in living systems—ecosystems.

But as a science, contemporary ecology sometimes ends up sounding as much like an intellectual pun as a search after truth. Look at it this way. Just as much of biology seems bent on reducing nature into neat categories that fit into some vast indexed library of science, so ecology works to reduce *the whole into one such category*. Don't believe it.

There are only three underlying rules for anyone wishing to become an adept at spiritual ecology. The first states: In a connected world, the whole is no longer the whole when it is a part.

Nature is no longer nature when it is a category of research. There lies the impasse. Contemporary biological methodology is still essentially reductive—no matter what that enlightened ecologist down the street from you has to say about it. The discipline has simply not yet invented either a language or a methodology that explains a holistic process without, first shattering it into its component parts, and second, assigning causes and effects to each now-separated segment. But is that what nature is, causes and effects? Ever smaller parts? Actually, the human mind alone, one small part of this scientific order, is itself composed of many other attitudes beside the objective scientific one. Somehow, the science of ecology sometimes reads like a translation of a Beethoven symphony rendered into English. Suffice it to say that we live inside a symphony and treat it as a language.

As you can infer here, I remain a holdout, largely unconvinced about what most people consider to be the unquestioned efficacy of the contemporary scientific method. But I also readily admit that science is always going to exist in a state of flux. In fact, I see much evidence that biology is currently involved in a drastic overhaul of its own methodology, at least as it relates to helping the human race live within its planetary limits. But how could it be otherwise? The biologists are no different than the rest of us. Like the aboriginal elder, many of them realize just how much they have forgotten about connectedness.

However, some of the most vocal of our scientific spokespeople continue to assert that the concept of spiritual ecology sounds too much like a contradiction—an oxymoron—like building weapons for peace. They say that environmental sanity is truly about sane science and sane politics leading to a sane society. By contrast, this book about dancing with poppies, dreaming with ants, praying with sharks, ceremonializing with yelloweye rockfish, peacemaking with deer, smacks of both naiveté and pantheism. It tries to elevate ancient aboriginal relationships to nature, which, even in their own time were merely localized and primitive, back into a place of primacy. It is a digression and can never be adopted generally.

How does one answer this assessment? I prefer the Cheshire cat approach that answers charges of self-contradiction by turning them inside out. Yes, it is all true. For example, spiritual ecology recommends a mundane spirituality as opposed to the heaven-based spirituality of many established religions. The adjective *mundane* fits our meaning like a glove. Webster's dictionary defines it as "worldly, of this world, as distinguished from heavenly and spiritual; earthly." In other words, the English language, itself, conceives of a spirituality within nature as an actual contradiction in terms. Consequently, any *spiritual ecology* worth its salt reflects a veritable revolution in the way the culture perceives (in this case, through its language) this long-suppressed courtship between spirituality and nature.

Nor do I disagree that environmental sanity is about sane science and sane politics leading to a sane society. But how do we acquire this environmental sanity? I, for one, suggest that the scientists and the politicians will only discover environmental sanity through a spiritual reconnecting to nature. Go sit on the Earth. Spiritual ecology is the modus operandi for achieving environmental sanity.

Which brings us to the second of the three rules that guide spiritual ecology: No person or group is the enemy. The challenge set before us is not another competition, let alone a holy war. Rather, we are confronted by processes and systems that are dysfunctional and patently dangerous within a limited world. As social philosopher Andrew Bard Schmookler points out, the fundamental issue is less moral evil than spiritual ignorance.[2]

Which leads to the third and final rule of spiritual ecology: Human beings do not own the Earth. This timber, this property, this Earth, this life—these and all other things are not *ours*.

I agree that some of the basic tenets of spiritual ecology sound naive. On the other hand, all of us have learned to cope with dysfunctional systems making demands upon our lives in a dangerous world. It is for that reason alone that I, for example, often feel naive not to accept a marketplace mentality that drives seemingly sane scientists and sane politicians to support the virtual annihilation of dolphins from the Eastern Pacific in the pursuit of tuna-flavored cat food. Or that charges more money for recycled paper than it does for cut-down-the-forest paper. But I still boycott the tuna companies. I still use recycled paper every chance I get. And yes, spiritual ecology may seem a digression, but only in the same way that a gut reaction to uncontained progress is perceived as an unpragmatic digression.

Likewise, when critics rail that a pantheistic philosophy can never be adopted generally, I have to agree with them. But then, this writing does not strive to promote that anthropological, academic category called pantheism. Rather, pantheism, itself, seems a splendid example of the mistake in perception that so often shadows academia. There is the joke about the anthropologist visiting a certain African country to study pantheism. But he could not find even one person who called his religion "pantheism." One has to wonder what Luther Standing Bear would make of his own spiritual connection to nature being called pantheism or animism. Or regard the much more probing conclusions of anthropologist Paul Reisman:

> Our social sciences generally treat the culture and knowledge of other peoples as forms and structures necessary for human life that those people have developed and imposed upon a reality which we know—or at least our scientists know—better than they do. We can therefore study those forms in relation to "reality" and measure how well or ill they are adapted to it. In their studies of the cultures of other people, even those anthropologists who sincerely love the people they study almost never think that they are learning something about the way the world really is. Rather they conceive of themselves as finding out what other people's *conceptions* of the world are.[3]

Another long-dead Indian chief, Seattle of the Duwamish tribe, has recently emerged as one of the most profound spokesmen for these "other people" who shared a deep interconnectedness with nature. Upon the occasion of surrendering all of his tribe's ancestral lands to white settlers, he commented: "All things are connected like the blood which unites one family. Whatever befalls the Earth befalls the sons [and daughters] of the Earth.''[4]

Old Chief Seattle did not warn that people living 150 years in the future had better learn to carve demon masks and eat camass roots and dance around with feathers stuck to their behinds in order to survive. It seems a mean-spirited distraction to distort what is actually a savvy relationship to nature by judging it as some outdated "primitive" philosophy in competition with our own. As Reisman points out, wisdom is not a game of basketball with tall moderns battling short primitives. Actually, to saddle such persistent wisdom with names like pantheism and then label them a digression, seems a monumental non sequitur—like saying that perception and gut reactions can never be adopted generally. Seattle's words are timeless, which leads to another, perhaps more ominous image:

> When the last Red Man shall have perished, and the memory of my tribe shall have become a myth among the white man, these shores will swarm with the invisible dead of my tribe . . . at night when the streets of your cities and villages are silent and you think them deserted, they will throng with the returning hosts that once filled them and still love this beautiful land.[5]

Do you ever see them, these victims of an American holocaust already dead for seven generations or more? Seattle implies that they are dancing through the streets of our cities in the hope that somebody, anybody, might still be able to pick up on their ancient celebration of the interconnectedness of all life. Seattle seems to be implying that we shall start to see the ghost dancers when we practice spiritual ecology.

In turn, this book takes the point of view that Seattle probably knew what he was talking about. So spiritual ecology attempts to resurrect those timeless ideas about loving this beautiful land in the Duwamish sense of *coevolution*, and then updates them into a mindset and a mood fit for the times we live in. That's it: spiritual ecology offers nothing but an updated mode of perception. We need some new bones and rattles to help us read the very same signs that Chief Seattle saw so clearly 150 years ago. Some of his images now appear so utterly prophetic that it almost seems that he was able to tune into a network news broadcast seven generations into the future.

If he *was* able to hear today's nightly news, then there is an overabundance of signs from which he might have chosen. For example, the greenhouse effect is now upon us. And although the jury is still out on how this is going to affect us in the distant future, everyone seems to agree that profound changes are in the air. Some tell us that the temperature may rise four degrees Fahrenheit within our own lifetime. Others avoid the sober emphasis on numbers and simply say that the planet is burning itself up and we have no way to get off. Still others describe it as a natural process of balance come home to lay claim to our own abuse of the Earth. Jeremy Rifkin, for one, has predicted that sometime during the 1990s, some momentous series of natural events will carry the full impact of the greenhouse effect into the consciousness of one and all. Other doomsayers suggest that we must start preparing for the end of Western culture as we know it. Strong stuff.

What is going to happen? Actually, there are several possible outcomes. The violent storms and extended droughts we already notice may lead to mass starvation on continent-wide scales. Or perhaps that four-degree rise will melt the polar icecaps, causing the Netherlands and Manhattan to drown. Or for that matter, is the budding greenhouse effect already responsible for what some doctors are now calling an *epidemic* of skin cancer? On the political front, some governments will almost certainly lose whatever flimsy hold they have upon their citizenry, while other governments will continue to obscure the issues to the point of absurdity, postponing action because it means such an obvious restructuring of political priorities. Call it *idiocracy*. Meanwhile, some will simply close their eyes and assert that these changes are the latest in an ongoing series of divinely inspired punishments.

Although the greenhouse effect is literally visited upon us from on high, it is not as divinely high as some would have us believe. The greenhouse effect is the result of a straightforward transformation in the chemistry of the atmosphere. It was perpetrated by us, on us. If we feel a need to generalize it, then we must regard it as only one more symptom of the greater environmental tragedy being enacted during our own lifetime. We have trashed the environment, all of us, working hand in hand, day and night, for about a century now. Most unfortunately, all the signs warn that this trend is going to continue unabated into the immediate future.

Given that last dismal pronouncement, we need to start restructuring our relationship to the Earth right now—not next year. We need to attenuate the present damage, as well as to continue to live through whatever momentous changes are in store for us. These alterations in habit and perception must either start with us or the circumstances are almost certainly going to impose environmental, social, and political changes from without. Can we afford not to change? Expand your consciousness outward and try to imagine the environment that would greet your own grandchildren. And their grandchildren. And their grandchildren. Can you—can we—*afford* that?

Chapter One

🌿

How to Noster

Whenever the forum of Iroquois tribal government held a council meeting, they first spoke an acknowledgment of obligation:

> In our every deliberation we must consider the impact of our decisions on the next seven generations.[1]

Thereafter, any vote among the living council members also included an equal vote for the needs and dignity of those who would live 150 to 200 years in the future.

The Iroquois would have probably agreed with Marshall McLuhan when he wrote that the medium is the message. In this case, the generational format of their council essentially defined a long-term relationship with the land. The rights of future generations never became an *issue* of policy because it was, instead, the actual *context* of policy. Conservation became the context upon which both their government and their culture was built.

Thomas Jefferson was said to have drawn much inspiration from the structure of Iroquois democracy in the process of blueprinting our American system of government. It makes one wonder about things that might have been. For example, how would our lives be different today if Jefferson had included the rights of the seventh generation in the Bill of Rights? Potentially, we might not have had a greenhouse effect looming over our lives today.

Our present-day culture plows through the environment like one of its own giant earthmovers, ill-adapted to base environmental policy upon anything much beyond the needs of the current fiscal year. We teach our own children that their own intuitive recognition of that forgotten interconnectedness—best expressed through less logical and more emotional channels—is a naive, childish fancy; we "educate" it right out of them, and leave it to the objective methodology of science to define our relationship to the land. But this way of perceiving nature transforms the community of life into a supermarket of information, most elegantly depicted as facts and statistical models. There it resides under the supervision of those who understand the mathematical models, under the control of those who sponsor the biologists.

If the medium is indeed the message, then it seems fitting to redefine the science of ecology to mean this tongue twister: the human linguistic translation of nature's nonlinguistic, holistic processes. In other words, whereas ecology should mean that we are what we live inside of, it actually means that we are what we translate. Science translates the life-filled wholeness of nature into an objective, intellectual relationship. But poppies or sea turtles or condors don't see it like that, don't "speak" of it in such terms. Listen for a moment to the condors. They seem to be telling us that we may have hired the wrong crew for the job. Any starry-eyed study of "the all and the everything," as Gurdjieff inadvertently defined ecology, seems far better served by philosophers, shamans, and poets. These dreamers have always possessed a methodology capable of describing the whole because they do not also try to stand outside of it.

Permit me to boldly suggest that the culture's relationship to nature will improve dramatically on the day that Senate subcommittees about land use start consulting with native American shamans, poets, and deep ecologists as a matter of course. Improvement will come when we elevate our poets, musicians, shamans, and philosophers to the critical position currently occupied by our scientists and politicians: that of defining and explaining nature for the rest of us. So commences the central nagging argument of this book.

Our poets and philosophers have been trying to wrest that responsibility away from the anthropocentrists for some time now. That effort is known as the environmental movement. We have social ecology, bioregionalism, the Green party, permaculture, environmental law, soft technology, deep ecology, and—move over Beethoven—spiritual ecology.

This text owes a great debt to the trenchant philosophy of deep ecology and makes all due obeisance to the compassionate writings of Arne Naess, Bill Devall, and George Sessions.

Deep ecology is a philosophy that grants inherent rights and freedoms to all beings—especially the freedom from excessive human interference.[2] Howeve,r that adjective, *deep*, has always confused me because it tries too hard to imply a secularized version of what the deep ecologists themselves comprehend as a *spiritual* relationship to nature. Too often, the term *deep* serves as a kind of adjectival disguise, shielding the deep ecologists' blatant metaphysical intentions from something they obviously mistrust: organized religion.

The founders of the deep ecology movement seem rightly concerned that the term *spiritual* is presently being held hostage by fanatical fundamentalists of all kinds. Why would anyone want to muddy the meaning of their own heartfelt cause by saddling it with such an ambiguous word? So they chose *deep* ecology rather than *spiritual* ecology, essentially as a matter of semantics. Yet despite the masterful disguise, deep ecology still implies a basic spiritual connection to nature.

This disguise generates another result. Deep ecology is most often defined in divisive terms, intrinsically opposed to the *shallow* ecology supposedly espoused by our governments, our land managers, our environmental lobbyists, our fishermen, and all the "others." Shallow ecology places mankind first (anthropocentrism), while deep ecology places nature first (biocentrism). Deep ecologists separate themselves from shallow ecologists because they believe that all those establishment types are fated to fight the same environmental battles over and over again, although they occasionally make temporary gains. In the realm of pure content I find myself agreeing with this controversial map of the environmental subculture. Truly, there can be no great healing of the planet until the humans adopt and adapt to a biocentric standard.

Unfortunately, the *form* (as opposed to the content) of the deep ecology movement has crystallized into a self-righteous opposition to all those less-evolved, shallow beings of the planet. I, for one, cannot believe, as the deep ecologists insist I must, that the likes of the Sierra Club are actually the enemy. I walk into any redwood forest anywhere, and prefer to offer a silent, humble thank you to all the three-piece-suited lawyers who work so hard to save the trees.

In the realm of form, spiritual ecology diverges from deep ecology by adopting *connectedness* rather than divisiveness as its operating standard. It bespeaks a level of human consciousness that makes the effort first to witness and then to pattern itself after the interconnecting processes already immanent within nature. We get connected when we act connected.

And although dictionary literalism would assert that spiritual ecology is an oxymoron, I find the two terms, spiritual and ecology, to be refreshingly redundant. If the word *spiritual* is like the word *whale,* then the word *ecology* is like the word *ocean.* It is the fluid within which our spirit swims.

Because ecology purports to explain the connection between the parts and the whole of nature, it seems spiritual by default. Not never-fail-to-go-to-church-on-Sunday spiritual; not wear-an-amethyst-crystal-around-your-neck spiritual. Rather, I feel that I live in a state of perpetual mourning to learn that the last condor, named AC-9 of all things, has been taken to the San Diego Zoo, of all places. Or I learn to revere a deer by permitting one to share my garden and so find crazy ecstatic joy in her presence despite the fact that she eats up all my raspberry canes. Sublimity found in a deer, and without drugs, mind you. Or I invite a Tibetan lama to interact with wild orcas primarily because both species deserve such a metaphor. Or I fall down on my hands and knees to observe the demeanor of yellow jackets, not because I desire objective information about their behavior, but because they are my neighbors and I want to live at peace with them. Or more stridently, I send my best wishes to those activists who put their lives on the line to block the path of a bulldozer that is about to smash a logging road through the last of our first-growth timber. In fact, I send my best wishes to any and all activists who set out to improve the world of my own seventh generation.

Ours is a possessive pronoun. As Erich Fromm writes, possessiveness is a function of the love of control. The possessor misunderstands the nature of life and so ends up acting as an agent of death.[3] But the relationships inherent within spiritual ecology are not about ownership. Well then, what if I were to say that timber, property, earth, and life are *us*? No, unfortunately, that is not quite it either. *Us* is a noun and nouns are objects. The relationship I hear is, rather, dynamic and connective. It is a verb, one that expresses the *vibrant unity* that is us. Permit me some poetic license to dredge up the Latin pronoun *noster* (meaning our) and recoin it as a verb: I noster; you noster; he, she, or it nosters. But this verb is something both special and unique to the English language. As a verb it is singular and plural, past, present, and future tense all at the same time. The long-dead ghost dancers and the seventh future generation noster in the very same tense. I noster means the same thing as we noster. In effect: You are us, we are them. It may even be used as an occasional adjective, such as in *noster biology*.

Put another way, spiritual ecology does not place the human race first. It does not place the earth first. In fact, it doesn't place the seventh generation first, either. In matters pertaining to the biota, making distinctions of rank seems akin to exclusivity and selfishness. There can be no such clear-cut distinctions, no firsts, because there are no seconds, no thirds, no any other level. The categories drift together. We have found the enemy and he nosters.

Of course, there is already a name for all of this; and it is called *cosmic consciousness*. Unfortunately, at the present moment, cosmic consciousness spins through the cultural jukebox like its sibling term, *spiritual:* two old tunes in search of a contemporary beat. And while most everyone accepts this cosmic consciousness as a fundamental spiritual truth, very few of us actually have any idea what it means to live life outside its oppressively long religious shadow. I ask my daughter Claire, at four years of age, "What does God mean?" and she offers a profound answer that sums up at least part of the culture's relationship to cosmic consciousness: "It is a bad way to say gosh." In such a spirit, this writer admits to an inimitable wariness of both the trappings and the traps of highfalutin religiosity.

But of course the creed of spiritual ecology borrows much from establishment religion. One might even describe its central premise as asking that we start to love nature as Catholics love Jesus, as Protestants love Heaven, as Muslims love Allah, as Jews love their Law, as Buddhists love Enlightenment. The difference is, of course, that spiritual ecology is not a religion. However, realize that at least some branch of every organized religion already embraces its basic tenets.

For our purposes here, we might simplify the issue of established religion and consider that there are really no more than two basic categories: first, the inclusive, internalized, and implicit; second, the exclusive, externalized, and explicit. The *inclusives* teach that we read the sacraments and ethics as implicit signs along the path of personal and social revelation. The *inclusives* both borrow and respect the ideas about divinity from all the other spiritual pathways. Spiritual truth is both universal and immanent, no matter which name it chooses to register under. Every religion offers sects and individuals who follow this path.

Likewise, just about every established religion also possesses an exclusivist orthodoxy as well. The *exclusives* equate spirituality with all things outside our world. Consequently, our poor souls were never meant to nourish and be nourished by this green Earth. When we extol a grand external salvation awarded on the merits of our ability to rise above nature, we often avoid a responsibility to life on Earth. It means, for example, that the exclusives do not invoke a connectedness to the environment as a valid path leading toward the light of their own personal salvation. Because the seventh generation is nowhere to be seen, some sad part of my own being has come to equate the exclusives with the extinction of species and the destruction of eco-systems. In effect, something both compassionate and humbling seems sliced right out of the heart of spirituality.

As the Dominican priest Mathew Fox has written in the provocatively titled "My Final Statement Before Being Silenced by the Vatican":

> Mother Earth is in jeopardy, caused by the anthropocentrism of religion, education, and science during the past three centuries. A new beginning is required, centered on the *sacredness of the planet* . . . [but] worship that bores people is a sin. Worship is meant to *awaken*, to challenge, to delight and to empower. We believe all adults can touch the divine child that exists within us.[4]

In other words, while desiring to discount the religiosity (meaning religion as affectation) of any specific religion because it proves to be so dreadfully mutable and exclusive, we also start to perceive the *eternal spirituality* of religion. In the history of civilization, a life in Spirit has always offered one very practical method for hearing the whispers of the seventh generation. Again, listen to Mathew Fox's "Final Statement":

> The survival of the Earth depends upon "reinventing our species" (Thomas Berry) so that we live more harmoni-ously with Nature. The new cosmology that science, art, and mysticism unite to teach is the ancient spiritual and ecological lesson: all things are connected.

Ultimately, this spiritual ecology exists as an heir to religious longevity, and provides the only relationship to nature that also exists in the same time scale as nature herself. For example, listen to the words of ecologist Joanna Macy as she describes an unorthodox program to deal with the obscenity of nuclear waste:

> . . . it would require a community empowered with such dedication to guard the centers of radioactivity we be-queath to future generations for thousands of years. In my

mind's eye I could see surveillance committees forming at today's nuclear facilities. These Guardian Sites are centers of reflection and pilgrimage, where the waste containers are *religiously*[5] monitored and repaired, and where the wisdom traditions of our planet are the source for contexts of meaning and disciplines of vigilance.[6]

Actually, I can imagine that this program could someday lead to the previously hypothesized congressional hearing in which shamans, poets, and artists are seen sitting on both sides of the bench, consulting with each other about the responsibilities inherent within this concept of a nuclear priesthood. As it stands, this proposal automatically invokes the participation of the seventh generation.

Spiritual Ecology aspires to demonstrate how we might perceive across generations, both forward and backward. It asks us to support the ghost dancers as well as the nuclear priesthood. It invites us to venture out into nature and attune ourselves with the migrating songbirds, who provide some of the loveliest accompaniment to the generational dance. Listen! Their songs carry a message from the wounded rain forest where the birds make their winter home. How has that message changed since the glory days of Chief Seattle? For that matter, how has it changed over the past year or two?

In that light, consider this book about *Spiritual* Ecology to be a "how-to" manual about remembering how to connect with nature. I have written a book that shares with you my own misguided assumptions, as well as my own exciting revelations as I relate to nature. That also means that I care not to attain the status of new environmental expert on the block. I am not a missionary promoting some New Age environmental priesthood. In fact, I confess right here at the start that I can pollute and degrade with the best of them. Actually, I am not unlike you—one person, one tiny part of an enormous problem, who is determined to take dead aim at the solution. On that authority alone, I offer these anecdotes and metaphors as simple images pointing toward a new potential. I offer them in all due humility, hoping that some of the examples herein may serve a few others as they serve me.

By inference, this book also attempts to provide cryptic instructions about how to hear the very faint melodies of songs sung by the seventh future generation down the line: the progeny of sea turtles, deer, songbirds, Douglas fir forests, orcas, and human children. If Chief Seattle could so clearly hear the songs of his own seventh generation, might we not do the same? The metaphor of music making is especially potent because, of all our own human creations, it is perhaps music that inspires us best to feel the beat of our own heart. This book endeavors to offer a kind of environmental aerobics, a song and a dance that we ourselves join, accompanied by the chorale of our own past and future ancestors playing on their own bones and rattles. Strong preventive medicine. Good dancing.

This means that *Spiritual Ecology* offers an attunement rather than a linear discourse. It does not purport to offer competition to the hundreds of pessimistic books grappling with environmental strategies that lead to hard choices. What I here place before you tries to keep it simple, asking that you grapple with only one important choice—embrace the seventh generation or do not embrace the seventh generation. I attempt to flesh out that choice with anecdote and imagery, reflection and paradox. But do not sit around and ponder any single message too long and too hard. Attune as you would to a symphony, as you would to the songbirds at dusk, as you would to whales singing their melancholy songs in frequencies beyond the range of the human ear. Learn to attune as if by osmosis.

And bear with me. I am well aware that this writing may sometimes lead you down a mirror image of that same path traveled by experts who translate symphonies into objects. In other words, it is just as much of an illusion to translate objects into symphonies as vice versa. Likewise, I apologize right here at the start for offering absolutely no assurance that this book is actually going to teach you how to hear the whispery tunes sung by the seventh generation. I readily admit that, on a certain level, these are conjecturalized songs sung by unborn people and heard through a made-up, inscrutable process called *tuning os-mosis*. Nonetheless, the seventh generation is undeniably out there. Take a deep breath. Use your imagination. Dream them up for yourself.

Chapter Two

The Mirage of Nature

Six of us are camped where the MacKenzie River meets the ice pack of the Arctic Ocean; where the shallow delta (100-mile wide), heats the flowing water to a very unpolar 70 degrees. A flat, verdant oasis of estuarine warmth set down in the heart of the arctic tundra, this magnificent delta country is framed on the west by the very substantial northern terminus of the Rocky Mountains. To the west, the south, and especially along the convoluted lips of the northern ocean, the vistas seem endless, providing no sense of distance whatsoever. Only a fool dares to wager just how far away those shape-shifting dots and spires popping up along the far edge of the sea might be, not to mention *what* they might be.

Actually, the tallest landmarks in sight stand about a mile to the southeast: Very substantial two-legged beings, sandhill cranes squawking and gliding about the horizon in courting pairs. Up and down they bounce, touching wingtips, bobbing necks, squawking at the top of their lungs like some hard rock crooner; courting each other across an interminable meadow of fluffy cottongrass that makes them look, through binoculars, like long-necked dinosaurs slow-dancing through dry-ice "smoke" of American Bandstand.

The continual squawking of the cranes makes the six of us feel that our perceptions of the environment have started to travel back in time. We squint and furrow our brows; gaze upon a more distant flock of cranes as they glide to land upon a tree stump. The shimmering forms along the horizon first coalesce into a modern nuclear submarine. Time passes. A few days later someone calls them a Victorian flotilla. Finally, a week or two later we all agree that they look exactly like a herd of woolly mammoths marching across the tundra. And by that time we are starting to feel stranded, regressed in a community of six rumpled cavemen utterly dazzled by the hocus-pocus of our own baffled sensibilities.

We are a group composed of 3 musicians, a sound recordist, a photographer, and a boat skipper venturing to the shores of the Arctic Ocean to spend two intense weeks studying and documenting the possibility of interspecies communication between human musicians and beluga whales. Six seekers negotiating a fragile truce between our own late-twentieth-century professional self-images on the one hand, and the childlike reality of relating to whales from the platform of this arctic beachfront paradise. Six adults, each blessed with a midnight sun halo of mosquitoes that keeps us looking more beatific than a Renaissance Madonna, more veiled than an Arabic wife, and more aware of our extremities than any mere yogi. The otherwise simple act of walking from one's tent to the campfire takes on the dress-up significance of a high school girl getting ready for her first prom. Or this simple reminder: "Don't forget to wear two pairs of socks, the first one tucked under, the second one tucked over your elastic-bottom pants." Some insist that the cold weather protects this land from human encroachment. That's not true. The mosquitoes do it.

Actually, it is only the female of the species that seeks the red blood of vertebrates, a fluid as essential to the reproduction process as any that the male mosquito is able to conjure. The sly and artful dance that commences when the human partner flails his arms about his head, and which finally concludes when a victorious female partner zips off to some local sinkhole to lay her hemoglobin-enriched eggs, is nothing less than a magnificent example of interspecies sex. Meanwhile, the male mosquito is vegetarian.

This is the sexual act at its most excruciating. And the first day in camp was our worst. Actually, it was so bad that I, as project leader, started to wonder what I was going to do if one of our party cracked under the strain of living with two or three hundred mosquitoes constantly buzzing within inches of his face, wrists, and ankles. But things progress, and by the third day each of us was starting to feel like the world's greatest authority on mosquito protection. For one thing, we had discovered the proper fitting of the mosquito-proof face net. These headcoverings worked fine, except for the matter of breathing comfortably. By the third day we also realized that a fifteen-knot wind worked best because it kept the mosquitoes at ground level. In time, we learned to dress and breathe according to the fashion dictates of the offshore breeze.

By then, we had cast aside our ineffectual herbal lotions in favor of a "miracle" repellent called DEET. But this reputed miracle demanded its due. One of our members drew a heavy silence by asking if our growing hallucinations might be caused by the powerful pesticides contained within the repellent. After all, the liquid feels just like applying polyurethane to the temple of one's body. (I later learned that DEET is absorbed right through the skin, into the bloodstream. The British journal *Lancet* lists slurred speech, staggering gait, agitation, tremors, convulsions, and even death, as documented consequences of heavy DEET use.[1]) We sought to control the discomfort of mosquitoes; but in a world determined by connectedness, there is no such thing as controlling nature. At best we tip the balance toward or away from a healthy world. In this case, to poison mosquitoes quickly is a way to poison ourselves slowly.

Here along the lip of the Arctic Ocean not a condom, not a piece of foam, not a soft drink bottle, not a beer-can holder is anywhere to be seen. Each day I explore further down the beach, eyes fixed on the ground, diligently searching for even a trace of litter as if it were the arctic researcher's equivalent of the Holy Grail. What am I doing? Have I flown into one of the last vestiges of true wilderness left on Earth just to spend an hour each day searching for telltale signs of civilization? The beach is always clean— immaculately clean. I worry that the fate of my already tenuous hold on the late twentieth century will be determined by the number of gum wrappers I can turn up. But there's not one in sight.

We six have mounted a field project to interact with the beings of this wild land, but we cannot escape interacting with the illusions about this land as they exist in the minds of human beings. Some part of my brain seems to question whether any place without litter can actually be considered a part of contemporary planet Earth. Instead, this place seems like a vast museum diorama depicting North America in the year 20,000 B.C. If so, then what am I, the museum goer or the exhibit? The answer to that question varies from day to day, entirely dependent on how well I am able to connect.

On the fifth day of our two-week-long adventure, three of us motor our inflatable boat along the coast to the half-mile-wide west channel. There, like Robinson Crusoe celebrating Friday's footprint, we find our first sign of Man. In this case it is an abandoned Inuvialuit beluga hunting camp. How bizarre to find some solace in ancient sardine tins, scattered shotgun shells, a ratty nest of nylon rope, and a huge cooking pot used, no doubt, to render beluga blubber to oil. But the treasure of this camp is a twenty-foot-high lookout tower constructed almost entirely of huge driftwood logs. On this treeless plain, such logs must have floated all the way from the edge of the boreal forest a thousand miles upriver.

I take my turn climbing the ladder to the top of the tower. The almanac has told me that the MacKenzie River is the single longest river on the North American continent; not quite as long as the combined Mississippi-Missouri, but longer than either one alone.[2] Still, I am unprepared for the vista that unfolds before me. There is no "other side" to this delta, only channels the size of most large rivers, drifting off into still more channels. I peer across the west channel with the eyes of a Verrazano surveying a virgin Hudson River back in the sixteenth century. Why stop there? The recurring sense of time flowing backward has clouded my mind again. It is as if I remember the Rhine, the Danube, the Tigris, the Nile, the Indus—any and every large river before which human tribes ever squatted on their haunches, pointed their sticks at the wet earth, nodded their heads in accord, and decided, yes, here is where we shall build our civilization.

The MacKenzie River in July is like a prehistoric version of any of those other rivers. Green with wildflowers and scrub willow blooming to profusion in the overly rich bottomland, it also seems the polar opposite of any of those other modern rivers. I reach this conclusion because the west channel is still wild, offering several species of large mammal, none of which strides upon two legs. Mostly, it offers no other sounds than the pleasing gurgle of water, the constant drone of mosquitoes.

There is, of course, a sound reason for all of this tranquillity. Within five weeks, by late August, the brown husks of cotton grass, woolly lousewort, and buttercups strewn across the flat prairie of the delta will be quite frozen under a heavy morning frost. Within a few more weeks, the peaty topsoil will have frozen all the way down to the underlying permafrost. The sandhill cranes, snow geese, and whistling swans will have concluded their annual task of bringing forth another generation. One brisk morning, they will have caught a promising updraft toward that eternal source of diminishing warmth and headed 3,000 miles south to Wyoming, Nebraska, and Texas. By the time the birds arrive there, in early October, the air temperature along the west channel will be below zero degrees Fahrenheit; the river will be solid ice. Likewise, the fifty-mile apron of shallow, muddy liquid we have deluded ourselves into calling the Arctic Ocean will be frozen all the way out to the permanent ice pack. This warm, arctic Riviera of early July will have become a solid white terrain without seams.

The belugas will also have left the area long ago, gone west and then south to the relatively ice-free waters of the Bering Sea. Near there, during the cold December of 1985, more than a thousand of the white whales found themselves trapped in the ice at one of the fjords along the coast of Siberia. Local fur trappers ventured out on the ice to provide food for the stuck belugas, but within a week, forty of the whales had died, suffocated when their breathing holes iced over. The Soviet navy responded to their plight by sending an icebreaker to crack a sea lane through the strait. This was soon accomplished, but for reasons of their own the whales refused to swim to safety. Inevitably, the ice started to close in again. "Then," as one of the icebreaker's crew later related it, "someone recalled that their kin, the dolphins, react very well to music. Several melodies were tried out, and it turned out that classical music was to the taste of these arctic belugas."[3] Evidently, the music of Beethoven blared out from the ship's loudspeakers. This time, several hundred belugas followed the icebreaker for twelve miles through the fjord and into the Bering Sea—freed by the melodic appeal of Beethoven, only to return next spring to the MacKenzie delta.

By April each year the belugas start to push their way north through the ice-free leads of the Bering Strait, then east across the Chukchi and Beaufort seas—10,000 whales set on a crash course toward the warm oasis of this, their freshwater nursery. The newborns get to spend a secure month lolling about in a 5,000-square-mile lukewarm bathtub where the depths rarely go deeper than six feet, and where the entire sea bottom is composed of nothing but soothing mud.

Most auspiciously, this year the beluga whales showed up just hours after our arrival. Two of them had sailed past our makeshift town like aquatic pied pipers to blow a welcoming tune on their instruments. You could hear them from a quarter-mile off, bugling and snorting—three-foot wide, gray-white oblongs chugging through the shallow muddy ocean, looking like hippos wallowing in some African waterhole. They pushed themselves up from the mud, gave a toot, slid back down without a splash, sped off just under the surface, and then repeated the same rumba step all over again until . . . gone! Unfortunately, we were not yet ready to greet them halfway, still struggling as we were with the burden of unassembled equipment and unrelenting mosquitoes.

We were still assembling gear and fearing insects when the whales returned the next day. I lay in my tent quite mesmerized by the pitter-patter drizzle of flying mosquito bodies as they bumped up against the outside fabric. I heard the brassy bleat, once, then a second time. I pulled on my mosquito net, unzipped the interminable layers of tent zippers, stepped outside, rezipped everything, stood up to gaze offshore, and nodded to the rest of the group. The six of us watched the six of them, a family of white-on-white whales straining their pliable necks above the surface to scan the shoreline. This time they appeared like a band of nude, Rubenesque mermaids at the bath. There was even a baby among them. Was it the large male who let out a long sliding wail that sounded like a trombone blowing dixieland on a hot summer afternoon?

Except this sighting did not occur in the afternoon. It was after eleven at night, but still bright enough to wear sunglasses without drawing a comment. Last summer, while scouting beluga whales near Nome, Alaska, I noticed many of the local folk were out in the yard barbecuing dinner at midnight. Actually, the two photographers in our party stated a preference for the reddish glow that emerges during the wee hours. Imagine how such a three-month hiatus from night would affect the culture of any large American city. It would almost certainly signal an end to unemployment—until, of course, the three-month-long continuous darkness set in during the opposite half of the year. Here in the north, in an environment filled with grizzly bears, wolves, and moose, the summer sun also offers no small measure of security. There is no night for anything to go bump in.

A whale appeared briefly the next morning as well. It tooted a few times and then vanished. I lay in my tent half asleep, yet felt buoyed by their presence. I made a mental note about the male's distinctive air vocalization. It was easy to speculate about the various answering sounds an interspecies communicator might make to entice the belugas closer to camp. That melody sung by a bevy of overweight mermaids had lulled me into a complacency distinguished by one more arctic illusion. I named this one, *wellbeing*. You see, like any veteran pied piper, the belugas chose to disappear.

And we never saw them again.

The reason for their disappearance was later explained to me as stemming from the same greenhouse effect that had barbecued the Great Plains all that summer. Supposedly, this also sent flash floods to the MacKenzie Basin. The inordinate amount of mud spewed into the delta kept the beluga whales twenty or more miles offshore for the rest of the brief summer, well away from our magazine-writing, sound-recording, still-photographing aspirations. It was a reminder that we cannot leave the twentieth century behind—not the gear, not the attitudes, not the effects. Though we fly 400 miles above the Arctic Circle and finally drop down into a land without human footprints, we cannot escape the excesses of the human experience. Wilderness, itself, has turned into a contradiction in terms. It may not exist anywhere on Earth outside the human dream for simpler times.

With little promise of belugas in the offing, three of our party decided to escape back to their usual lives after one week on location. They left one bright morning, climbing into the belly of a float plane, carried up until the roar of the single engine turned into a buzz, then a hum, and finally was gone. As a legacy, they left the quieter three of the group, quieter still during another week spent around the clay firepit, dubbed the Beluga Cafe. Now, even the most mundane of our activities seemed uprooted from normal reality, as if we had transformed ourselves into characters on a poster for a grade B adventure film. But by now this landscape no longer seemed as alien as Mars. No, the environment was definitely of this Earth, if not also of our minds. We were the extraterrestrials set squarely inside our own conceived actions, otherworldly homesteaders squatting upon an Earth constructed from images pulled from the most perplexing dreams of our childhood.

Four more days pass. I sit at the campfire all alone this afternoon, watching an expanse of cirrus clouds slide across the sky on its way to a meeting with the sea ice that lies over this horizon *here* if not over that horizon just beyond it. Does that make any sense? It does to me, for it serves my own sense of accuracy to hedge in describing anything pertaining to distance, time, or perspective. Yesterday, for example, I spent three long hours motoring the inflatable black-rubber boat over the bumpy, windy ocean. Every distant white cap looked just like a beluga whale surfacing for air. In fact, not one of those distant puffs was what my eyes had hoped them to be. After about an hour of chasing after nonexistent cetaceans, I turned off the motor and lay down flat in the boat just to give my eye-brain coordination a well-earned rest. Suddenly, as if congealing right out of the rubber of the boat, a hundred or more mosquitoes flew in for the attack. In some bizarre travesty of reconciliation, I found myself relishing the presence of this uninvited company. Any company.

The presumed authorities on the subject of beluga populations must suffer from the same malady of mirage-making as myself. The guidebooks seem to relate fairy tales, emphatically assuring me that at least 10,000 beluga whales migrate into this shallow delta each July to nurture their newborn in the tepid, gentle waters. Yet not one whale is anywhere to be seen in this other habitat we call the real world. But wait, what is that dot undulating and writhing along the borderline of the ocean? A single tree magnified by the kinetic lens of contrasting air densities? Another sandhill crane couple bobbing up and down on some tidal islet? Perhaps a second horizon, the reflection off the pack ice that looms fifty miles farther offshore. Or, maybe it's the ghost of adventurer John Franklin,[4] setting a course along that historical mirage forever known as the Northwest Passage. How will the greenhouse conditions affect that icy passage?

Now I sit at the Beluga Cafe, nearly two weeks after our arrival, not yet privy to information linking excessive mud to the disappearance of the whales, and wonder if the members of that pod that last showed themselves ten days ago were actually straining their necks to locate those places where humans might dwell. After all, this MacKenzie delta is the theatre where a 10,000-year-old human-beluga blood drama is enacted annually. Our own small band of musicians and writers may be the first group of humans to arrive on this part of the delta whose primary tools for relationship are neither harpoons nor rifles. Later after our trip, I shall learn that the whale hunters camped twenty miles west of us were having no better luck locating their quarry than we were in locating ours.

Under certain conditions, the aboriginal hunting of game species should probably be permitted. However, let me add a few caveats. The hunters must depend upon that animal and that hunt for cultural as well as physical sustenance. In other words, the relationship between human predator and his prey has to provide a reaffirmation of both the aboriginal identity and the emotional qualities that define an individual within that tribe— and as distinct from the homogeneity of world culture. It must define a closed circle.

As Barry Lopez has noted:

> The mind we know in dreaming, a nonrational, nonlinear comprehension of events in which slips in time and space are normal, is, I believe, the conscious working mind of an aboriginal hunter. It is a frame of mind that redefines patience, endurance, and expectation.[5]

By contrast, most of the Inuvialuit beluga hunters live out a large percentage of their year in the thoroughly modern towns of Inuvik or Aklavik. Those among them who live off the land do so as trappers. They utilize the notorious and horrific leg-hold trap to provide furs to the world's fashion brokers. Yet despite much bellowing among the trappers that none of their various catches are endangered species, and that the trappers themselves are the best environmentalists because they stand to lose the most if any fur species go into decline, they seem unable to grasp the essential fact that the issue here is not one of conservation, but of animal rights.

Nor can the worldwide protest against trapping be rightly construed as one more glaring example of the white man depriving the Indian of his traditional rights. This is, instead, an ideological battle that is being waged between two grass-roots factions, one economic, the other moralistic, both of whom employ the paper weapons of public opinion campaigns and legal minutiae to persuade men and women to wear (or not to wear) the furs of northern mammals upon their fashionable backsides. This is not to imply that the very poor trappers of Arctic Canada, most of whom also happen to be Indians, do not suffer the consequences of their jobs being shut down. But these jobs are always going to remain vulnerable to the uncertain tides that define a world economy.

The question of the beluga hunt goes much deeper. For hundreds of years, the Inuvialuit relationship to their own sustenance was essentially a spiritual matter. The humans only killed the animals in order to survive, and never killed more than they required. Food was a sacrifice and a gift, a bequest from the spirit of the slain. This prompted the formalization of a ceremony of attunement between the human predator and his prey. Hence, the ancient Eskimo who killed a beluga whale had to refrain from doing any work or having any sex for the following four days because that was the precise amount of time the animal's ghost lingered near the carcass. Likewise, no one in the village could use a sharp object for fear of wounding the ghost, or make a loud noise for fear of frightening it.[6] If by accident the ghost *was* offended, then bad luck or even death might rain down upon the village. This resulted in still more ritualized injunctions.

Some choose to call this superstition, and so find easy grounds to dismiss it. But whatever we call it, we need to recognize that these beliefs of an interconnection between man and whale created a sense of responsibility in the villagers. Whales were not killed indiscriminately, which insured the preservation of the species. The preservation of the whale insured the preservation of the people. I choose to call this mode of relationship *spiritual ecology*, because it describes humans and animals existing as interdependent and coevolutionary members of the larger ecological community.

The Inuvialuit creed shared more with the traditional relationship between the buffalo and the Sioux than it did with the relationship between a modern hunter and his whale. Unfortunately, the modern Inuvialuit beluga hunt, this noble and sometimes desperate attempt at retaining cultural tradition, suffers on several fronts. First, the critical need to hunt the beluga to feed the aboriginal village has essentially vanished, replaced by the generic village supermarket selling Mexican tomatoes and Iowa pork chops as it does everywhere else in North America. Significantly, some of the locals point to the faceless modernity of the market to argue that the beluga hunt serves to reinstate traditions otherwise in decline. No one argues against this cultural hunger.

Second, all of the hunters rely entirely upon the modern rifle, and only utilize the traditional harpoon at the very last to secure a severely wounded animal to the boat. And they all use motor-boats, which permit a hunting party to zoom right up on a pod and start shooting. For those critics who find dubious traditional merit in the current reliance upon high-powered guns shot from the platforms of high-powered boats, the hunters retort that they, themselves, are not interested in becoming museum relics. Instead, they are a modern-day people striving to define an identity that melds the best of two worlds. When I met these hunters in person and listened to their good-hearted yet very passionate descriptions of an experience that obviously means very much to them, I heard them say that the beluga hunt exists today as a vital bridge across the chasm of a century of disruption brought upon their aboriginal birthright.

Except that it is not. In fact it is a brutal, bumbled massacre. The most telling point about the experience is that the hunters may actually lose a greater percentage of wounded animals *today* than they did before the advent of firearms. This occurs mostly because the traditional harpoon always tethered an animal to the boat. Unless the line broke, the animal was secured no matter what else happened. Guns, on the other hand, offer more power, but no such security. Based on statistics gathered between 1972 and 1975, one scientific observer, W. J. Hunt, estimated that the modern killed-to-lost ratio was about 40 percent.[7] This translates as four whales lost for every ten killed. Most significantly, it does not take into account the many whales that were wounded and yet somehow escaped.

Confusing the issue, some apologists declare that the bullet of choice is hard pointed, implying that the hunters seek a *humane* kill by penetrating deeply into the vital areas through five to eight inches of blubber. But this explanation makes no sense. If the animal is killed outright, then the body immediately sinks out of sight in the muddy, coursing waters. Unless a harpoon has also been stuck at some early point in the proceedings, the body will not be tethered to the boat and it will never be recovered. In fact, the modern beluga hunter relies upon a soft-pointed bullet because he shoots, not to kill but rather to wound—to impair the animal enough to get within harpoon striking distance. These bullets expand on impact to rip a huge bloody crater in the animal. As one observer has described it:

> In one case 40 rounds were fired at a large male before it was killed. I could clearly discern 27 wounds within about 30 cm. of the eye. . . . In another case, a hunter expended 60 rounds at a whale that he was ultimately unable to secure because he had used up all his ammunition.[8]

Now I sit alone at the campfire called the Beluga Cafe and contemplate the pain of whales as meted out by the pain of native hunters who employ a modernized version of an ancient hunt in a desperate measure to retain a last, final vestige of their cultural manhood. Yet I do not mean to gloss over the fact that the meat has always been the prize—whether the meat of seven generations ago or the meat of next week. To quote one famous description of northern attitudes: "I have one thing to say about this land. The only thing I like to eat is meat."[9] But meat or no meat, I cannot escape the conclusion that this contemporary hunt serves as a valve through which the locals vent their frustrated anger at a world gone awry, a world where formerly crucial ceremonial events like beluga hunts have lost their primacy. It is a world closer in spirit to the massacring of the buffalo by sportsmen shooting automatic rifles from trains, only to leave the carcasses to rot, than to the Sioux shooting those same buffalo from horseback, and then utilizing all the varied body parts as essential elements in their own survival.

If it were otherwise, why would the actual killing of these gentle and vulnerable creatures seem, somehow, more important than the capture of the carcass? If it were otherwise, why would they not use the harpoon at the start, as in the old days before rifles, instead of mutilating the cherubic naked white bodies beyond recognition with forty or more rounds of ammunition? In truth, these beluga hunters suffer from the same crisis of perception as any other modern people. They are operating within a system that has been rendered dysfunctional. And they are trying to cope as best they know how.

These local humans seek to retain an important remnant of a holy culture through the profaned medium of a ceremony out of context with their own postindustrial lifestyle, and so find nothing but one more mirage bobbing along the Arctic horizon. I fantasize a group of Inuvialuit hunters sitting around their own version of the Beluga Cafe. One of their party suggests that, this year, they put aside their soft bullets and their fast motorboats and, instead, seek out a single beluga whale, to be harpooned from the platform of a skin boat, and delivered to them through the adrenaline rush of a Nantucket sleighride, which is how whalers described the whale's pulling their longboats. But why stop there? What if these hunters, many of whom are also musicians, were given the opportunity to play music with the belugas every summer? Maybe that is why I, interspecies musician that I am, came here in the first place.

I sit alone this afternoon because one of our trio, Mickey, complained of cramps all morning and so decided to amble miles up the beach in an attempt to exorcise his muscular demon. I can see him down the beach, a good two miles away, reduced to nothing more than an exclamation point moving from left to right. He tramps along the peaty shore clad in an orange-scarlet suit turned monochrome by a trick of haze and distance. Suddenly, I am disoriented by the ghost of someone very close by who is whistling "We Are Marching to Pretoria." When Mickey returns to camp I will learn that, Yes, he had been whistling all the while—whistling "Waltzing Matilda."

Last night, the three of us had taken the inflatable boat a half-mile up-channel, where we spied large hoofprints impressed in the beach mud. The improbable distance between front and back prints led us to believe that they belonged to a moose. One of us mentioned that a bull moose might stand nine feet at the antlers. The thought of such proportions sobered us to pensiveness; we were suddenly diminished to the size of a primordial rat out to steal eggs from the local dinosaurs. So, four hours ago, my second companion, Jonathan, set off into the bush in the hope of spying a moose before the moose spied him. In this case his prize is not to be eggs, but rather some wildlife photograph filled to the brim with misty light and mammalian fortitude.

Given the dead flatness of this terrain, doesn't it make sense that any moose would be easily spotted from a great distance? Of course the reverse also holds true: a moose can see a human being from a mile or more. Not to mention smell, hear, taste—an entire shopping list of perceptual faculties developed to perfection by any large mammal capable of surviving in this land where 95 percent of the human beings carry rifles. That is the very reason Jonathan feels it essential to lug a fifteen-pound shotgun around with him all day long. The magic words are: *Just in case.* Just in case the reverse occurs and the moose beholds him first, and from a short distance as well. Then what? A snort and a charge from the nine-foot creature, to be quickly followed by a profound, life-altering explosion. Dropped on the spot. Knowing my gentle companion as I do, I have to believe that he would be scarred for life if he were forced to kill a moose, especially if it turned out to be a cow protecting its calf.

In his spiritual history of the conquest of North America, *Beyond Geography*, Frederick Turner depicts the destruction of aboriginal Indian culture by Europeans as a holy war. Ultimately, the conquerers never found satisfaction in these wild and verdant shores because the European tradition from which they sprang was founded upon a concept of the Earth as devil. Their culture had long been spiritually bankrupt. Based upon the medieval terror, of Crusade, and the Renaissance intolerance, of Inquisition, now translated into a holocaust for a new continent. This holocaust started at the beginning of the conquest, as attested by the very first log entry Columbus made upon meeting the Arawaks, on October 12, 1492:

> They should be good servants and very intelligent, for I have observed that they soon repeat anything that is said to them, and I believe that they would easily be made Christians, for they appeared to me to have no religion.[10]

By comparison, the spirituality of the native cultures—the *disguised* no-religion of the long-extinct Arawaks included—was essentially based upon a deep respect for the land, for community, and for a sense of place.

Turner's essay reaches a sobering if not monumental conclusion: the merging of European intellectual prowess with native American spiritual ecology was and is the single greatest lost opportunity in the history of the world. As it is, the legacy of the conquest provides us with little beside speculation about what might have been.

I mention all of this because, now, I sit supremely alone in this heady wilderness environment for the first time in ten days. What else to do but rhapsodize a cloud of mystical grief over what I construe to be another grand lost utopian opportunity every bit as monumental as Turner's own. What tragedy do we passively accept; that the Peaceable Kingdom of Edward Hicks' painterly imagination exists nowhere on Earth except as the universal leitmotiv of the literature of our children? More to the point, how has it come to pass that the weapon is the most common instrument employed by human beings to relate to the other wild beings of this planet? As we Europeans annulled the spiritual contribution of the Indians, so we also annulled the spiritual contribution of the animals.

For example, the grizzly bears in this region are routinely shot on sight. Thus, over any meaningful period of time the bears who ventured closest to human beings, for whatever reason, were the ones who were shot first. That is, those bears exhibiting any measure of curiosity or outgoing behavior were the first to be done in. Likewise, only the stealthiest and most fearful of the species survived. If there had ever been even a few token "ambassador" grizzly bears who sought out human contact as dolphins still do today, then no one will ever know about them unless they read between the lines of the local mythology. Actually, the continuous killing of bears by humans in this area goes all the way back to the Paleolithic period. And although the ancient Inuvialuit concocted elaborate ceremonies to apologize to the spirit of any bear about to be slain as food, the essential relationship remained based upon killing. So the bears became what we made of them: they coevolved into creatures both fearful and stealthy. We live with this legacy today.

Given the basic adversarial context of this relationship with nature, Jesus seems a shrewd environmentalist when he explains that the meek shall inherit the Earth. In other words, the pejorative image we impose upon nature in order to justify control also provides the underpinnings of our spiritual undoing. Can anyone doubt that our physical undoing lags far behind?

Or to interject a note of optimism, how differently humanity might relate to the natural world if each individual life, whether human, animal, or plant, were primarily perceived as a *harmonic* component of the whole. Even the traditional hunt for food could take on the attributes of a ceremony of attunement. For example, the northern Athapaskan people had a concept called Hunting with Dreams:

> They camped at the place he dreamed about and one of his sons killed the fat moose he was told of in his dreams. His son came back from the hunt and they went out to get the moose. The other family went with them then. . . . The son asked his father, "Aba [father], how did you come to dream that I would get that fat moose? You dreamed right."[11]

To practice this hunting with dreams turns the idea about higher animals and lower animals right on its head. The wild creatures are now perceived as our mentors because they live so much closer to the natural harmony. Furthermore, this ceremony of attunement offers yet another example of how to noster, because it connects across time as well as across species. It is a hunt mounted in the spirit of preservation, and thus offers an attunement to the seventh generation as well. We permit those future generations to do something more constructive than simply hang their heads to mourn the eventual passing of the large mammals from the MacKenzie delta. Could some new outburst of human spirituality transform our senses to attune better to the vibratory field of nature? Is that what spiritual ecology means?

As I put on another pot of water to brew the third cup of hot chocolate in three hours, my mind goes deeper and deeper into the perambulations of this grand speculative opportunity. Suddenly, and seemingly without reason, I stand up and turn around to gaze across this prairie that goes on forever behind our beachfront camp. There stands monochrome Mickey in his mosquito suit, a good two miles down the coast, still whistling and moving away from camp. Forty-five degrees to the south my eyes alight on the usual sight of two sandhill cranes stalking each other through the reeds like tall skinny elves in love. Sixty degrees more and my eyes strain to capture two round and brown shapes gamboling through the smoke of the cotton grass meadow. They are definitely four-leggeds: brown bouncing balls set upon the cartoon of a lyrical horizon.

I strain my eyes to bring the two beings into closer focus. Grizzly bears! They have to be. Ironically, and despite my own better judgment, the part of me that yearns for communion with wilderness takes over. A faint smile cracks my lips, while the wisp of a heavy weight seems to lift from my shoulders. Now I sigh, squint ferociously, and start playing with the angle set between my eyeglasses and eyes, trying, just this once, please, to find a sharper image out there on the tundra. Aldous Huxley reminds us that the structure of the human eye does not permit us to sense every part of an extended area as clearly as it senses one small part.[12] The resultant strain erects a barrier between the sensing eye and the perceiving mind. In this case, no matter how hard I try, I cannot make those bears look as clear as they do in the National Geographic television specials. Actually, I can barely identify them as bears at all. Round, brown, bouncing; those are all the attributes I am able to discern. So instead, paying further obeisance to Huxley, I *flash* my eyes, meaning that I glance quickly at the place where the balls bounce, then close my eyes to let my brain reconstruct the image that fell for an instant on the screen of my retinas. Supposedly, when you stop trying to see, seeing comes to you. Does that also mean that when you stop trying to see a mirage, the mirage turns real? There is a widely held belief among traditional peoples, that the part of an animal we see is not the real part but only a disguise, an outfit put on when it comes time to visit our world.[13] Once home again, the animal takes off the costume, and changes back to its true form, which in some ways is exactly the same as a human's true form.

When this seemingly bizarre conception of animals starts to sink in, it puts an unmistakable damper on what might otherwise have been an edifying visit to the zoo, or an evening spent watching those televised nature specials. Suddenly we realize that almost none of us has ever even seen a *wild animal* in the traditional sense of the term. Furthermore, this nature that we moderns perceive as a *resource* or as a *panorama of separate species*, traditional peoples perceived as primarily a neighborhood.

But who has actually observed this masquerade party aspect of the animals? Actually, after two weeks spent in the mind-altering silence of the Arctic, dosed with hot chocolate and mosquito repellent, I feel ready for any revelation. So I flash my eyes and try to perceive two undisguised bears who, for their own part, continue to render themselves visible and then invisible at will.

What's the use? I get up from the plastic five-gallon bucket that doubles as a dining room chair, and start hunting around the cook tent for the voyeur's binoculars that should be somewhere nearby. I seem no more capable to see them than I am the bears. Jonathan, our own moose man, took them. He also took the camera with the telephoto lens and the shotgun with the telescopic sight. More alarming to my own inner sense of survival, I stare at all the loose food lying around the Beluga Cafe, and start to giggle. As it is, the presence of two grizzly bears frolicking like Magellanic Clouds around the Milky Way of this camp kitchen, has to necessitate a certain degree of care.

I finally figure out how to achieve a better view: by standing on the bucket filled to the brim with peanut butter and parmesan cheese. The bears disappear behind some bushes, then reappear to start digging up the ground. They are moving across the prairie like bulldozers, ripping up the fabric of the groundroots to extricate whatever rodent or vegetable goodness lies underneath. It will go on throughout the summer and fall. They will eat and eat and eat, and then wander off one day to dig a hole, place themselves within, give a good yawn, and fall asleep for seven months.

The romantic who resides within my own clogged brain pushes me to believe that the reinstatement of Eden, whether personal or general, wholly depends upon the outcome of this chance proximity between human and bear. And I would wantonly push my body out across the meadow, arms outstretched, just to greet these emissaries of wildness in person. Didn't an old hunter once swear he'd seen Johnny Appleseed frolicking with a bear family?

Luckily, the sober side of my brain clicks into gear. I throw some more driftwood on the fire, get it going good and smoky, and then walk two hundred yards away from camp, along the edge of the beach. When my separation from the kitchen seems adequate, I turn toward the meadow again to plot the bears' status. I stare and stare, flash and flash. But they are gone.

Orange-scarlet Mickey finally returned to camp voided of his demons; equipment laden Jonathan arrived within another hour without a single mammalian photograph to his credit. Both smiled and chuckled as I related the description of this recent ursine event; although, not surprisingly, neither one of them actually believed that I saw what I said I saw. After two weeks of experiencing nature as an ongoing series of optical illusions, how could I be sure that what I actually saw was not a caribou, a bush, the shadow of a cloud flowing across a brown patch of ground? So what else to do but tramp across the meadow in search of grizzly evidence. And there, not more than 150 yards from the camp kitchen, Jonathan uncovered the splendid proof we all sought. Proof that, although objective observation may not prevail in these climes (if it lives anywhere else either), its mirage still offers hope that our senses function as we have been taught they must. There before our six human eyes, steaming in the glow of late afternoon, lay solid evidence that a bear had eaten, digested, and relieved itself.

The next day, between the ionizing spasm of a violent Arctic thunderstorm, a riverboat pulled into camp to take us and our disassembled gear toward home. We rode 100 miles upriver to the civilization offered by the delta town of Inuvik. Significantly, none of our expectations survived the trip. And we are all the better for it.

In conclusion, you may well be wondering why I have chosen to place this account of my own dysfunctional senses at the beginning of a book purporting to offer expert guidance on the matter of perceiving nature. Here, only a short way into this *how-to* book, I have intentionally cast serious doubts on my own limited ability to utilize the senses to perceive such things as distance, food, vegetation, whales, horizons, bears, history, and much, much more. It is as if this nonexpert had gone out of his way to undermine a very shaky edifice of personal expertise.

In fact, if this chapter has described any kind of expertise whatsoever, it is in the realm of patience and perseverance. Thus, in the *how-to* sense of learning to perceive the interface between human and nature, *Waiting for Godot* is as apt a corroborative text as any of the works offered up by the likes of Darwin, Bateson, E. O. Wilson, John Muir, Theodore Roszak, or Aldo Leopold. The I Ching says it best: "perseverance furthers."

Chapter Three

How to Pray for the Enlightenment of All Sharks

A recent newspaper story described the controversy that resulted from the harpooning of a gargantuan 2,800-pound great white shark off the coast of Connecticut. A local shark aficionado, Peter Benchley, author of *Jaws*, compared the killing to "going out and shooting dogs." The commercial fishermen, no doubt nonplussed by this attack against their livelihood, countered by inviting Benchley to join them out on the water sometime so "he can judge for himself if there is no sport involved." Finally, a biologist attached to the state's natural history museum joined the fray by defending the fishermen's seizing "a once in a lifetime opportunity," calling their catch a "prize"—a valuable addition to the museum's permanent collection.

We are thrust into the cauldron of a classic controversy between commercial interests and establishment scientists on one side, and animal rights activists on the other. Here is a microcosm of the entire environmental debate, a soup pot within which public debate swirls and bubbles without ever seeming to locate solutions to satisfy all parties. It is the stuff of a thousand new books and articles each year. Armies of authors research ever-thickening heaps of statistics, dredging precedents up from the depths, cannily delineating arguments based on ethics, museum attendance, the economics of commercial fishing. They distill, dilute, and dilate the formulas and arguments to prove that sharks, or rain forests, or pesticides are plentiful or scarce, helpful or hurtful. Finally, they attempt to assemble their facts into some meaningful literary recipe fit both to grab the attention of the reading public and to elicit some measure of positive change. If these books and articles share anything in common, it is this: those who write them and read them undoubtedly subscribe to a fundamental *objectivist's* viewpoint.

But let's get both personal and simplistic: I stick my own head in the sand a moment, then pull it out to declare that all those who employ the objective viewpoint are attempting to translate their own personal, educated perceptions about the slippery truths inherent in nature into accurate numbers and cogent arguments. As strange as it may seem, there lies a significant part of the problem.

Look at it this way. These writers and theoreticians usually consider themselves to be *experts*. More important, somebody else considers them to be so as well. The experts create a very effective mystique. And the society, the tribe—we, us—listens to its experts before it listens to those others who offer an *other* point of view most often described as opinion. Borrowing adjectives from the deep ecologists, is the point of view of a shaman, or a poet, best described as a shallow opinion, as opposed to the deep opinions served up by the experts? What do the experts say about it?

They tell us that the numbers we utilize to organize our relationship to nature serve as important *signposts* along the highway to change. Therein lies, perhaps, the greatest value of the objective view of nature. But the experts rarely tell us that statistics are passive, utterly pliable, able to be bent and stitched together, glued and torn apart, reordered and reinterpreted in so many varied and sometimes opposing ways as to become useless as indicators of anything much beyond the point of view of their interpreter. If the interpreter is good, then the statistics are useful. But who assigns these values of good and useful, as opposed to bad and useless?

Actually, that question describes the greatest abuse of the statistical finding. It is possible to consider statistics as cogent *numerical opinions*, some person's reasoned advocacy of the important points within a greater objectivist's perception of nature. If the interpreter chooses his numbers well and argues his case logically, then the statistics may move you. You ascribe power to them. You alter your lifestyle accordingly, or at least abide by the rules passed by lawmakers who were moved enough to pass new strictures that tell you to do so. But, on a larger scale something seems awry. If statistics are so dependent upon their interpreter, then quite possibly they do not exist as indicators of externalized objective reality any more than do the opinionated human beings who concoct them.

What occurs so often, at least within our own system, is that exploitive interests wander through the very same labyrinth of statistics as the preservationists. They grab at this number and that fact to turn their vision of the minotaur of endless information into a tamed beast of a conclusion that often proves a point exactly opposite to that of the environment watchers. I repeat: the patterns that seem to illuminate one or another objective point of view, emerge instead as an outgrowth of the point of view of the pattern maker. Objectivity emerges as the human perception of the way *humans* perceive things to work.

Not such a risky statement if you are a Tlingit shaman, or for that matter a quantum physicist. Unfortunately, neither the commercial shark fishermen nor the museum curator who collaborate to kill sharks merely because they are big, have yet caught up with what's really happening. If there is a criticism hidden within this depiction of the process of expertism, it is not about the fact that the process exists. Rather, it is that we ascribe too much power to a version of reality that does not seem to be helping us deal with the problems that beset us. The problems are legion.

Philosopher Gregory Bateson wrote that most of our present use of information excludes context.[1] One cannot perceive a thing-in-itself without also distorting it. Likewise, the world is not a collection of such *things*, unique to themselves, but rather a dynamic network of relationships bound together by communication.[2] By contrast, those who subscribe to a version of objective reality that insists upon reconstituting the slippery truth as substance and quantity seem not unlike the denizens of Borges' infinite *Library of Babel*, who search forever for *the Man of the Book*.[3]

On some shelf in some hexagon (men reasoned) there must exist a book which is the formula and perfect compendium of all the rest: some librarian has gone through it and he is analogous to a god. . . . Many wandered in search for him, for a century they exhausted in vain the most varied areas. How could one locate the venerated and sacred hexagon which housed him? Someone proposed a regressive method: to locate book A, consult first book B which indicates A's position; to locate book B, consult first a book C, and so on to infinity. . . . In adventures such as these, I have squandered and wasted my years.

Too many treatises about humanity's[4] relationship to nature emerge as neat, enumerated statements about the way the experts view this process, this verb[5] called nature, when it is repackaged as an object, a noun. This noun declares that our world is a bundle of resources that are outside ourselves and utterly available. Over the centuries we have manipulated our ingenious prehensile thumb around the new object of nature, built up our strength to the point that we currently exert maximum control over our possession. Consider the fact that the English noun "nature" ascribes no contextual difference between living nature and dead nature. Fishermen and curators catch a shark, kill it, stuff it, mount it, yet still refer to their handiwork by the name shark. Schoolchildren file past the shark exhibit all day long and learn that the main difference between a living shark and a dead shark is mostly the level of fear we bring to each. One can only wonder if we might benefit by generating as many names for the human manipulation of nature as Eskimos have names for snow.

Of course life is not a black-and-white affair and so there are more than two sides to this argument. At its best, the objectification of nature aids this human animal, you and me, to achieve relative miracles. In all humility, and despite my own injunction to noster, you and I are also the winners in this ongoing race called progress.

None of us stands outside the culture and so none of us is absolved of our contributions to the environmental crisis. I, for one, am not privy to any special wisdom or holiness. I too am moved to a state of wonder by the latest tidbit of scientific data pertaining to the breeding habits of black holes, or the pounds per square inch exerted by the front tooth of a great white shark. I too have to stop and marvel at the wonders of this personal computer in front of which I strap myself several hours a day to write books such as this. But just as I admire the PC, I also abhor the out-of-context-with-the-environment strip-mining techniques that provide the rare-earth materials that comprise the guts of the box. Just as I use my fair share of paper, I still feel justified in railing against the mismanagement of resources that leads to the utter destruction of the old-growth forests. However, I also acknowledge that this book may sometimes appear to stray from the fine line I have drawn between cultural and personal motivations. It sometimes transforms this writing into a room filled with broken glass, and shows this author to be a barefoot boy within.

In other words, I get as confused as the next person by subscribing to mutually exclusive points of view simultaneously. Here is one of the great existential issues of our time—as well as the engine that drives the most devastating argument leveled by the out-of-context exploiters against the holier-than-thou preservationists. I use a car, a refrigerator. I benefit from strip mining. I am it. I noster. What about you? So this writing does not purport to preach to the converted, simply because none of us is environmentally chaste or enlightened. The environmental purist exists no more than Borges' Man of the Book exists.

Tibetan Buddhists employ a spiritual path known as the bodhisattva. The bodhisattva, the compassionate one, knows the path to enlightenment but consciously chooses not to enter until the whole world is also enlightened. He devotes lifetime after enthusiastic lifetime to offering a helping hand to others who falter from the path. The environmentalist's dilemma is a passive version of this active concept. None of us can be absolved from exploitation until exploitation itself ceases to be the modus operandi of our culture. But how do we turn this passive dilemma into an active vehicle for change? The answer may seem complex; in truth it is simple: By starting to act a little bit like a cross-generational bodhisattva. By spending this lifetime learning how to protect the seventh generation.

To recapitulate: Our societal network already connects each of us to every other. On the one hand, that truism signifies that every one of us is a despoiler. We drive our cars down to the corner grocery store and spew vapors into the air that warm the atmosphere, causing certain rivers to discharge vast amounts of mud into their tidal estuaries, provoking beluga whales up along the lip of the Arctic Ocean to bear their young fifty miles farther from shore than they did last year. On the other hand, societal connectedness also implies that each of us is a potential bodhisattva; each of us can help every other one of us to alter his or her perceptions. We start with ourselves. As such, the crisis of the environment is also a crisis in personal perception.

My first book, *Dolphin Dreamtime* (first published under the title *Animal Dreaming*), touched upon this question of the perception and misperception of the natural world. I had set out, many years ago, to participate directly with animals by attempting to play music with them. And although the work of communicating with animals has long since developed into an actual career for me, my original interest started out with a simple intent: I wanted to play music, explore wilderness, and be helpful. Inspired by this basic aim, I found myself becoming increasingly adept at producing situations that placed me, as well as a few other musicians, in the domain of wild animals. And as one short answer to all those correspondents who write inquiring how they too might get involved in this work of interspecies communication, I offer simple advice: go do it.

It was only after much experience that I started to seek *results*, and, on those rare occasions when I communed with an animal expressing a certain degree of enthusiastic humility I sometimes achieved them. However, this was no case of pied piper musical virtuosity, no outrageous grantsmanship to keep the work bubbling, no scientific wisdom to insure credibility. None of that. Just enthusiasm and humility, mixed together with a generous measure of naiveté. This working method was then cut and shaped to fit the specific sensory behaviors of such creatures as orcas, buffalo, and howler monkeys, to name just a few of my animal collaborators.

Back in the late 1970s, during what might be called the middle period of this ongoing work, my own intentions became almost entirely goal-oriented. Given enough sweat and ability, what I considered to be the Rosetta stone of improvisational music would eventually permit an *interspecies vocabulary* to emerge. Likewise, my main subject became the very vocal, large-brained orcas who inhabit the inland waterways of western Canada. But before I ever came close to those objective goals, something else got in the way. In the process of exploring the potential for this human-orca dialogue, I caught a glimpse of a natural universe quite unlike anything I had expected.

I came to believe that there was no code to crack, no foothold upon which to devise some ingenious transitional computer language. In fact, there was no *language* whatsoever. Unless, of course, you take into consideration the high-tech implications of *holophonic echolocation*, a dolphin's potential to send three-dimensional sound-pictures to its mates. Such a "language" probably does exist, although cracking that particular code may have to wait until some future administration in Washington frees up all the money now spent on defense—it would take that kind of technological commitment. But who needs it? Certainly not the cetaceans.

Just as music is not science, neither is interspecies communication through music science. Of all the things that our culture tries to manipulate into objects, music may be the least accommodating. It is not an object, it is a real-time experience, a flow in which musician and listener are mutually immersed. In terms of a research project about interspecies communication with several species of animals by means of music, the original goals no longer made any sense. For a while, the work of my fledgling organization, Interspecies Communication Inc., seemed a half-science seeking after big science. Naturally, all of us involved in the work also entered into a period of transition and adjustment.

Personally, I became far less interested in the *science* of the interspecies relationship—answering the hard questions about any animal's ability to communicate with human beings, let alone with me—and more interested in the *art* of the relationship. An artist also asks questions. But instead of utilizing rigor and skepticism to provide experiential answers that exist in a direct causal relationship to those questions, he or she focuses upon a medium that provides the experience directly. The artist works to convey a perceptual message in a manner that requires no operational definitions, and no rigid rules of correspondence to expel the subjective perceptions of his or her own consciousness.[6] And whereas a scientist thrives on absolute answers expressed as numbers, an artist thrives on process. A scientist seeks to expand humanity's frame of reference; an artist seeks to expand humanity's depth of insight.

If, as I submit, the environmental crisis is a crisis in perception, then artists must be permitted the same access to nature as now permitted scientists. After all, it has long been the artist's task to transform the way we see our environment. Or, to stretch a point, the orcas themselves seemed to be offering an unmistakable critique of the human condition: human beings did not need to rethink things, but rather, *reperceive* them. In that light, consider this description of how art was treated in ancient China:

> A painting was not exhibited, but unfurled before an art lover in a fitting state of grace; its function was to deepen and enhance his communion with nature.[7]

In my own case, the more I played music with orcas, the more I found myself swallowed up by process. And when I sought after surety, that which scientists call the replication of data, I rarely achieved anything beyond a temporary confirmation assuring, in effect, that the musical dialogue I achieved today was not going to be replicated tomorrow. The few answers I learned (or achieved or found) were not answers in the important sense of universality. At best they answered one particular question arising from one particular frozen event. I was not playing music with orcas so much as I was interacting daily, and on a peer level, with one or two highly evolved *individuals* who happened to be orcas. A few of those whales seemed as obsessed by the process as I was, while the rest of them expressed only a mild interest.

When the wild orcas started to be transformed in my own mind, not as animals, but as *people*, they also seemed to be taking off their orca suits. Occasionally, I found myself getting so caught up in the music making that I caught a glimpse of what it meant to take off my own human suit. What did I look like? I'm not sure, although it felt a bit like the invisible orca/man. Whatever the appearances, we two species soon started to communicate on a much deeper level. In that light, permit me to share one message those wild individuals taught me: Captive animals, no matter how individual they may seem, almost never take off their costumes. If they did, they would cease to exist, and essentially vanish into thin air.

Ironically, the orcas also taught me what it means for a human being to be an artist. They could improvise chord changes at will, indulge in complex rhythms, invent melodies. Significantly, they would only play with me when I did not also try to control either the situation or them. The less structure I imposed upon the music-making events, the more I found myself making giant leaps from concepts about individual orcas to all orcas, to all of nature. Unfortunately for documentation's sake, the more I leaped about, the more of a challenge it became to explain this process to a nonparticipant. What exactly was going on out there with the whales? I could not clearly say. So I started recording tapes of the human-orca interactions. If it was happening, then presumably you would be able to hear it for yourself.

Unfortunately, out on the boat, late at night, interacting with wild whales through music, everything I experienced offered deep and abiding context. Nothing was meaningless, everything became grounds for revelation—even the crackling of shrimp issuing through the underwater sound speakers like so much radio static. But if everything sounded so evenly potent, what distinguished the good tapes from the merely mediocre?

Evidently, the good tapes were also good examples of Bateson's idea about things-in-themselves. They all shared one essential trait: the key elements of a real-time experience had been successfully preserved in a form that made them accessible to an uninitiated audience. They were now embodied in an artifact that froze a fluid relationship between species into magnetic patterns on a cassette tape. When we generalize about translating contextual relationships into media records, we encounter another example of that insidious crisis in perception: any and all of our "real life" documents about nature are not nature. The experience of nature is not what it seems to be when we listen to orca tapes, see it on television, quantify it through statistical analysis, or objectify it through our scientific papers. We have become so complacent that we accept a disguised version of nature for the genuine experience.

But occasionally we humans find a way to take off the distorting glasses. At those moments we become acutely aware of the narrow distorted character of our thoughts about nature. In other words, we humans may come closest to expressing slippery truth when we utilize a slippery medium such as music to express it. Interacting with animals through music offers one way we may occasionally entice nature to take off her very ingenious disguise. What does she look like underneath all those human numbers and all those human thoughts? Who dares to say for sure, although she certainly looks alive even when she certainly looks dead.

This kind of interspecies research shares far more with the accidental art of John Cage, or a vision quest into the southwest desert, than it does with the United States Marine Mammal Commission or even any oceanarium show you may have seen. Or for that matter with the work of those who conduct controlled language experiments upon monkeys in cages and dolphins in concrete pools. They seem to me to be practicing an insidious form of interspecies boot camp. Laboratory research on animals—whether that means injecting rats full of cancer cells; or training bottlenose dolphins to kill an enemy, as the U.S. Navy wants to do at the Bangor, Washington, submarine base; or foisting on chimps and dolphins human linguistic concepts, as is done at the Yerkes Institute or Kewalo Basin—is an arrogant form of science that seems akin to a medieval inquisition. It displays the pursuit of knowledge as outright cruelty, and so ends up satisfied with a body of information *about* life that is utterly devoid *of* life.

But I was describing my own path toward growth. Another personal milestone along the way: I became a father. My elder daughter Claire, four and a half years old as I write these words, still calls them "aminals" and "hippopopitus," but her heart and her senses are capable of reaching out to the environment of our own front yard in wise ways that make me yearn for simpler times. After all, it is the children who teach us that the only complete experience of nature includes dreams, myths, and totems—all of the projections of wildness that reside so pervasively within our own minds.

As my two daughters refreshened my own sense of wonder, they also nudged awake a deep fatherly concern to protect their vulnerability. So, for example, this writing spirals out from what wise Henry Thoreau called the *preservation of the world*. Young children are quintessential sponges, soaking up every human foible placed before them. Luckily, they also project the eternal optimism that resides within each of us teaching us adults to tilt toward idealism—how things really ought to be done—and tilt away from the pragmatic way things really are done given the current exploitive state of human culture.

I continually ask myself a key question about life during the age of the greenhouse effect: How are all the children going to live in twenty, forty, or even two hundred years? I hope they will never lose the idea expressed in so many stories: that all the animals within nature, including the human animal, are part of a big, extended family. That is one hint about undisguised nature perceived as an interspecies neighborhood. It is a pervasive idea of childhood, yet how quickly some of us have forgotten it. But take a child out into the wilderness, and that elusive perception turns into daily experience. So, for example, my own ongoing studies with the orcas have developed into a project for families: human families relating to orca families in an interspecies neighborhood. The children, more than any of the rest of us, make it so.

Natural philosopher, Paul Shepard, argues that a child learns to make categories by categorizing animals.[8] At twenty months, my younger daughter Sasha knows the names of about thirty animals, out of a 200-word vocabulary. But she is also learning, for just one example, that wolves are evil, black, hairy devils who disrupt the lives of industrious pigs and eat sickly grandmothers. Somehow, it seems important not to deny her these classic tales of childhood, although we also admit that they no more represent the spirit of the wolf than a nuclear power plant represents the peaceful atom. As parents, we feel a responsibility to bring in other images, such as the stories about the beautiful, glossy-coated wolves who inhabit the Alaskan wilderness. We take the time to compare and contrast the two images about wolfness, and so instill an essential lesson of balance. But fairy tales work their magic in self-contradictory ways. For example, that articulate arbiter between myth and consciousness, Marie Von Franz, has commented that fairy tales are nothing less than any society's expression of the beast known as *anima*[9]:

> The anima tends to manoeuvre a person into a situation which is meant to be without issue. To be in a situation where there is no way out or to be in a conflict where there is no solution is the classical beginning of the process of individuation. . . . In psychological language the situation without issue, which the anima arranges with great skill in a person's life, is meant to drive him into a condition in which he is capable of experiencing the Self.[10]

In this sense, the big bad wolf is just as easily apprehended as a big bad human wearing a wolf costume. This is the big bad wolf responsible for shooting real wolves from airplanes in the Alaskan bush, the one who blinds the eyes of rabbits to test women's eye mascara. And assuredly, baby Sasha understands this paradoxical purpose of myth making much better than those animal rights advocates who would have us ban such stories as a gross lie about wolves. After all, most tragically, the big bad wolf expresses an important truth about human beings.

Listen and you may even hear the big bad wolf whispering the answer to that question about life and the greenhouse effect. There really is no way out of a conflict in which there is no solution. The greenhouse effect drives us into a condition in which we are finally capable of experiencing the self. Or put another way, we have to alter the relationship to our own anima—the life principle—if we are ever to rehabilitate the environment. Once again, we are being coaxed to perceive the world anew. When we comprehend the environmental crisis as a crisis in perception, such emergencies as the greenhouse effect necessarily turn into lessons that reveal how we, ourselves, have to change.

Look about you. The environment is burning up in a hundred, a thousand places, worldwide. But there is no fire escape here, no "out," no other solution than a shift in knowing who we are. The human race—meaning you and me as well as that determined and well-meaning Brazilian engineer who believes he is clear-cutting the rain forest to provide capital for his country's debt-ridden economy; and the whale harpooner who believes he is just trying to support his family while offering fare for the very gourmet Japanese people; and the patriotic factory owner in Cleveland who believes that he serves his own workers by not refitting his smokestacks to contain a problem that primarily affects another nation's distant wilderness lakes; and the pregnant Sudanese mother who believes she is just trying to have a family because she has born twelve children, all of whom have recently died of starvation—we all did it. We are all *continuing* to do it. And in our planet-wide, species-wide perceptual whitewash, no one is ever quite culpable, because *everyone* is culpable.

The perception of perception is a complex and tricky business. For example, we currently believe that there are approximately 21,000 gray whales in the Pacific Ocean. Someone in a position of authority may someday decide that the formerly endangered grays are not only no longer an endangered species, but that there are now enough of them. 21,000 means *enough*, and so some (how many? who decides?) could become available for harvest. Enough? Enough. *Enough!*

I do not mean to be sarcastic. Nor do I mean to lead you down the path of a reductio argument.[11] Rather, watching my eldest daughter recently made me remember that when I was five years old I used to lie in a field of tall grass, staring up at the clouds, repeating a word over and over again, until it finally lost its meaning and became only a sound. My only desire here is to repeat this word *enough* enough times until the semantics that pretend to explain this twentieth-century relationship between humanity and gray whales, begins to float away in a surrealistic cloud.

Obviously, a tragedy lies waiting within the mutable figures known as expert findings. At some point in the future, some whaler somewhere may be able to conjure up enough statistics to propose that there are enough available stocks of gray whales. Thus, he will propose (why is it only men who ever propose such things) that gray whales be harvested for their blubber. His rationale: that there are not only enough gray whales, but actually, there are quite a few too many of them. We need to harvest them to provide enough food, enough jobs, enough capital. Again I shout: *Enough!* In the past hundred years of this objectivist costume ball, the human perception of the semantic whale (or the semantic laboratory rat, or even the semantic "expert") has not indulged any other relationship. Most intriguingly, when the numbers finally do speak, it also means that the experts themselves are exonerated. (Experts invoke the rules, and the current rules cherish models of population dynamics that encourage human primacy more than they cherish gray whales. The seventh generation might just as well not exist. They won't unless we change the rules.) Semantics renders the experts responsible and not responsible at the same time.

Unfortunately, the culture is going to continue to find salvation in this anthropocentric vision of responsibility at least into the immediate future. At least, that is, until the environmental beacons—the greenhouse effect, the ozone holes, the pollution, the extinctions—start to blind us with ever-increasing obviousness.

Meanwhile, objectification will continue to provide the engine that feeds the end run of this, our proud humanity, as we gallop across the face of the Earth in search of ourselves. Together, humanity and objectification, the one flesh and blood, the other a spreadsheet of counts and comparisons, copulate to reproduce each other until neither another point of view nor another species has any room to assert itself.

It is in such a cold discouraging light that I volunteer one more anecdote. This last example offers a radically optimistic perception about our own place within nature. As this chapter was initiated in the cause of sharks, let me shift from gray whales and back to sharks again.

I spent the summer of 1986 immersed in musical communication work with orca whales on the fjords that separate Vancouver Island from the mainland of Canada. Members of the expedition were drawn from many walks of life, including a very refreshing Buddhist lama, born in Tibet, and then living in the city of Vancouver.

Just before breakfast one morning the two young boys in our group, David and Auri, drew the attention of the adults to the beach. There, just a few feet from shore, a good-sized dorsal fin cut lazy circles through the water. Was it a salmon? Possibly, but if so it was a very large one, easily fifty pounds.

The lama stood on a rocky promontory just above the place where the rest of us had gathered. He seemed to be chanting, fingering his beads, staring transfixed at whatever manner of beast swam attached to that fin. Finally he walked down beside me and asked if there was anything special he needed to know about using the camp dinghy. He wanted to row out to that fish. To the lama's mind, that animal was in trouble and needed some help. No, he had no intention of physically intervening. His mission was not at all veterinary. Rather, he hoped to spiritually prepare the animal for whatever life or death fate was in store for it.

At that moment the fish turned on its side and veered just a few feet from where we all watched. It was a shark, probably a six-gilled shark, about four feet in length. The animal's under-side was now shown to be completely lacerated, with pieces of flesh hanging like streamers. Had it been caught up by a fishing net, and then released? That was the obvious explanation. But then, there had been no commercial fishing activity within a good two miles of camp. Someone asked if the shark might have been the victim of those same frisky orcas who played in our cove for more than an hour last night. Possibly. After all, both dolphins and whales are known to pick up a fish as a plaything, throwing it up in the air the way a cat plays with a mouse.

The lama climbed aboard the dinghy, zipped up the orange life jacket that coordinated splendidly with his flowing red robes, and started to row. He cut a peculiar figure, facing toward the bow but rowing stern-first, back and forth, always hovering just above that dorsal fin. Every so often he would stop rowing, lean over the gunwale, finger his beads, and then speak directly into the water as if involved in deep spiritual consultation. After an hour he returned to shore and dragged the boat up onto the beach. His first words were, "That shark is in a bad way." Then he emphasized the central point of his voyage, "He will hear us if we pray." I never did, although he did all day long.

Over the course of that gloriously sunny day, the lama could be seen walking down to the tide line just to look after the whereabouts of that shark. At three that afternoon, he found me again, this time to report that the shark had finally disappeared.

Several hours later, toward dark, the lama and I decided to take a walk along the beach. In actuality it was more like a guided tour that one enjoys inside the great museums of the world. Every few feet he would ask me to please stop to study a human face or animal or monster that presented itself within the contortions of one or another of the gnarly driftwood logs that littered the high-tide line. Suddenly, I stopped in my tracks, groaned once, and directed the lama's gaze to a nearby tide pool. There lay his congregation of one, our friend the shark. The creature was obviously dead, and already quite stiff. We bent down to examine its streamlined contours. Suddenly, the lama turned inward and started to murmur a death prayer in his native Tibetan. The chant spoke of a long journey about to be undertaken. As such, it offered up a set of clear directions—a road map as it were—to aid the shark in its travels.

The lama stood up and sighed deeply. "Oh well," he chuckled. "I guess that one didn't make it." Without any further ado, he continued on his walk, quite content over a job well done. Actually, I was quite surprised to find him so utterly devoid of mourning.

Now, so much later, I cannot shake the impressions made by the deaths of two sharks. One of them, small and insignificant by most human standards, lay stiff in a tide pool, where no doubt the flesh slowly began to ooze out through holes in the sandpapery skin. I see a raven, or perhaps an eagle, come from the sky to pick the carcass clean. Finally, the remains are picked up by a storm wave, to be devoured by the sea itself.

The other shark, a 2,800-pound great white harpooned by commercial fishermen off New York, even now lies embalmed and mounted behind glass while a long line of awestruck schoolchildren parades past. This shark has become transformed into a monument, not so much to sharks as to the human sensibility that chooses to perceive nature through its own modeled handiwork. This is a monster shark of ponderous numbers, possessed of so much weight, so much incredible distance between the two walls of its jaws. The taxidermist has utilized every trick of his craft to imbue this costume of a shark with all our expectations about sharkness. So the razor-sharp teeth are bared to the gums, perhaps in unconscious tribute to those days long past when human beings cowered in fright before the sheer power of an unleashed nature.

Finally, I see the lama. Perhaps one day he too will walk through the doors of that museum to come face to face with that display of a model who was once a shark. As always, his own relationship embraces a compassion for the death, as well as a reverence for the life of that being. I imagine him once again turning inward, to chant the same prayer he murmured on that fine sunny day beside the tide pool.

Chapter Four

The Slippery Truth about Yellow Jackets

It's been a dry summer here in the San Juan islands of Washington, a dry year, a dry two years; the kind of weather that persuades the wasps to arrive in full force. The predominant ones in this area are yellow jackets. I have been cutting a joint into a board with a Japanese saw: a sharp-toothed, spatula-shaped tool that permits one to slice through wood with extraordinary precision. The yellow jackets are obviously attracted by the sweet smell of fir sawdust. One at a time they have buzzed right up to my sawing arm, right through the invisible boundaries of my personal space until—no doubt motivated to revenge the screams, tears, and welts meted out to my eldest daughter who has been stung three times over the past week—*swish:* some reflex causes me to start wielding the saw as a weapon. My ears register the slightest "tick" as springy metal whips up against the hard cuticle of insect skin; "hzzz," the saw blade momentarily vibrates into song before, "thud!" it slams against the dry mossy ground. Finally, after four or five blows I pause a moment to survey the results of my vengeance. There, just beyond the frontier of my bare feet, lie six yellow jackets in total disarray. Two have been dismembered, wings and body sections strewn across a foot or more of ground. Two more lie whole but unmoving, their skins broken, a dark liquid beading out from breaks in their thoraxes. The last two are still alive, obviously stunned, but quivering at a rate beyond the ability of my eyes to capture.

More yellow jackets appear. This time, their advance registers like a buzz saw ripping through my insides, and again I react: Tick, hzzz, thud—the carpenter's samurai blade springs into service. Within moments the bodies of fourteen more yellow jackets lie broken against the two-foot wide strip of ground that has become our battlefield. Yet this is no victory. As one squadron gets annihilated, I already hear the sympathetic vibrations of fresh recruits racing toward the apparent enemy, namely me. If anything, the battle grows ever more lopsided.

An entirely new mood arrives on the wings of this new horde. Is it my imagination, or do they actually buzz less ferociously? Mostly, I cannot help but notice that these replacements appear quite disinterested in either the sawdust or in me. Instead, they zoom directly into the hub of their fallen comrades, urged to action by some new and quieter task. This change in tactics forces me to drop both my guard as well as my saw, and so peer downward directly into their midst. Closer and closer my eyes probe, refocusing several times to let this vast mass of a giant finally perceive a glimmer of the universe that is the insect's domain.

Lying on my side, face rubbing against the moss, I behold an epic spectacle of yellow jackets. They drop down out of the sky one by one, land upon their fallen comrades, turn them this way and that to find a good strong grip, and so lift them bodily into the air. Are the yellow jackets rescuing one another? One of the purported saviors hovers a mere centimeter from the ground, attempting in vain to gather and match up the various parts of a dismembered comrade. I can only fantasize that this airlift, this potential mission of mercy, will eventually conclude back at the nest, where the wounded soldiers will be ministered back to health by yellow jacket nurses and yellow jacket orthopedic surgeons and even yellow jacket pharmacists capable of secreting enzymes and hormonal potions that serve as the social insect's version of medicine. So my mind conjures up a vision of a wasp field hospital, the hymenopteric equivalent of a M.A.S.H.

As I watch, ten, fifteen, and finally twenty or more of the sleek black-and-yellow insects land on the moss, buzz quietly, and then go about the business of carrying away their kin. Somehow, a creature who displays such compassion for its mates deserves a better deal from me. With that sentiment well in tow, this giant chooses to relent. He stands up, postpones his original ambition of sawing some boards, and strides away from the battle.

Battle? Is that what it was? Not very likely. Now I wonder if the yellow jackets ever had any real interest in my flesh whatsoever. Furthermore, I've always known that my daughters get stung because they're frightened by the threat of the wasps, and so flail at them with their little arms. In retrospect, it seems a classic case of interspecies miscommunication: the yellow jackets get flailed, my daughters get stung.

Later that same day, in retelling the story of the altruistic yellow jackets to a friend and colleague, I am unabashedly accused of inventing a scenario that, in fact, exists nowhere in nature. Certainly wasps are *altruistic* by a biological interpretation of that term, meaning that the individual gives up its independence, its daily activities, and many times even its life for the benefit of the group. But a wasp field hospital? You've got to be kidding.

Genuinely confused by this alteration in my perspective, I decide to call upon the expertise of an entomologist, a scientist who studies insects. Introducing myself over the phone as an insect aficionado, I ask him to please interpret my description of observed yellow jacket behavior. He pauses as I conclude my tale, clears his throat, and then quickly repeats the scolding already meted out by my friend for attributing human qualities to the actions of an insect. "Wasps do not *care* about one another as we humans occasionally do. Nor do they exhibit, well, compassion either. In fact to be really honest about it, compassion is not even a term within the biological lexicon."

Instead, the entomologist chooses to explain the wasp behavior in terms of pheromones, those chemical smells and tastes that make up the form and content of yellow jacket communication. Certain pheromones mean defense, others signal food, and so on.

Some of the most elegant studies of insect communication, including pheromones, were done on that distant cousin of the yellow jacket, the weaver ant.[1] It was discovered, for example, that when a worker weaver ant chances upon an intruder, even at a considerable distance from the nest, she stops foraging for food and begins to fight, while also releasing alarm phero- mones. If the adversaries are numerous, some workers break off from the fight and immediately return to the nest, all the while laying an odor trail to and from the battleground. Back at the nest, they recruit other workers by jerking their faces back and forth, toward and away from the nest mate as a further statement of the incipient problem. It seems significant to add here that these same workers utilize a very different kind of dance, a side-to-side, face-to-face, antenna-waggling dance, when com- municating the presence of food to other workers. This is a distinctly different type of motion than the toward-and-away, call-to-action dance.

The entomological researchers, one of whom is E. O. Wilson, the distinguished father of sociobiology, limit their speculations about the depth of weaver ant communication to the guarded comment that antenna rubbing may transmit the actual odor of the food, while the invader dance resembles the movements employed in fighting. But Donald Griffin, from whose book, *Animal Thinking*, this example is taken, wonders if the con- sciousness issue need be dismissed so ungenerously. He remarks that the intruder dance may just as easily be interpreted as an intentional pantomime. Likewise, the two differentiated commu- nications are just that, communications, expressions of animal consciousness. Thus the two dances convey to the recruited ants two distinct messages about what is to be done at the end of the odor trail. Griffin adds that his colleagues err on the side of anthropocentric absurdity when they argue that it is nothing but coincidental that the fighting dance actually succeeds in prepar- ing the ants for fighting rather than food gathering. It seems the same ingrained thinking that leads our nuclear industry to state that it is merely coincidental that the building of nuclear weap- ons also prepares human beings for nuclear war.

The recruitment of ant workers includes yet another feature that suggests that the animals are first thinking, and then acting upon those thoughts. Rather than immediately setting off down the odor trail, some of the ants on the receiving end of the recruitment gesture instead turn to other workers and repeat the same gesture, *even though they have not been directly stimulated by the invaders.* In this manner, a maximum number of recruits is enlisted very rapidly. In other words, this second line of communicators transmits a message learned only from a communicated signal, not from a pheromone itself. So on down the chain.

The prevailing scientific view about the matter describes these actions in some detail, but then strictly enforces a code of silence about interpreting it. In a way we are led back to one more example of the subjective/objective impasse from the last chapter. Griffin is declaring that traditional entomologists seem predisposed to believe that ants cannot display consciousness, even if that is what the evidence suggests. And by being so adamant about disallowing any interpretation of rudimentary consciousness in observed ant behavior, these investigators are primarily offering the rest of us a very strong statement about the predetermined limits imposed by their science. Once again we are presented with a presumably objective point of view that works especially hard to demonstrate what are actually the *subjective* limitations of its own objectivity.

Griffin's book takes serious issue with these prevailing scientific views about animal consciousness:

> Recognizing that most communication between ants involves chemical signals, which would be almost impossible to decode if they are at all differentiated, we should maintain open minds about the possibility that these simple distinctions among recruitment messages might be only the more easily detected components of a versatile system of chemical communication. I am extrapolating here far beyond anything that these scientists or their colleagues have suggested. When asked how they know that these ants cannot entertain any conscious thoughts, the scientists usually fall back on the prior conviction that insects are genetically programmed automata and that their brains are too small to permit conscious thinking. *Evidence* of differentiated communication has not yet altered this deep-seated conviction.[2]

As with ants, so with honeybees. Scientists observing the components of honeybee communication have established that their complex waggle dance (art form?) communicates (language?) sun position (astronomy?), a system of measure (mathematics?), direction (navigation?), and even the *desirability* of the food in question (adjectives and/or adverbs?). Furthermore, the waggle dance is not only utilized to locate food, but can also be used to communicate the location of a water source to cool an overheated hive (thermodynamic engineering?), or even the location of a materials source to repair a damaged hive (architecture?).

Lastly, there is an intriguing version of the waggle dance that impels the bees to commence a once-in-a-lifetime swarm.[3] "Join together," commences the song that drives this dance. "Form into a well-drilled unit, protect the queen (listen to the beat now), go forth from the hive, venture into the world, and search for a new hive cavity with all the right attributes."

However, if we subscribe to the prevailing noninterpretation of insect communication, the queen must be the only one privy to these "right attributes" because not one of the swarming bees was even born when the last call was made. But how else could the bees learn it? If, for example, one were to explain this waggle dance communication in terms of instinct, then it almost seems analogous to a human child's emerging from the womb not only cerebrally and physically prepared to acquire language, but also possessed of the syntax and vocabulary of a specific language already at his disposal: French babies born speaking French. But if the waggle dance is *not* instinctual, then it signifies that the queen must be a kind of insect professor, who teaches an actual grammar about "right attributes" to the workers.

Griffin points out once again that most scientists deny that the language of honeybees can be called a language at all, because there is no evidence that the bees are able to judge whether or not their dances *symbolize* anything in their surroundings. Nothing has been demonstrated beyond the fact that the *human* researchers are able to extrapolate the connections implicit in the dances. In other words, if the bees were shown a replica of their own dances (a televised Honeybee Bandstand?) they would not be able to tell whether the signals accurately represent, for example, the distance and direction to a food source they have just visited.[4]

Here we are faced with an example of the *Bambi syndrome:* scientists cannot accept the reality of animal language or animal consciousness until an animal possessed of certain key attributes of both *human* language and *human* consciousness appears on the scene.[5]

In this case, unless the bees are able to comprehend their dance *outside of its essential honeybee context,* the scientists will continue to declare that the waggle dance is not fit to be called a language. By inference, there is no cause to suspect consciousness either, unless the animal is able to demonstrate a perception of itself outside its own life context. So goes the prevailing sentiment about language and consciousness as espoused by the scientific heirs of the industrial revolution.

According to this definition, language is not only the medium that communicates the objectification of the world, it is the message as well: it *is* the objectification of the world. One can only wonder if these same entomological critics were shown a segment of the real American Bandstand, with Dick Clark, would they be able to discern the fundamental sexual signaling going on between teenage dancers, although it was a rite of passage they, themselves, once visited?

On a more subjective level, I give my eyeglasses a good symbolic cleaning before pronouncing the very opinionated judgment that these experts our culture chooses to explain nature to the rest of us see nothing but genetically programmed robots where I perceive, instead, a hotbed of writhing, sentient insect beings. I mourn those very sentient beings presumed dead. Who is able to resurrect the Lazarus of nature?

So weaver ants, so honeybees, and so yellow jackets. When I swatted those wasps out of the sky, knocking the living daylights out of them, the blow indubitably caused them to spray a chemical field across the battlefield of my front yard. The original pheromone probably "said" food (the sweet fir sawdust). This primary smell was then, no doubt, coupled with an alarm aroma sent off by those wounded during the subsequent assault. "Yum, yum! Help! Help!" wafted the aroma of the pheromones over the quiet breezes of late summer. The yellow jackets who arrived in the second assault continued to send out the mixed message. But now the call for food probably began to predominate the airwaves. The reason was simple. Being scavengers and predators, these yellow jackets arrived to find an incredible windfall of victuals, namely, their dead and dying brethren. No personalities here, no friendship, no conscious choices, no insect airlift, no individual emotions as we understand them. No thoughts manifested by a mind inside a brain as, ostensibly, are our own. Consequently, no empathetic qualities upon which to hang moral comparisons with human society. No, just meat! Witness the simple rote behavior of the social insect. In zoom the wasps from every direction. "So," concludes the entomologist of my own phone call, "your observations are way off the mark. The insect world is even more—how shall we say?—'ruthless' than our own."

I can only wonder if zoological convention would scold the entomologist for utilizing the same descriptive anthropomorphism for which he had earlier scolded me. I had described the "compassion" of the wasps. Now he chooses to sum up what he believes to be their mindless behavior as "ruthless." But to be fair about it, he is not unaware of his use of such a word, first excusing himself before using the term. The forbidden expression is utilized by such as he to describe an insect's ethology to such as me; chosen for no other reason than to shoo away my own crazy ideas; exercised only to enforce his message about the utterly cold neutrality of a wasp's heart in language, no matter how flawed, that I can understand. It is his polite way of declaring that my own layman's observations about yellow jacket behavior are patently worthless until such time as my observing embraces both the objective methodology as well as the precise language of entomology.

Do I dare complain? After all, without a commitment to methodological convention scientists might never have discovered the many-layered beauty of such nuggets as the waggle dance of honeybees. Call it objectification if you must, says he, but the structured pursuit of knowledge is essentially good. Ultimately, we need it to progress.

But this is a two-edged sword because a perception of the world based upon objectification is also a consciousness without context. Many point to this peculiarity of contemporary perception as the singular stunning achievement of our species; the quality that distinguishes us from all the rest of nature. For one trivial example, we are unique because we alone can watch our own dance up there on the TV and know that it is us. Or was us, if the show was taped last week.

This investigation of the honeybee's waggle dance makes me wonder how many other scientific studies about animal behavior and *intentionality* have been stripped of all references to animal consciousness. If we insist that animals cannot possess the attribute of consciousness, then we must recognize that we are conforming to the precepts of one particular school of traditional science. However, we must also realize that the evidence suggests we may be deluding ourselves, just as the Renaissance Church deluded itself by refusing to accept the heliocentric worldview offered by Copernicus.

That which distinguishes also separates; any triumph achieved by the old worldview inevitably generates failure. The human race cannot long endure its self-imposed separation from nature. When an overpopulating human race forgets how to relate to grizzly bears without rifles, the bears soon turn into an endangered species. When we separate our car exhausts from the nursery behavior of beluga whales, we soon end up puncturing a hole in the ozone. On a personal level, we forget how to give credence to the deep intuitive yearning for integration with nature.

Nonetheless, this yearning for connectedness continues to break through the surface of the society. It is the incubator in which the entire environmental movement is nurtured. Unfortunately, a society that perceives itself separate and above nature too often transforms our yearnings into mere fragments of connectedness. For one painful example: the environmental movement diligently works to save forests while it often raises its own operating funds through mail campaigns that utilize massive amounts of new, not recycled, paper.

Or for a more generalized example, does the sheer amount of facts and information generated to explain nature ever satisfy the deep yearning for connectedness with nature? The lama would probably answer, no, they are two very different things. Yet our science too often seems set on a course to achieve the status of Laplace's "great Intelligence," who knows the position and velocity of every atom in the universe and therefore can predict all future events forever?[6] In other words, the yearning for connectedness is very different from the yearning for knowledge. Yet because our society designates objectivist science to define and explain nature to us, too many of us equate the yearning for knowledge with the yearning for connectedness. They are, however, different needs stimulated by very different perceptions of nature.

Unfortunately, merely to comprehend the absurdity of Laplace's "great Intelligence" is never going to provide the transformation that the situation demands. This comprehension leads to changes based upon moderation and attenuation. It seeks new models to temper what it understands to be a kind of contemporary overenthusiasm. For example, continuing with our current model of the environmental movement: new organizations spring up every day to counteract what everyone understands to be a de facto emergency. But most of them end up sticking one more finger into what is a very leaky bureaucratic dike, without also delving into the mindset that created a deficient dike in the first place. I do not mean to disparage these attempts at saving this or that animal, this or that ecosystem. Without the polarized infrastructure of checks and balances, the buffalo, for example, would almost certainly be extinct today, the first-growth redwood trees only a memory.

Social advocate Jeremy Rifkin explains it well: the environment is not the issue of our lifetime, because it is the context.[7] The root problem that exists between humans and nature is not one of scale, but rather one of perception. Likewise, a perception *of* scale leads to a responsibility *for* scale. Gregory Bateson goes so far as to call the contemporary perception of human knowledge a crisis of the mind. And then says this:

> The only way out is a spiritual, intellectual, and emotional revolution in which, finally, we learn to experience, first-

hand, the interlooping connections between person and person, organism and environment, action and consequence.[8]

For example, von Frisch's entomological explanation of the waggle dance was never meant to describe a relationship between bees as much as it meant to describe the contextual relationship between bees and those human beings who utilize the methodology of scientific data collecting to observe them. I, for one, prefer to call it a mystery and not a dance. I long for mystery in my own life, just as others no doubt, long for answers. Perhaps the single greatest lack of contemporary science is its inability to provide a sense of mystery to our lives. Instead, mysteries exist only to be solved. By contrast, spiritual ecology promotes mystery—not as a know-nothing counterpoint to modern education, but rather as a primary method for changing our perception of nature.

On that note, permit me to expand the beehive into still another dimension. Among the Masai people of East Africa, honey wine is brewed by a man and a woman who must remain chaste for two days before as well as throughout the entire six-day period during which the wine is fermenting. Should this couple commit a breach of chastity, not only would the wine be totally undrinkable, but the bees who produced the honey in the first place would fly away.[9] The first time I read this account, I took the obvious anthropocentric bait and interpreted the bees' departure as a bad sign, something to be avoided at all cost. But do they fly away because they are indignant, or because, contrary to whatever the Masai may believe, the act of human sex has somehow liberated the bees from the slavery of producing honey for another species? An act of conception, of nurturing the next human generation may thus be construed not as a wrong, but as a balancing of the transgressions perpetrated against nature by the current generation.

I do not mention this account of Masai beekeeping only to offer my own unorthodox interpretation of a complex set of metaphors. No matter which explanation we accept, we have also started to treat the Masai bee myth as a source of mystery. I have chosen not to neutralize its import by finally confiding that, after all, this anecdote is just a fairy tale—the big bad wolf now appearing in the sexy guise of a copulating Masai couple. Rather, I ask that we attempt to apprehend a generalized version of the global human-bee relationship by stitching the Masai point of view to any of several other bee myths, and then stitching the two of them to the contradictory scientific points of view taken by E. O. Wilson and Donald Griffin, who both cite the "evidence," one stating that bees are communicative, the other that they are not. But that seems akin to stitching a piece of a Masai robe onto a scientist's field fatigues. In fact that is the whole point—all these versions need to be coexistent if they are to form a gestalt reality. All together, they define the human relationship to bees. We might even imagine some bright young entomologist coaching the Masai couple to heights of rapture just to document the resultant waggle dance.

But back on the telephone, the wasp scientist finds little humor in the bizarre gestalt incursions I insist upon stitching onto his exclusivist discipline. His emphatic stand makes him sound like an entomologist from central casting: Entomology, if not the first or only word, is absolutely the last word on insects. All we know about insects is a result of a careful and quite objective observation. My own feisty view about the yellow jacket universe (not to mention honeybees, ants, and Masai), is worthless as an actual perception of reality. In a word, I do not know how to perceive.

Likewise I am left speechless by a professional insect man similarly caught by the spiderweb of his own unyielding paradigm. Here we are faced with an expression from a very entrenched sect of biology that also expresses itself as an exclusivist religion. But does that also mean that a Masai winemaker, or a child, a Gregory Bateson, a poet, or for that matter, anyone unversed in the zoological scriptures remains incapable of first observing, and then describing nature? This unasked and unanswered question worries me no end. I have the uncomfortable feeling that this professional describer of nature is practicing a kind of *observational fascism*. To paraphrase physicists Bohm and Peat:

> We increasingly ignore the wider context that gives things
> their unity. In fact, this spirit is now spreading beyond

science, not only into technology, but into our general approach to life as a whole. Understanding is now valued as the means to predict, control, and manipulate things.[10]

How can any of us grasp the subtleties of animal behavior unless we are able to utilize all of the tools contained within our own acoustic version of the pheromone, namely human language? After all, our speech is certainly an extension of the mind's own ability to think and grasp ideas. Can we expect to deprive our language of its symbolic, metaphorical, moral, and emotional context, and then honestly expect that our consciousness has not been vacated as well? Voided, just like the personality of a yellow jacket. No doubt this particular entomologist would answer that only by cleansing our language of its mixed messages can we ever expect to perceive nature as it is. Actually, many biologists subscribe to the notion that words don't do the job at all. They describe the machinations of nature far more accurately, at least from their viewpoint, by boiling down observations into mathematical equations. Yet if that be true, then the visions of children and poets are necessarily flawed, meaning that they are not worth considering in any "serious" discussion about nature. Our policymakers subscribe heartily to this notion. They consult only the "experts" when making decisions about the exploitation or preservation of nature. To repeat an earlier example, they tell us how many gray whales are really enough. The poets and the mythmakers are out of the loop altogether.

Perhaps the entomologist would almost certainly resonate with this essentially meditational approach to nature if it were nought but a personal and religious matter. And no matter how crucial the spiritual approach may be to the general health of the individual, it is nothing but individualistic and subjective. In a word, it does not describe reality. That also implies that objective reality only shows itself when we mask an essential aspect of our whole being. We wear only one small part of our human-being disguise, and so do not utilize all the parts within ourselves. Instead we base our reckonings about nature only upon the separated rational part.

The objective viewpoint cannot perceive the context of the whole because the objectivists, themselves, insist upon utilizing only a part of their/our whole being. That is why, for example, the term "science of ecology" is an oxymoron. And had I thought to ask him about it, I feel sure that the entomologist might have answered that the scientific description of nature would be exactly the same if Venusians, instead of Earth-humans, were making the assessment. But what does that mean? Do the bees communicate or not? Perhaps it all depends on what part of the human disguise you choose to don at any particular moment. Or perhaps it means that the description of nature remains the same under all circumstances, with one significant exception: when modern human beings are making the assessment.

What this objectivist viewpoint renders in the real world is a perceptual buffer placed between our conscious thoughts and our very important gut connection to nature. Over the past few centuries that buffer has metamorphosed into a weapon set in place for no other reason than to defend us from our own feelings; from our own rightful place within the community that is nature. How easy to use that sterilized weapon to capture and finally imprison a nature devoid of our own heart! Without that weapon, we might never have been capable of destroying so much, of participating so little. And of course, the animals, now little more than the objects of our objectivity, are endowed with neither motive nor choice. They have been divested of their poetic lucidity. That, of course, is the not so subtle verdict rendered by the professional journals in which science is published, where verbal precision purports to be law.

By the end of my phone conversation with the entomologist, I was left more dissatisfied than before; but not by any continuing inability to comprehend the mystery of the yellow jackets. No. In fact I started to grow rather fond of that particular mystery. Rather, I now grew confused by this expert's dogma. As I heard him explain it, none of the human emotional models by which we appraise our own world seems even to apply to the rest of the animals. Yellow jackets are not saints, nor are they even faintly compassionate. Rather, they are just like the language of science itself: amoral and neutral.

On the one hand, I respectfully acknowledge the entomological description of yellow jackets to be a very potent body of facts. On the other hand, just like a honeybee sharing the wealth, I have waltzed very far away from the current zoological stance that equates the gathering of data with truth-telling, which it is not. Entomology's yellow jacket is not my yellow jacket, although I certainly acknowledge that former creature as the yellow-and-black striped wasp that utilizes pheromones so deftly, the one that stings my daughters so "ruthlessly."

I returned to sawing wood the very next afternoon. Yes, the yellow jackets flew in once again for a taste of human sweat and sawdust. This time, however, I felt quite unwilling to swat them out of the sky. The reason had as much to do with field hospitals as it did with pheromones. That is not to say that I refused to accept the story that the wasps were cannibalizing their mates. Of course they were. But on the other hand, despite the cannibalism, I still clung to my mysterious vision of yellow jacket saints. I remained a firm believer that nature is profoundly more complex and more independent in action than we know: if an animal is observed manifesting the same mechanical behavior ninety-nine times in a row, on the hundreth occasion it may, instead, start practicing medicine.

None of our observations are objective. They are all just opinions that add up to the same amount of truth as any one of them alone. Likewise, any two unique observations generate a third viewpoint that is necessarily different from either one alone. How else can any of us ever hope to comprehend the profound mystery that is yellow jacket intention? Not that I have suddenly been filled with the final word on yellow jacket diplomacy, yellow jacket compassion. Rather, for the first time, I have bent down far enough to the ground, and far enough away from the experts, to scrutinize the insect universe on my own. That observation, and even more, that communion, has served to still my hand. Perhaps we act more objectively when we cling to our poetry than to that miserly catalog called data. That is the truth, as best we can know it.

One final note. Some researchers, addressing the incredible challenge of translating dolphin whistles or chimpanzee signing into English, sometimes describe the enormous intellectual gap that exists between these large-brained mammals and ourselves by stating that it is like learning to talk to an extraterrestrial. Actually, compared to a yellow jacket, dolphins and chimps seem more like members of my own immediate family, friendly and familiar. If we are to believe that dolphins are "extraterrestrials," in effect the ultimate strangers, what does that make the yellow jackets? Mostly, it makes them more in need of a good press agent. Perhaps that is the ultimate purpose of this anecdote. I have been dragged, against my will, into the role of an apologist if not an enthusiastic promoter of yellow jackets. Yet I offer no excuses that this, my first press release, is neither effusive nor worshipful. I think of my swollen daughters and reject the idea outright. Instead, let it serve as nothing more than a respectful account of a small shift in perception. I doubt that the yellow jackets, at least the sentient yellow jackets of my own imagination, could ever ask for anything more from us humans.

Chapter Five

⚜

The Case of the Pain of Whales

On San Juan Island, Washington, a researcher was granted a permit by the U.S. Marine Mammal Protection Agency in 1986 to shoot "cookie-cutter" darts into forty-five orcas over a period of five years. The quarter-inch wide, three-quarter-inch deep sample lifted from within the skin and blubber of the whale was to be analyzed to evaluate the level of pollutant chemicals as well as determine the genetic relationship among the whales sampled. The researcher hoped "to provide direct evidence that the gene pool of orcas is much smaller than could be determined by simply counting fins."[1] The forty-five constitute about half of the current population of orcas who reside in Puget Sound.

Not surprisingly, the issuance of the permit generated perhaps the greatest amount of protest around the Sound since the various oceanariums of the U.S. west coast mounted their orca capture operations a decade previously. The objections ran the gamut from a defense of the basic right of these whales to exist without suffering any more threat from human invasion, to the issue of whether or not the science involved had any lasting merit beyond serving a Ph.D. candidate in his quest for a degree. At the heart of the controversy lay the fact that these whales are seen and loved by hundreds of thousands of people. The very image of a scientist poised on the deck of a boat with bow and arrow aimed at the hide of one of "our orcas" was a matter of intense concern, notwithstanding the science involved. After a decade of fighting commercial oceanariums, and the entire nation of Japan, the impassioned whale watchers of the Pacific northwest had no hesitation whatsoever about doing battle with this well-intentioned graduate student who presented his study as being to the whale's ultimate benefit.

Both the Marine Mammal Protection Agency and the researcher tried to allay public criticism by accentuating the permit provision stipulating the presence of an *expert* on board whose job it would be to judge any negative reaction on the part of the darted specimen. If such a reaction was observed, then all parties agreed that the project would immediately be terminated. Yet, unfortunately for the project advocates, that secondary image of some "objective observer" with special access to the pain of whales opened up another can of worms. What within the orcas' behavioral store, the critics wanted to know, was going to constitute a negative reaction?

The whale might ram the boat. Or perhaps it would veer away from the archer at high speed. In turn, some students of orca behavior worried that the departing orca might simply keep on going, leading its entire pod away from the darting area for a long time to come.

Those who doubt an orca's ability to make such long-term decisions might consider that oceanariums used to capture orcas by driving them into shallow bays around Puget Sound. But the orcas soon figured out their persecutors' plan, and simply refused to enter any shallow bodies of water, no matter how brutal the capturers became.[2] In fact, the whales had not been seen in the preferred capture site of Pedder Bay for an entire decade.

There are many examples of cetaceans reacting succinctly to harassment from humans. Near Maui, researchers documented humpback whales shunning a former nursery site soon after commercial waterskiing operations started up. And in Alaska this same humpback stock had been well documented in its outright exodus from Glacier Bay. The issue in that case was presumed to be aggressive and noisy whale-watching boats. Power boats were banned, and the whales returned. In both incidents, the whales communicated a clear message that the humans were able to read.

But what if, in the case of the darting research, the message were not so clear? What if, for example, a darted whale, formerly friendly, stopped venturing within a hundred yards of boats and instead drew the line at 300 yards? What if this subtle change in behavior went unnoticed for an entire year? Would anyone be able to state unequivocally that the new pattern sprang directly from the dart? And given the off chance that such a conclusion was reached, would it be enough reason to terminate a project already well underway?

Or consider the dramatic case of the gray whale who surfaced just underneath a whale-watching skiff, spilling all the occupants into the sea. One man suffered a heart attack and died. Some longtime observers of gray whale behavior concluded that the huge animal was just acting frisky. There are many documented instances of grays venturing right up alongside small boats to give whale watchers the opportunity to stroke their gnarly skin. Other commentators disagreed. After all, the species was once called "devilfish," a name given them by nineteenth-century whalers who often witnessed the grays capsizing their longboats.[3] Whom do we believe? Here was an outwardly similar display observed in two separate episodes 150 years apart by humans who held very different intentions toward the grays. Who was the expert willing to pool all the information at hand, and then render an objective verdict about gray whale behavior?

The last chapter focused on the ways that the objective point of view colors our own personalized relationships with nature. This chapter focuses instead on the objective point of view as it influences the public domain.

Objectivity, as it is utilized by the Earth sciences of this late twentieth century, treats us as gods: as if we were somehow able to view nature from the outside looking in. This separation makes us invincible, justified in manipulating and eradicating animals and environments in the name of that just cause known as the pursuit of knowledge. To utilize just one example: objectivity permits the medical research community to name a rat a *specimen,* which then justifies the injection of carcinogenic pesticides into the rat's body until it expires. The human master dressed in his white lab coat designs an ingenious computer model, takes precise notes, publishes his results in a worthy journal, and so adds his results to that ever-expanding ream of information concerning the flesh of mammals wracked by tumors. How easy it then becomes for the observer to throw his used-up specimen into an incinerator to make room for the next rat on the assembly line. But what have we learned from the rat's sacrifice?

We have learned the precise amount of that poison (which we already knew was never meant to be put inside the body of any living creature) that it takes to kill a rat. We then extrapolate and come up with the equivalent amount required to certainly kill a human being. In most cases, the chemical finally wins a qualified approval permitting it to be utilized within the ecosystem in certain strengths below that amount.

We end up spraying it on one or another of our growing foods, and thus poison the soil, and the insects, the birds, and the rats, and maybe even a few unborn farm workers as well. The food is harvested, scrubbed, and packaged in some processing plant, and fed to ourselves and our children. Eventually, every creature living on this planet ends up with residues of those same chemicals inside his or her body. However, let it be known that no researcher has yet accumulated enough information to pinpoint the complex connections that probably exist among all the varied residues reacting and interacting with one another inside all the wildly varied living organisms strewn in its path. Given the immensity of the task, no one disagrees that such a study would simply be impossible.

Meaning, in effect, that our objectivity chooses its criteria for safety as a function of the equipment, the techniques, and possibly even the political clout of the testers. In that light, our objectivity is at best a qualified objectivity—what might just as easily be called subjectivity. Meanwhile, every single day more chemicals pass the tests and are "safely" sprayed onto our food and into the soil. But these new tests demand more experiments upon more and more rats. We are finally confronted with an endless chain of little murders perpetrated in the name of health, but which actually end up causing big and very slow murders all over the planet. In sum, laboratory experiments on animals primarily teach us just how shortsighted and unethical we have become in our pursuit of information.

The lesson to be gleaned from the orca-darting program is far less apparent. In fact, before rendering a verdict about the expert hired to judge the pain of whales, we first need to consider at least one more case of human/whale interaction. This one involved the orca pods that reside just a few hundred miles north of San Juan Island, in Johnstone Strait, British Columbia. During the summer of 1983, a fisherman was seen taking pot shots at two orcas. Both animals were wounded, neither one died. In the days that followed, local researchers seemed to agree that not only those particular animals, but in fact the entire extended family of whales went into retreat whenever humans attempted to draw near. Once again, the whales communicated a clear message that the humans were able to read. But as the days turned into weeks, the message grew hazy. The ability to discern it became more dependent on the methodology utilized by the observer. Those scientists employing *invasive* techniques— zooming upon the whales in motorboats, following the pods for hours at a time, and so on—now noted that behavioral patterns had returned to normal. But those researchers who employed *benign* techniques—observing from a stationary base, permitting the whales to initiate contact, and the like—continued to note changes throughout the entire next summer. One longtime researcher has stated categorically that the entire extended family of whales, that unit we call a pod, never did recover from the shooting.[4]

It seems relevant to mention here that most of the scientific researchers who choose to study whales in either United States or Canadian waters must first receive government permits that actually license them to *harass* the otherwise protected whales. It also means that those agents who grant such licenses (scientists all) believe that scientific research is just about the only pursuit that justifies legal harassment.

In actual practice, that works out to mean that behavioral research and harassment often define interchangeable terms defining the same process. Naturally, those researchers who harass the most also argue the loudest that they cannot collect the important data about orca behavior unless they are permitted to observe the whales on a regular basis, meaning from motor-boats. Significantly, the benign researchers, those who patiently wait for the whales to initiate a visit to a stationary observation point, have started to put pressure on the motorboat researchers to give the whales more room. As in the case of the humpbacks of Glacier Bay, there is some evidence that the orcas of Johnstone Strait are not quite as prevalent in the area as they once were. But, why should they be? Their staple food of salmon exists in many other places where they do not also have to contend with four or five noisy research boats chasing up their backsides all day long. All summer long.

It also seems pertinent here to restate the second of the three general rules of spiritual ecology: No one is the enemy—only systems are dysfunctional. Thus, the invasive school biologists are by no means the villains of this piece, no matter how tantalizing that conclusion might seem at first. Instead, consider science as one cultural expression of the anima placed in our path for no other reason than to allow us to see ourselves as we are. It was set up that way in the beginning; a methodology out on a fact-finding mission to gather, and then cook up information about the world into a form palatable to our species-specific (and too-human) brains. A thumbnail history of this fact-finding mission seems in order.

Sometime during the last two centuries, the society at large began to worship at the source of all its newfound technological power; a power, I might add, largely fueled by advances in science. Naturally, the scientists waxed enthusiastic to serve this cause of social progress, and science redefined itself as a pro-vider of the seemingly endless stream of artifacts that the culture demanded. In return, scientists were given carte blanche to find ever more ingenious uses for all the varied resources offered up by nature. Nature was eventually defined as our own private resource. The pace continued to accelerate, until finally we lost sight of all we had wrought. At some juncture along this rise to power, the human species began to affect the "resource" of nature. Something had gone awry.

In recent memory, a few signposts have emerged from the clutter to demand that we start to question whether our own great success is not in fact our own greatest failure. Perhaps the most insistent of these illuminating signposts has been the white glare and raining afterglow cast off by nuclear weaponry. Even today, nearly a half-century after its inception, the atom bomb remains the ultimate metaphor of the folly of power. Because mastery does not often offer wisdom in its wake, very few of our ingenious gadgets, whether we call them drift nets, disposable diapers, or the peaceful atom have helped us cope with the spoils of our technological endrun. It is finally dawning on us that, just like the demigod Prometheus, we are quite chained to both our status and its privileges.

For example, adherents of behavioral biology's *invasive* paradigm sincerely believe that they are discovering and gathering information that leads to knowledge and truth about the natural world. Yet from the hindsight of our own future—for example, the year 2140 of my own seventh generation—it may very well seem obvious if not utterly tragic that this logical and objective methodology did not gain knowledge, but instead *invented* a mechanical description of the Earth that existed nowhere in nature outside the twentieth-century mind. It was a restless mind, reeling in its own power. It was a mind marching under the banner of progress although increasingly aware of the devastation left in its own wake. Yet no matter the consequences, this mind remained self-assured and the master of its own fate, possessor of a civilization and a spirituality disconnected from any sense of equality or collaboration with all other beings.

If the distinction between *invasive* on the one hand and *benign* on the other seems overstated and arbitrary, then let it be known that it heralds a major paradigm shift within field biology. As such, the differences between the terms have triggered an ongoing and sometimes emotional debate within the halls where behavioral science is discussed.[5] In the case of the pain of whales, those biologists who employ an *invasive* methodology seem primarily human-centered, inspired by an intellectual and career calling to gather information *from* the whales, *exclusive* of the whale's needs. They seem primarily motivated to achieve published bylines in one or another of the parochial journals that both serve and define the scientific community. Contrarily, benign researchers are whale-centered and thus inclusive in their research; they are primarily motivated to protect the local community of whales while also healing the environment.

It seems important to emphasize here that this new *inclusive* spirit is slowly growing in stature within the biological sciences. It is very slowly overwhelming the old exploitive mode, while painfully transforming the discipline into a planetary healing profession. In other words, whatever worldview may have formally forced the virtual exclusion of compassion and participation from our biology, it is now perceived as time to discard that viewpoint, no matter how useful or entrenched it may seem in other ways. The greenhouse effect, to mention one signpost, absolutely demands it. We begin to base our ecological decision-making process less upon utility and dispirited information, and more upon the recognition of such criteria as environmental healing and animal wisdom.

The actual healing commences when we, biologist and nonbiologist alike, see our own selves plainly reflected within the wounds inflicted upon the Earth. As that reflection deepens within each of us, we also grow more capable of perceiving the need for action. This critical motivation to utilize the biological sciences to actively heal the planet, might be called a *noster biology*. I define the term as a science that feels compassion for the seventh generation.

In the case of the pain of whales, the paradigm split demonstrates its critical significance when we realize that the field methodology of choice deeply affects any researcher's ability to observe the whales. If the whales do not choose to congregate near a land-based station, then some forms of benign research cannot exist at all. Thus, benign research might best be understood as a method that permits the whales the role of active *participant*. By contrast, an invasive researcher is nearly always able to motor up on an orca pod to carry out whatever study he/she wishes to undertake. The whale is treated as an object without inherent right, a source of information, a *specimen*.

Here's the catch. One ongoing study has started to show evidence that the orcas do not vocalize as much when there are noisy motorboats nearby.[6] This means, of course, that whatever data an invasive researcher is able to buy through the power of a fast motor, he or she must pay for with a diminishing amount of whale signals. It may seem almost too obvious to a layman, but this also implies, first, that the observers are neither invisible nor separate, and second, that the whales have been exhibiting conscious choice all along. In other words, years of accumulated acoustic data serve primarily to depict the orcas as they *invent a response* to the presence of loud motorboats in the vicinity. The behavior that is ascribed to whales reflects the behavior manifested by researchers. The process of gathering information has actually invented the information. There are no observers, only participants. So much for specimen science providing the keys that unlock the mysteries of animal behavior.

The darting program certainly fits into the invasive camp. A crew motors up alongside an orca. An archer draws a bow, shoots a tethered arrow, yanks it out from within the whale's skin, and reels the cookie-cutter back to the boat. Meanwhile, another crew member watches for any immediate response. This latter individual, the so-called objective observer, he who is hired to judge the pain of whales, will thus be privy to any short-term and outwardly dramatic communication on the part of the whale. But inevitably, the subtle long-term variations on that theme must elude him.

Under the burden of such a cursory survey, it seems that the program might well benefit from the added input from a simultaneous study employing the techniques of benign research. Unfortunately, these Puget Sound orcas often travel in a tight formation, far and wide across an expansive body of water that is constantly brimming with humans following them in motorboats. The value of any research that must wait for the whales to visit a stationary base would be very limited. The question has also arisen as to whether the traveling behavior of these Puget Sound orcas may have been developed by the whales in response to the very real harm of nearby motorboats. Ultimately, invasive research kills benign research.

By comparison, at least some of the Johnstone Strait orcas can be seen just about every day because they reside within a relatively small semi-wilderness area. This is exactly the reason so much benign research is practiced there, including the unraveling of orca language, as well as the intricacies of interspecies communication between human and whale. Many of the Johnstone Strait researchers are quick to point out that the environment of Puget Sound is simply too busy to permit any kind of long-term benign study.

It also seems relevant to add that, out of seven research groups strung out along the fjord of Johnstone Strait, six of their leaders cosigned a letter sent to the Marine Mammal Protection Agency on the very eve of the darting decision, pleading that the permit not be granted. Yet despite the fact that the letter reflected a veritable roll call of active orca researchers, the permit was granted. The sole abstainer was a man whose own permit had been rescinded just the year previously for unnecessary harassment of orcas in the cause of collecting data. The ever-widening split in field methodology now unveils a political schism within the scientific community about what does, and what does not, constitute valid whale preservation.

Given all the confusion and subjectivity in this debate, it seems fair to conclude that no human being is capable of rendering an objective judgment about an orca's subtle and long-term reaction to a cookie-cutter dart—especially an expert in marine mammal science. Ultimately, we are left with the classic tale of *Rashomon*: witnesses to the same incident each report a different string of events, recall an entirely different defendant, favor a different verdict.

Yet the director of the darting program continued to defend his project by stating that the darting would most likely have no effect on the orcas whatsoever. For example, he claimed, when fishermen in Alaska repeatedly shot at orcas with high-power rifles, the whales still refused to turn away from the longlines to which they were headed. And of course, how much more devastating is a bullet than a mere dart. Unfortunately, to declare that the shooting of whales (who spend so much time out of sight, underwater) has no effect on them because no effect was observed by humans, would seem akin to fatuousness if the scenario were not so otherwise gruesome.

One must also look askance at the intentions of the Marine Mammal Protection Agency. They attempted to safeguard the Puget Sound orca population and mollify a suspicious public by proclaiming the merits of an expert whose job it would be to judge a reaction. Who was this expert? Certainly not one of the benign orca researchers in Johnstone Strait who cosigned that ineffectual letter protesting the granting of the permit. And what reaction? The whale's reaction? The judge's reaction? Some of us might extrapolate the whale's reaction and the judge's reaction to be the very same reaction. But what does that mean in the real world? As R. D. Laing has written:

> One tries to get inside oneself
>   that inside of the outside
>   that one was once inside
>   once one tries to get oneself inside what
>   one is outside:
>   to eat and be eaten
> to have the outside inside and to be
>   inside the outside[7]

The invasive researchers obviously believe that they can isolate the symptoms of "pain" through a cursory observation of behavior and then pronounce a judgment. The benign researchers, who have always been more concerned about the living whales than the research objectives, contend that any real "judgment" has to be based upon empathy and compassion. But as the yellow jacket scientist informed us earlier, these concepts do not even exist within the lexicon of invasive research. In fact, I take some license and hear the invasive researchers answer that there is no validity in the benign approach because it is unscientific, and is thus . . . well—unscientific. They may be right. Ironically, where empathy and compassion hold sway, there could never even be a whale darting program in the first place.

On the more ephemeral level of semantics, invasive solutions that are put forth to solve our various environmental problems necessitate a level of order based wholly upon control. In the invasive lexicon, solutions *mean* control. However, if we start from the premise that a wild nature, not a tamed nature, is what is good, then the solutions we find can never solve the problems, because, in effect, they *are* the problem. And if we choose to believe George Orwell when he wrote that semantics manipulates nature, we might conclude that the deeply ingrained semantic perception of solutions has subtly manipulated our ethics in a manner destructive to wild nature. Solutions are no more solutions than *enough* gray whales is *enough*. In his 1987 address before the United Nations, Mikhail Gorbachev seemed to be hinting at the very same conclusion:

> Life is making us abandon established stereotypes and outdated views, and it is making us discard illusions. It would be naive to think that the problems facing mankind today can be solved by the means and methods that were applied or seemed to work in the past.[8]

Just as the traditional biologist perceives the whales as a complex quasi-machine, so a noster biologist perceives that same whale within the context of a healthy planet. Consequently, the solutions offered up by benign research teach us that everything within nature is interconnected. It achieves this balance by mapping the relation between human and whale (or human and rain forest or human and greenhouse effect) without applying boundaries between subject and object. It finds pattern within unpredictability and creativity where systems are creative.[9] We ourselves become the only context of change, the only grounds for a revolution in perception. Noster biology offers the promise of guiding that transformation because it does not pretend to stand outside of it.

Here is a new biology that sends a small group of young scientists into Costa Rica to learn how best to replant trees where the forests have been cut down. A noster biology that devises experiments to demonstrate to what extent humpback whales are affected by the sounds of motorboats within their calving grounds. It includes the studies in energy efficiency conducted in California's Imperial Valley, where cattle wastes are being used to generate electricity for 20,000 homes. Or the biologists who have prevailed upon the government of India to stop all human encroachment in the Andaman Islands because of its unique ecosystem. A noster biology that, essentially, protects the rest of nature from our own worn-out excesses.

And in the case of the Puget Sound orcas, it looks as if there will never be a darting program. The Sierra Club Legal Defense Fund sued the Marine Mammal Protection Agency. A more subdued description of the event than the version given here was utilized as a key affidavit in the defense of orcas. Another judge, a federal judge, found for the plaintiff and revoked the darting permit altogether, stating that the potential harm to the orca population far overrode any potential benefits of the program. She concluded that the Marine Mammal Protection Agency erred in granting such a permit without first seeking an environmental impact study.

Rumor has the young man archer journeying off to South America, where he commenced his darting program under the auspices of the Argentine government. Unfortunately, another persistent rumor says he is patiently biding his time in order to reapply for a permit once the dust has settled.

Chapter Six

❦

Activism

January. Traveling south along the Baja coast in the Sea of Cortez with two grizzled American fishermen in their spaceship of a powerboat; eyes fixed on the mountainous shoreline, searching for that elusive cove that appears so appealingly sheltered on the two-dimensional surface of a nautical chart. The wind has come up like a fury, from flat calm to howling gale in less than fifteen minutes. We swing around the designated point and into a beautiful bay that sweeps back into the cactus-filled arroyos of the Sierra Gigante. Ted, the older of the two retired gentlemen, taps Ben on the shoulder as he spies something bobbing up and down between the rocky reef and the lee shore. Is that an animal struggling in a net? Ted zooms the boat in for a closer look, and starts cursing at no one in particular as he identifies that bulbous head as belonging to caguama, the green turtle that is so fast disappearing from the oceans of the world. The boat lurches again as Ted maneuvers into position beside the net. I follow Ben up onto the foredeck to get a closer look at the thrashing creature. But before I am even able to judge the extent of the turtle's entanglement, Ben has reached into the water with jack-knife in hand, and starts slashing at the monofilament cords.

I react with silent shock at the urgency of Ben's response to a problem whose solution might have taken so many other forms. Certainly, I too want the turtle freed, although I might have chosen to move a bit slower in dealing with what I consider to be a complex situation. Not a single word has passed between us.

Ben pulls and slashes, trying to free the turtle quickly. Is it my imagination, or does he seem to be relishing his act of destruction every bit as much as he savors the role of liberator? Can there be any doubt that he does not want this net to be used ever again? The set of his face seems to support a still deeper suspicion that he is also lashing out at the net's invisible owner, who may or may not have actually been poaching protected turtles. So, finally, he vents his anger at all wildlife poachers, everywhere. No matter where they may try to hide.

But, what about the poor fisherman, Ben's unwitting victim, who might have spent a week's pay to buy this fifty-yard-long setnet by which he wrests his meager living? Strung as it is, perpendicular to shore, I suspect that the device was set for a less ambitious prize: the grouper, bass, or pompano that frequent all the nearshore reefs along this coast. Catching a turtle may have been nothing more than an accident, although certainly a welcome addition to the family cook pot. I quickly scan the shore, hoping that the fisherman is not currently sitting behind some large boulder, watching through the crosshairs of a shotgun as Ben tears up his net. No, not much chance of that. This country is wilderness and this net is probably visited no more often than three times a week.

The turtle is bleeding from several wounds where the monofilament has cut into its flesh. Suddenly, my own mood shifts. I am awakened to the fact that except for our own intercession, this turtle would have probably drowned within the hour. Something clicks into gear. Old Ben's energy has flagged, he is totally out of breath. I take up his jackknife and begin to slash at the net. One strand at a time pulls away from the turtle, as Ben carefully guides the weighted net up toward me. Finally, the two of us heave together and lift the entangled turtle right out of the water and up onto the deck. Neither one of us pays the slightest attention to those soulful eyes, or that heavily patterned carapace. No, we just cut and untie, cut and untie, and finally the turtle is freed.

We push the thirty-pound animal onto its back while we decide what to do with it. Ben's hands are bleeding from handling the monofilament, I'm chilled and starting to shiver.

The wind is howling like a banshee. Ben and I look at the reptile, then at one another, and start giggling like two schoolboys caught up in some devilish prank. Too exhausted to think straight, I start pushing the destroyed net back over the side. What am I doing? That net is still deadly! Such a drifting tangle of monofilament is what is known as a *ghost net*. It hangs just below the surface for years, picking up hapless fish, turtles, marine mammals; sinking only after the negative buoyancy of the dead animals finally counteracts the lift of the plastic floats. And when the animals that have been caught in its web finally rot free, the net floats right back up to the surface again where it may catch another generation of hapless victims. I grab at the vestiges of monofilament but it's already too late. The net quickly slips out of sight if not also out of mind. I feel distraught, ready to jump into the water to retrieve it. "Don't worry about it," offers Ben. "It's still tied to the reef. Let the fisherman deal with it." More to the point, Ted, our skipper, is in no mood to wait around here for even a minute longer than he has to. He immediately fires the mammoth engine and zooms the boat a half-mile farther south before stopping. I pick up the heavy turtle with two hands and, like some interspecies shotputter, heave it into the water. The animal sinks, but then finally surfaces fifty feet farther out to sea, swimming away from the boat. Elation! We have saved a life! Significantly, hardly a word has passed between the three of us during this entire operation. It is as if we had been following a routine we accomplished every day.

And what of the turtle? In a day, a week, a decade will it end up in some other fisherman's net? Or perhaps in that same net? Do turtles learn from their mistakes? Might this incident have taught the caguama to avoid all such two-dimensional *things* that drape their tentacles in such neat checkerboard patterns?

Now the motor really shifts into gear and the boat slices through the swells like a jacknife through a fishing net, zooming up the coast at thirty miles an hour. Any turtle unlucky enough to get caught in our path would be chopped open like a skunk broadsided by a truck.

As we plow our way up the coast, Ben starts to talk about his own feelings. He is absolutely sure, has no doubt whatsoever, that the net was strung in that manner for the sole purpose of catching turtles. He believes he has a moral duty to free any sea turtle, destroy any turtle net, since "everybody knows" that the animals enjoy full protection under Mexican law. This individual turtle is also the representative of a species existing on the brink of extinction. And even if it were not granted quasi-legal protection[1] by the Mexican government, we would still be morally justified if not obligated to save it whenever presented with the opportunity.

And while human laws everywhere assert that some government somewhere will ultimately exercise control over the fate of those turtles who transiently reside within their own so-called national boundaries, I feel forced to stutter out my own plea for preservational anarchy—adding that, personally, I have never been able to accept the idea that any country owns its wild animals. The threat of extinction makes its own laws, demands that everyone join its police force. And if the ownership of wild animals must be a given, then give it to no one else but the seventh generation.

Yet, it is not any thought of future generations, or even turtles that continues to gnaw at my conscience over the next several weeks. Instead, I am unable to erase the imagined expression on the face of my fisherman adversary as he comes in a day, a week, to inspect his precious net. Similarly, I cannot help but fantasize a "what if" scenario: What if the fisherman had motored around the point of the cove just as I stood on the bow heaving his dismembered net back into the sea? How ironic— saved by the power of a fast American gas guzzler.

In my fantasy, the invisible poacher becomes an opaque participant in a cross-cultural collaboration. We are an improbable team, he and I, fated to first catch and then set free a turtle while synchronously buying, carrying, setting, and finally destroying the fishing net. Would my own act of mercy have served any purpose, to his way of thinking? Would it have generated anything other than a bitter anger toward the three self-righteous gringos motoring down his coastline in their expensive boat? Probably not. Although, of course, anger or no anger, the turtle would still be free. In the end, I freely admit that I feel more buoyed by the vision of a free-swimming turtle than I feel dismay for the Mexican who unwittingly became my fishing brother.

Unwitting action leads, unfortunately, to some unsettling conclusions about living the life of an environmental activist. For example, long ago, while attempting to save dolphins at Iki Island in Japan, I learned that lasting changes in environmental consciousness only occur when the locals themselves learn that it is to their own benefit to protect the environment in which they live.

At Iki, the fisherman reacted to an American activist who freed 100 animals as if the savior was nothing except a robber. Thus he was tried and found guilty by a Japanese court of law on a charge of theft, of stealing dolphins, who were fishermen's *property* by virtue of the irrefutable fact that they had been entrapped in the nets of fishermen.[2] Those dolphins would assuredly have been put to death the very next morning, their bodies ground up into fertilizer and pig feed. So this deed perpetrated by a foreign activist unquestionably saved the lives of a hundred dolphins.

This liberation also generated an international media event. The liberator, in an act of high art, had taken what everyone believed to be a cut-and-dried debate about dolphin stocks, and rearranged all the issues into a nonlinear metaphor about *changing the rules*. The international community was forced to perceive the issues in a new way. But the locals, who lived quite outside the domain of this global media event, reacted in a knee-jerk manner to what they perceived to be an insult to local hegemony. Not only were *their* rules not changed, but a few of the fishermen actually went out of their way to kill more dolphins than before. Unfortunately, as time passed, and the Japanese federal statutes were changed to accommodate the new international rule, nothing emerged to sway local sentiments concerning the need to continue to kill dolphins.

I reach this conclusion only because the fishermen themselves were never anything but the dupes of the event. The dolphin liberator had never really tried to include them in his very public program for change. Consequently, of all the potential lessons implicit in the metaphor about changing the rules, the Japanese fishermen learned this one best of all: it is still quite all right to kill dolphins, although from now on we do best to keep the slaughter out of the news. Otherwise, the fishermen knew they'd get burned again.

Yet the liberator's ecosabotage did succeed in imposing limits on the dolphin slaughter because it prompted the rest of the world to advocate an essential neighborly respect for migratory dolphins, who are the property of *all* nations and thus *no* nations. Conversely, the actual changes that resulted from this act of dolphin liberation were achieved by insulting both fishermen and government in front of the cameras of the entire Western world. A change from without if there ever was one.

And there lies the great dichotomy implicit within any act of ecosabotage: this *external* act of dolphin liberation *did* affect the dolphin slaughters. That liberator may have actually saved an entire species in that part of the world. Just exactly the same way that Ben, Ted, and I alienated a poor Mexican reef fisherman while saving an endangered turtle. In other words, all the Americans in this story end up saving something or other, without any of us really translating our own deep spiritual love of immanent nature into an idiom fit to touch the heart of a Japanese or Mexican fisherman. We treated the symptoms without offering any measure of self-prevention, protected one system by insulting another. On that important level, we failed where we also succeeded. Ultimately, there is but one tenacious moral to be gleaned from this two-sided parable: once again, we see that the crisis in the environment is a crisis in perception.

Now, years later, sipping one of Ted's margaritas in the cool shade of a tent pitched within the serene desert that is Baja California, I cannot help but reconstruct the confused desperation of the Iki islanders in the tense aftermath of that courageous but partially counterproductive act of dolphin emancipation. A decade after the incident occurred, I do not know how to answer when someone asks if the dolphins are still being killed in the

Sea of Japan. The fishermen learned their lesson well. They have become experts at keeping the lid on what they perceive as *their own* affairs.

Any evangelical attitude imposed from the outside that preaches either a hard and fast rule (you are *not allowed* to kill dolphins or elephants or wolves, etc.) or spiritual materialism (the alternative will make you *better people*), fails to offer any lasting rationale for change. No reform program can ever hope to elicit the enduring support of the majority of people if they feel shut out of the decision-making process. Likewise, imposing the good in the form of a conflict, no matter how good we may believe it to be, makes the locals dig their heels in and resist.

You may well ask what other approach toward changing the rules could any foreigner have taken at Iki Island? Spiritual ecology offers one path. It starts from the premise that any destruction of an ecosystem is also, by default, fundamentally destructive to the destroyers as well. It is to the exploiters' best interests to change—not because they are good if they do, and bad if they do not, but because nobody can survive for long living in their own physical or emotional garbage. We should have collaborated with the fishermen to devise strategies to prepare them for the world of the seventh generation. The Peace Corps offers one very realistic model of this approach.

But the fishermen's behavior at Iki Island represents only one category in what is an entire panoply of environmental idiocracy— rule by idiotic policy. Consider another common manifestation of environmental activism. In this case, those on the inside, meaning the people who believe they live and interact within an environment, end up in stiff opposition to those acting from without, most often represented by the forces of an impersonal state or economy. For example, even at Iki Island, the national government kept interceding from above, in the reprehensible act of nurturing a continuation of the slaughters as the birth of a new industry. This very confusing intercession occurred despite a growing *local* advocacy for human/dolphin coexistence.

When we generalize this model, we find that such external meddling represents a recurring pattern of environmental abuse committed by big government practically everywhere around the planet. The pattern is the same, no matter whether the government is democratic or communist, totalitarian or socialist. Look at it this way. Sea turtles, whose ancestry goes back several hundred million years, have dwindled to the point of extinction. This has occurred entirely within the past fifty years. If they were more human, they might want to know why books on modern political theory never discuss the implicit responsibility that big government must accord sea turtles.[3] From their hard-shelled perspective, contemporary human government—whether we want to name it a politburo, a supreme court, American freedom, communist oppression, China, Mexico, or anything else—has unequivocally failed the sea turtles. Social commentator Theodore Roszak, for one, has described this political blindness with great anger:

> We are finally coming to recognize that the natural environment is the exploited proletariat, the downtrodden nigger of everybody's industrial system. . . . Nature must also have its natural rights.[4]

It seems pertinent to probe a bit deeper into this recurring pattern. To do so I will use as an example the mechanical structures of democracy as it relates to nature. I choose democracy not because it offers any unique pathology, but simply because it is the system I know best.

Democracy rules by consensus. In the spirit of this shared power, it inevitably requires layer upon layer of proof and counterproof before any meaningful action is ever taken. In terms of the environment, there is a very positive side to this democratic coin. The orca darting, for example, demonstrated just how a group of common citizens, environmental activists all, might shout loudly enough to void a law handed down by the governing bureaucracy.

But there are 3 major problems facing every democratic system. First, with so many factions needing to assert themselves, each demanding a turn to express both voice and power, the momentum for change often becomes unbearably sluggish. Second—a trait common to every political system—those who actually hold the reins of power use more than a fair share of that power just to retain power. That translates to mean that those who are in control in the status quo are always going to possess more power (and more momentum to retain that power) than even the most vocal minority. Third, in terms of the actual wielding of power, the economic and the political spheres—capitalism and democracy, democracy and capitalism—are two sides of the same coin. We can thus restate problem number two to mean that a successful capitalist possesses more power within government than even the most vocal minority. And because power often exists in direct proportion to the size of business, big business holds more power than small business.

The interaction among these problems of democracy has proven itself an unmitigated disaster in terms of transforming our destructive relationship to the environment. I express an opinion shared by many others[5] when I declare that capitalism has always fired the exploitation of natural resources. Lumber, electronics, petroleum, steel, autos are just a few of the industries that make up the treads upon which democracy bulldozes down the road of progress. But almost every other form of government also grants an extra portion of power to those who would maintain the economic status quo. If there is any substantial difference among the diverse political-economic systems of the world, it is not one of *kind*, but a difference in *degree*. In a word, capitalism has fired the greatest success. For example, the perestroika policies of Mikhail Gorbachev reflect the accomplishments of capitalism perhaps better than the rantings of any American jingoist.

But such success is bittersweet, a paradoxical kind of success that, incidentally,[6] degrades the environment more than any other motivating factor within human culture. For example, consider a statement made by a Washington State apple grower that seems to echo the apple-growing methods of Snow White's wicked witch as much as it does modern agriculture. This grower has just learned that the public has organized a boycott against his product because of a report linking chemical spraying with cancer in children. Acknowledging that children's health is a serious concern, he finds no irony in defending his own need to use poisonous Alar because: "We are forced to grow the very best fruit we can."[7]

Referring back to problem two above, big business, no matter what banner it decides to wave from its flagpole, has accrued more power to retain its own destructive self-interest than any grass-roots environmentalist (working from an ethical base) can gather to stop it. And when problems one, two, and three interact, big business exercises its disproportionate power base to further slow what is already a sluggish rate of change. Sluggishness, an inherent trait of democracy, not only favors the status quo, but is also a basic tool for retaining power in the hands of the controlling group. Sluggishness perpetuates the status quo.

That is why, within a democracy, the burden of proof always rests squarely upon the shoulders of anyone demanding change. The *burden of proof* has nothing to do with righteousness and very little to do with expediency. It is best regarded as a default set of brakes utilized to deter or weaken policy changes that might affect big business and big government, no matter how obvious or how dire the consequences. So our neighbor the apple grower invokes the burden of proof in all due righteousness:

> Claims of health hazards have not been substantiated, and are not even close to being substantiated . . . the report [which actually offers evidence linking the chemical Alar to cancer; *author's note*] is witchcraft.[8]

The government, itself, often ends up taking either no action or, more usually, very slow action. So in this case, the Environmental *Protection* Agency, the government agency delegated with the responsibility to police the use of such chemicals, went ahead and kept the poison on the market. It decided to protect the economic interests of apple growers to the detriment of children who drink apple juice. But fortunately, at that point, something else started to happen. While such situations unquestionably turn government sluggish, they also tend to push the citizenry to direct action. Citizens very quickly lose confidence that government serves their best interests. In this case, the consumer simply stopped buying apples. In other words, everybody lost.

When growers realize they are losing *business,* they soon decide on their own to stop spraying. And when the growers have stopped using the poison, government finally passes laws that ban the use of that particular poison. Unfortunately, new poisons are often substituted for old ones.

The frustrating lesson is this: One of the very best ways to instigate a change in democratic law, especially as it relates to the environment of the seventh generation, is to act as if the government has no real power, and that *the people do.* When the leaders of government realize that their mandate to govern has quietly slipped out through the back door of citizens' direct action, they finally seize upon the first *expedient* action. They act quickly, just to get their power base back.

Given this process—the very ponderous relationship between government, its citizenry, and the environment—is it any wonder that we are daily confronted with the growing disobedience known as ecotage or ecosabotage? In the early 1970s, for example, someone calling himself The Fox plugged up factory smokestacks, and on one occasion diverted liquid toxic waste from a U.S. Steel plant into the chief executive's office.

Given the current state of affairs, what else is one to do? Does a good environmentalist stay law-abiding and work within the system? Obviously, the traditional answer is yes. Isn't that what government is for? Isn't that what democracy means? Isn't anything else simply lawless, an affront to democratic process? For example, why do citizens often feel unpatriotic or guilty, or both, when they organize boycotts against such as apple growers? Or for that matter, what fantasy about right and wrong might actually prompt some parents to prefer feeding potentially poisoned apples to their children rather than join the boycott? In another disturbing instance, journalist Noel Perrin describes how a group of conservative Minnesota farmers discovered that the power companies were about to lay several hundred miles of power lines across their properties, while also maneuvering to deny the farmers any legal recourse to express their strong opposition. Perrin begins his piece by asking a series of probing questions:

What if the system seems to be corrupt? What if the very people in the system who are charged with protecting the environment are the ones who betray it? What if the forest service itself builds roads at taxpayer expense in order to facilitate the clear-cutting of great swaths of our national forests? What if high officials of the Environmental Protection Agency simply announce that they've decided not to enforce the laws the environmentalist got passed? . . . Does the good environmentalist sigh a little and start gathering signatures? Go back to court again? Or does he turn militant, and stage a sit-in in the National Forest? Maybe even drive spikes in the great helpless trees?[9]

It's a hard decision either way. Those who continue to buy apples for their children's snacks might argue persuasively that ecosabotage is criminal. Yet others argue, just as persuasively, that ecosabotage is the only way left at this eleventh hour, and is an especially good response because it is a dramatic gesture that ends up recruiting more support for its cause.

I offer what may actually seem to be a fairly obvious prediction. The anthropocentric rationale built into the ground floor of the business-government structure is going to push a lot more people toward the cause of ecosabotage before it pushes a lot fewer. As time passes, ecosabotage has to emerge as a clear-cut path for people trying to protect the seventh generation from the excesses of the system. If things get bad enough, then this vigilante mentality could alter the system as drastically as any revolution. More hopefully, it will not need to do so because nature will have become part of the status quo.

The Colville Indians, who once lived along the shoreline of the Columbia River, tell a myth about the river monster, Nashlah, who has been eating all the people, human and animal,[10] who travel up and down the river in their canoes. The trickster, Coyote, comes to the rescue by allowing himself to be swallowed into the belly of the monster. He lights a bonfire from the detritus of former victims, while proceeding to cut up the monster's heart to both warm and feed all the half-dead animals inside. As the monster succumbs to his wounds he coughs up all the animals who are thus saved.

But this is only the start of the relationship between sea monster and Coyote. The second half of the myth recounts the resurrection of the monster. Nashlah is now accorded a strict admonition against killing anyone traveling on the river. Even the most dangerous predator is a part of the status quo and so deserves certain rights to live and eat. In this instance, our monster neighbor is permitted to shake any canoe that passes directly over his pool. Nashlah is now regarded as the mythological keeper of an actual rapids along the Columbia River. And finally this:

> The law that Coyote made still stands. The monster does not swallow people as before Coyote took away his big power. Sometimes he draws a canoe under and swallows the people in it. But not often. Usually the Indians take their canoes out of the water and carry them round the place the monster lives.[11]

And whereas Jesus preached that we should love our neighbor as ourselves, at best our own society only perceives humans, and a few humanized pets, as our bona fide neighbors. By contrast, the Colville myth strips Jesus's injunction of all its species-specific implications by including the ecosystem, itself, as the very foundation of neighborhood. The transgressor has been admonished, but also reeducated to find his own beneficial place within that expanded vision of neighborhood. The Indians use the myth to teach their children that they must portage their canoes around those rapids called Nashlah. The implicit lesson is that there are no external, preordained laws guiding behavior from outside the natural environment. Or, to be most precise, there is just one preordained law: that all species must act with great respect for one another. Rules governing actions are applied from *within,* and molded very carefully to fit the specific situation at hand. Whatever other laws we are able to discern here are molded and modified of the people, for the people, and by the people of the neighborhood to fit the people of the neighborhood.

And although Abraham Lincoln also preached that a democratic government is of the people, for the people, and by the people, in fact the Gettsysburg Address never meant to delineate anyone besides human beings as *the people* of this democratic American republic. By contrast, poet Gary Snyder has written:

> What we must . . . do . . . is incorporate the other people . . . the creeping people, and the standing people, and the flying people and the swimming people . . . into the councils of government.[12]

So the story of Nashlah strips Lincoln's phrase of all species implications; it includes *all* species/people as the very foundation of citizenship. This all-inclusive embrace offers us a faraway glimmer of a new kind of democracy based on very old principles. In this version of government, it is the ecosystem rather than the nation-state that becomes the wellspring of political consciousness. Human governments may still govern human activity, but now they are founded upon the inclusive precepts of spiritual ecology.

The boundaries of nation-states are mapped out to follow the natural borderlines of bioregions and watersheds. Constitutions provide rules to guide human behavior as it reasserts its fundamental connection to Gaea, the goddess who is Earth. The song of the seventh generation is sung as a national anthem. Indeed, here is a different vision of democracy, one that exists in total support of environmental activism—not as just another political faction among many, but as the actual context of government. A way of life that embraces all life.

For the human experiment to succeed into the next millenium, the paradigm of environmental salvation must issue from within the breast of each one of us. Easy to say. But, by what mechanism is this supposed to transpire? I, for one, tend to get fidgety when I hear talk about a new religion of ecology, and yet here I am writing a book titled *Spiritual Ecology*. A spiritual solution? Imagine the reaction of a rhino harvester in Mozambique; or a rhino horn importer in Abu Dhabi; or a Saudi rhino consumer shopping for a gem-encrusted rhino-horn knife, which has been de rigeur in the outfit of a well-dressed prince for almost a thousand years. Or for that matter, imagine the reaction of a

U.S. politician who votes down any and all measures to protect endangered rhinos because he is also receiving PAC money from mideast oil interests.

A spiritual solution? No, not exactly. Spiritual ecology offers instead a perceptual solution that can then lead to a spiritual change of heart. If a majority of the world population could learn to place respect for the Earth above its own material success, and if at the same time the *haves* who live in the so-called industrial countries could learn to replace mindless consumption with voluntary simplicity, environmental healing would occur rapidly.[13]

But whose time span do we use to measure how *rapid* the healing is? After all, this is no harmonic convergence of mere minutes. Nor is it even the global achievement of a billion people in 150 countries tied to a TV broadcast of the Olympics for ten days. Instead, I take a highly opinionated stab at the figures and say that environmental healing must last at least 100 years. That is the low human end of it. If the Bengal tigers, the blue whales, the temperate rain forests of Vancouver Island, or the California condors were capable of orchestrating this hypothetical revolution in consciousness, they might prefer 200 or even 300 years. Once again, we find ourselves setting our watch commensurate to the much longer time span expressed by the seventh generation. Joanna Macy advocates millenia. Furthermore, the entire human race has to agree to this healing with one selfless voice and with one unilateral action.

In that light, indulge me as I stretch an already overstretched myth. Although the story of the hundredth monkey[14] has been largely discredited, if enough of us dream it together, perhaps we can reinstate it. So, I heave a deep sigh and implore you to *believe* in the healing of the planet, for belief is a crucial mechanism in healing a planet or anything else. Simultaneously, and on a much more pragmatic level, those of us already committed to the healing must continue to chip away at the degradation whenever and wherever it shows its ugly face. We must continue to free both turtles and democracies. Tread gently. Go in fellowship.

I returned with some friends to that same area in the Sea of Cortez just three months later. We were a group of ten *norteamericanos* who had chartered a boat for two weeks and set sail from La Paz, Baja California, in search of interactions with friendly marine mammals. One evening late in the trip, six of us left the overcrowded nest of the boat to sleep on the beach of an otherwise uninhabited islet.

In the morning, one of our party, Chip, rows the boat's dinghy to shore to pick us up. His first words to us are disturbing. Late last night a group of local fishermen visited the boat to request that our Mexican skipper deliver a huge caguama to the university in La Paz. The turtle is destined to go to a biology professor who is conducting a long-term research project on the subject of turtle fertility.

Chip reminds us that these same fishermen had earlier granted us permission to clam along the reef just offshore from their village. Just yesterday they had given us ten gallons from their own precious store of diesel fuel. We were all outwardly grateful for their kindness. Now they want us to return the favor by delivering this turtle. Chip takes care to accentuate the crucial issue of *simpatico*, asking that each of us consider the cultural implications of the fishermen's request.

Christoph, who is an undergraduate majoring in environmental studies, is the first to speak up. He believes that we are obligated to deliver the turtle as a gesture in support of science in general, and turtle research in particular. Science is an important and positive cause that deserves our unmitigated support. In his estimation, this particular turtle may rightly aid the future cause of all Baja turtles. Furthermore, our affirmative gesture of neighborliness can only bolster any aspirations we may hold of returning to the Sea of Cortez in the future.

The rest of us aren't so sure. Mela expresses a gut reaction of nausea over the prospect of transporting a live and vigorous turtle down in the two-foot by two-foot hold of our boat for at least three, and possibly four more days. Mary Clayton, a nurse, reacts even more strongly to what she considers to be Christoph's naive presumption of benign laboratory research. She finds the very concept of animal experimentation to be repugnant. As a nurse she has seen her share of it, and, in conclusion, does not want us to show support for that methodology by offering our boat as a transport vehicle.

Norton asks about the particular research to be levied upon this particular turtle. Chip explains that the integrity of the head fisherman seems utterly beyond reproach. The man had spent several hours on board last night and it was very clear that he was a close *compadre* of our much-respected skipper as well as the first mate. But to answer the question, the fisherman had been out front in stating that the professor had never discussed the details of the research with any of the locals. The fisherman didn't have a clue as to the fate of the turtle once the research was culminated. To his thinking, it also seemed entirely beside the point.

I cannot help but speculate out loud on one potential scenario: the turtle is dissected by the professor for a room full of second-year biology students. Christoph objects to my fantasy and so proposes an alternative: the turtle is stripped of its eggs, which are then incubated in a lab to insure a much higher percentage of survivors. After all, scientists everywhere are working to insure the preservation of the endangered caguama species. Like Mela, Katy reiterates the practical issue of our boat's tiny hold: a stressed-out turtle that dies in transport serves no one.

Chip explains that our skipper wishes us to vote on the matter; after all, we have paid a lot of money for this charter. So we bring the matter to a vote. The "nays" win the day—the turtle will not be transported back to La Paz in *our* boat. Then a second motion is placed on the floor. If (and only if) the moment seems diplomatically correct, we will offer to buy the turtle from the fishermen with the stated intent of returning it unharmed back to the sea. We vote again, and the motion is passed unanimously.

Back at the boat, the skipper stares at me incredulously as I boldly announce that we, as a group, have agreed to pass on his offer to ferry the turtle to La Paz. He fumbles a moment to find his voice, and then reminds me in quicksilver Spanish of the great favor the fisherman had done us with the clams and the diesel fuel. The fishermen who stand beside him nod in agreement. I shake my head, thank the fishermen directly for their kindness, but then state that clams are one thing, and an endangered sea turtle quite another.

After an intense discussion in which the first mate appeals in vain to what he considers to be my obviously flawed spirit of *simpatico,* the visibly embarrassed skipper tells me that, yes, he will abide by the group's decision. The fishermen click their tongues in disappointment. I look at my hands. A full minute of silence. Finally, the skipper turns to the fishermen and asks them to get the turtle out of the hold. My jaw drops open; the deed has already been done? I'm glad I didn't know that before. Two muscular fishermen stride to the stern and grunt and groan as they try to extricate what proves to be the very largest green turtle I have ever seen in my life. It is easily five times the size of the one caught in the reef net three months earlier. This caguama could be that one's ancestor, counting a lifespan of a hundred years or more. We all notice that the reptile is much too large to fit into the hold in any other position but upended and diagonal; quite unable to move beyond thumping the walls with its single free limb. Now it is my turn to grimace at the skipper. How could he have facilitated such inhumane treatment?

Four fishermen grunt and pull and finally hoist the turtle out of the hold, over the gunwales, and into their own *panga* where it is unceremoniously deposited upon its back with a loud clatter. The head fishermen smiles up at me; job concluded; and hey, no hard feelings, okay? If we want to dig for clams, we can use his beach anytime. Anytime.

I smile back, and hesitatingly offer to buy the turtle. To this proposition I quickly add, "Just to set it free." The fisherman, a bull of a man in his early thirties, squints into the sun, emits a short friendly chuckle and slowly shakes his head: No, sorry, this turtle has been snared for the sole purpose of research. Actually, it is no longer his property to buy or sell.

From the tone of his voice, I am made quite aware that this ocean man gives much power to his collaboration with the distant university professor. He wants to know if I can understand how he feels? "Yes, certainly, I do understand, but can you understand how I feel."

He stares at me a moment without committing himself one way or the other, and then this, "We feel exactly the same. I agree with you, it is a shame that the once plentiful turtles are now so rare. Especially the big ones. I would not have caught such an *abuela* [grandmother] unless I felt that the professor might be able to make them return to their former numbers. And just in case you're interested, I am receiving no money for this turtle."

Unfortunately, and no matter what he, himself, chooses to say about it, the two of us do not feel exactly the same about it. The beach in front of his little isolated *pueblo* had been littered with the bones of too many recently killed sea turtles. Bones, but almost no shells, which are sold for guitar picks, combs, and bracelets.

There is nothing left to do. The two of us shake hands. No recriminations, no lectures. Soon he motors off with his crew and his turtle, headed directly for the *gringo* yacht that just set anchor a mile down the beach. But I cannot wish him luck, although he is sure to find some boat willing to transport the caguama across a hundred miles of inland sea to La Paz. If not, he'll just have to make the run himself.

Days pass slowly out here on the Sea of Cortez. Long hot and sunny days filled with vistas of exquisitely bizarre coastal land-forms, manta rays somersaulting from the water like so much giant popcorn in the kettle of the ocean, sea lions swimming right up to us as we explore the reefs that cluster along the shoreline. So also there are sweaty hikes along memorable uncharted beaches littered with the strewn skeletons of long-dead sea creatures, known and unknown.

Significantly, none of us is able to shake the phantom pres-ence of that old turtle. Had it not been for our own stubborn foresight, there it would lie, upended and thrashing one limb in the torture chamber of a storage hold. The wind comes up. A loose rope thumps against the deck. We look at one another and end up staring instead into the eyes of a dying turtle. We sail together across a shiny glass ocean, each of us thinking the same turtle thoughts. Finally, we arrive back in port. By this time, all the discussions have come down to one essential question: How might any of us be able to help the general cause of turtles? Discussions proliferate to explore the possibilities.

In my own estimation the prize goes to this one: Print a broadside in both Spanish and English that delineates the complex issue of turtle economics in the simplest language possible. Avoid fury. Include a list of all the restaurants in La Paz, Loreto, Guaymas, Cabo, Mazatlan, Puerto Vallarta, Acapulco, etc., that *do not offer turtle* on their menus. Plead for a boycott of all the rest. Send this list to travel agents everywhere. Likewise, post the broadside in each one of the acceptable hotels and in restaurants. Hand it to every *gringo* in sight. Yes, most ironically, focus on the *gringos*. Turtle meat has become scarce. The price has skyrocketed. The only people who can afford to order it are American tourists desiring to sample the novelty of a once-traditional cuisine.

Chapter Seven

The One That Got Away

Water excels in benefiting the myriad creatures without contending with them.

—Lao Tzu[1]

Every August a group of friends journeys to the straits that separate Vancouver Island from the mainland of Canada; a small crew of animal lovers bent on developing a long-term musical communication link with the orcas who frequent the area. And as is typical with so many other campers, we never fail to make a grocery stop at the last major town along the highway. Three weeks of food supplies are routinely gathered during a leisurely hour-long stroll down some supermarket aisle. Eventually the filled cart is pushed to the checkout counter, where the items are placed on a moving belt for the value assigned each one to be read off by machine. Finally, paper engraved with the portraits of old men or monuments to old men—that which we call money—is traded for three weeks of sustenance. The items are collected in paper sacks, carried to the car, driven north to the road's end, loaded into our inflatables and kayaks, and so carried over the water to a wilderness site, which, over the years has taken on the name of Orcananda.

We finally arrive in camp, set up our sleeping tents, construct a camp kitchen that looks like an assemblage of flotsam and 16-penny nails, and so start the three-week process of rationing our food into thrice-daily communal meals. A scrutiny of the produce used in preparing any single meal also serves as our camp clock. Produce that perishes quickly, like lettuce and peaches, is consumed during the first week or two. By the end of four weeks, we're all feeling quite grateful for the limp carrots and sprouting potatoes that add a final nutritional zest to the otherwise heavy tablefare of grains, beans, nut butters, and too much granola.

Let it also be known that every bit of food we carry in from the outside world is vegetable. Interestingly enough, this decision to haul no meat is not the result of any set policy. It is, instead, determined afresh every year by the project managers. Likewise, for ten years running the general consensus in camp has applauded these managers for having made the right choice. However, let it also be said that the path leading to this dietary agreement is anything but straightforward. If, for example, twelve people inhabit Orcananda wilderness camp at one time, then you can bet the store that there are twelve different philosophies guiding individual dietary preferences. The diners run the gamut from the purist vegetarian to the laissez-faire junk fooder; from those who prefer a meal of salads to the meat-and-potatoes kind of guy.

The individual food preferences of this tiny camp appear to be a representative cross section of the way the culture at large relates to its food. Yet if the most carnivorous of our party can survive quite contentedly without mammal or poultry flesh for the entire month, one has to believe that the entire civilization could just as easily transform its eating habits for extended periods of time.

I am one of those in camp who has altered his usual eating habits, albeit not as drastically as some others. So, let me don the cap of Everyman and describe my own changes in diet as one possible path that could just as easily occur generally. This seems worthwhile, if for no other reason than the fact that humanity's relationship to food-getting describes one of the most destructive forces currently loose upon the surface of the Earth. We are eating the planet without feeding it in return.

Our species eats the Earth in two related ways: directly, typified by the ancient example of North Africans overgrazing their goats in the scrub forests that eventually eroded to become the Sahara Desert; and indirectly, typified by the contemporary example of Nepali peasants devastating Himalayan forests to provide firewood for cooking.

Plant a commercial acre of soybeans. Three months later, the harvest of soybeans may end up feeding just a few beef cattle, which in turn can provide cholesterol-saturated protein for just a few people. But those same soybeans, if consumed directly, would provide the same amount of unsaturated fat and protein to *ten* times as many people. In other words, if we all decided to stop eating meat today, we would immediately preserve major portions of our environment from the destructiveness of grazing, while also increasing our own chances of long life.

Every year, new books are written that offer the latest ream of statistics proving that we need to change our diet. We read them, yet we do not change. I know half a hundred of those statistical implications by heart and could easily pepper this chapter with hints and cajolements about impending heart disease inextricably linked to environmental ruination. How can I presume to do so? I know the facts, yet I also continue to eat a small (very small) amount of meat.

I avoid most chicken because the birds are kept in inhumane cages; that induces stress in the birds, leading to poultry meat laced with undue residues of adrenaline. Worse still, feed-lot chickens receive a diet that contains generous doses of antibiotics and hormones. And finally, there are reports that conclude that 30 percent of all poultry bought in the United States contains *Salmonella* bacteria. In conclusion, I choose not to eat chicken for the same reason I do not eat much junk food: because, in effect, mass-produced chicken is junk food. And when we disconnect food from its primary worth, as sustenance for a healthy body, we also promote our own ill health. However, despite that, I still eat an occasional chicken when I am able to find one from a good organic source.

I have abolished red meat from my diet for the same reasons, to which I add another of some significance. Most of us never think about meat as anything but brown lumps wrapped in plastic. Here is one more noncontextual artifact, this one generated from the bodies of formerly living creatures who are raised, slaughtered, and sold as units of flesh. The pig takes off its pig disguise, now to be shown as sausage. But to eat the beast is to become the beast. In this case, to consume such a nonbeast means that one must also ignore a critical interpenetrating compact that exists between all creatures who participate in the relationship of predator and prey. Simply put, those little brown disks strewn across your pepperoni pizza were once a pig. When we disconnect food from its source, we end up promoting that very same pervasive separatism that disjoins culture from environment. Eat a pizza, promote disconnectedness. The crisis in perception rears its ugly head once again.

I have decided to make the bond that exists between eater and eaten real in my life by acknowledging my own role in what is both a murder (by me) and a sacrifice (by the mammal). Until the day comes that I feel adequate to the task of slaughtering that pig, that lamb, that cow, I shall feel inadequate to the task of eating the beast. But of course, that day is never going to come. Call me unreasonable, but that which I cannot slaughter with my own two hands, I choose not to consume. I do not even need to wield the axe myself. Rather, I only need to feel capable of such a violent act. I am not. Are you?

However, I admit it. My eyes, my nose, and especially my stomach do not always stay in line behind the vegetarian resolve set down by heart and mind. I offer no apology for the fact that once in a very great while I find myself succumbing to the lure of liverwurst, or hamburger, or bacon. But while others might call this my fall, I offer no common cause with some animal rightists who transform their strict vegetarianism into a kind of culinary class struggle that separates *them* from *us*. This is no religious inquisition, no food fascism. Nor does the gardener in me easily identify with the argument that differentiates plant sentience from animal sentience. Despite the legacy of Linnaeus, the life force cannot be so cavalierly separated into classes administered by a rule of hard and fast ethics. Such a categorization of gustatory worthiness seems part and parcel of the reductivist problem rather than the holistic solution. When we noster, we perceive the life force as a process of connectedness that animates the entire biota, whether beet or beef. And while the occasional use of animal flesh should never attain the status of a mortal sin, the gradual forfeit of the red-meat-eating lifestyle must be recognized as a fundamental dictum of spiritual ecology.

Perhaps a more fruitful argument would be based upon the relative fertility of the beings we choose to consume as food. A cow drops a single calf after a seasonal pregnancy. Furthermore, that calf gulps down prodigious amounts of food, and grazes across a sizable plot of land before it is ever ready for market. A farmyard chicken, on the other hand, drops an egg every few days for months and months at a time. Or finally, the beet demands a few square inches of soil and a few month's time to produce several dozen seed pods. The moral is obvious: eat more beets than beef.

There is another level of comparison. The beet raised commercially may be sprayed with chemicals that seep into the ground water, which ultimately affects much more than the compact turf of any single beet. Using this measure of comparison, the organically raised beet serves both the environment and the individual better than the sprayed beet. Another moral: eat more organic beets and fewer sprayed beets.

Were life so straightforward. Were this writing so straightforward. I started out by declaring, perhaps a bit too loudly, that we carry no meat into this wilderness environment. Now I am going to spend the next several paragraphs extolling the virtues of catching and eating fish. However, I warn you in advance that what at first may seem to offer certitude about a particular eating preference will soon break free from its tethers. When that happens I will summarize the entire issue of food-getting with a parable whose message is both tragic and unavoidable. Ultimately, the human quest for food describes one of the primary forces affecting the planetary ecosystem. There lies the crux of the problem of the murderer and the murdered, of the conflict between ourselves and our food. On such a gruesome note of introduction, I divulge that for years now I have been the dominant fisherman of this wilderness camp.

I venture out onto the water at least every second day in an attempt to augment the heavy, fibery cuisine with fresh salmon, lingcod, or yelloweye rock fish. And although the vegetarians among us are sometimes quick to point out that, indeed, we are not dependent upon these fishing trips for our survival, the success of these expeditions provides us with a major source of protein as well as our only real source of fresh food. So our camp menu is somewhere between that of a traditional hunting tribe—where the choices are few but almost everything is fresh—and the typical U.S. urban diet—where everything under the sun is readily available, while even the food we label as fresh is never less than several days old.

Freshly caught fish satisfies all the criteria I have imposed upon myself concerning eating or not eating meat. First, I have convinced myself, with possible good cause, that there is no environmental stigma attached to the catching and eating of a mere fifteen fish landed during the one month we inhabit this place each year. Second, these fish lay hundreds, thousands, even hundreds of thousands of eggs every season. Third, these fish are fresh and nearly unadulterated food. I add the adverb "nearly" because I have also been told that even polar bears contain residues of DDT and PCB in their livers, no doubt supplied by some riverine runoff half a world away. Fourth, I am quite capable of killing the fish myself, which I choose to do as soon as it is pulled out of the water.

Over the years of my fishing experience, the equipment and the prey species may have grown ever larger, but otherwise things have tended to stay within a simple and easily comprehensible framework. Then one recent summer, an event occurred that drastically altered my own predatory relationship to the fish.

I poked around the camp in the usual way, asking if anyone would like to join me for an hour while I attempted to catch the community's dinner. Gabriel volunteered first, offering to run the motor over and back to the fishing hole. Then Sandra volunteered, punning that I could use a good networker. We piled the tackle box, the rod and reel, and the oversized net into the inflatable boat, and proceeded to go a mile up the coast to a favorite fishing hole.

One was apt to hook any of several species. First is the lingcod, a slinky creature with a toothy crocodile's snout and the coloration of camouflage fatigues. The year previously I had landed a thirty-pound ling in this same spot. When the fish was sliced open during the cleaning process, a five-pound salmon fell out of its belly. I have since learned to free all such large lingcod. Not only do they not taste as good as a fish half their size, but also, the larger the fish, the more apt it is to be a reproducing female.

Second is any of several species of salmon including sockeye, coho, king, dog, or pink. Each variety is uniquely tasty, as well as a genuine thrill to land. But the prize of the five, the sockeye, is nearly impossible to hook on rod and reel; and the flesh of either the pink or the dog suffers drastically in comparison with the other three. However, cohos and small kings are reasonably easy to catch and thus become a dinner entrée frequently. However, salmon are also among the richest of all food fish, so we find ourselves unable to enjoy them any more often than every third night. We usually cook them over a smoky bed of alder, sometimes basting them with a marinade of butter, garlic, lemon, and dill.

Third is the six-gilled shark. Some swear that it is both edible and delicious, although the creature has never graced our own table. Two years earlier I hooked a six-footer, just about as big as any fish is apt to get in this environment. Because I was fishing alone, the shark proved to be much more than I could hope to handle. Foolishly and quite miserly, I attempted to release the fish by extricating the hook, trying to save a three-dollar lure instead of simply cutting the line. The shark rolled over, pushed off against the bow, and punctured the inflatable boat with its sharp dorsal spike. I immediately threw the fishing pole onto the floor while I looked at the slow-hissing hole. For its own part, the fish dove out of sight, dragging a hundred dollars worth of rod and reel along with it. That incident, more than any other, taught me never to fish alone in these waters.

It could have been worse. I could have hooked a halibut. More than one commercial fisherman has counseled me to carry a pistol or a gaff if I ever get serious about dropping a two-pound lure down along the deep sand banks that these dining-room table size flatfish choose to inhabit. The animal must, *must* be killed before any attempt is made to drag it into the boat. The legend of the beast includes stories of fish who slap so powerfully as to destroy entire boats, not to mention human life and limb. But toting a gun does not fit my image of what it means to go fishing. Nor does a gaff work inside an inflatable boat. Significantly, the charts tell me that there are no deep sand banks located within many miles of camp. Luckily, and despite my own fantasies, I have never yet hooked a halibut.

As I described the menu potential of each fish to Sandra, she answered each with a resounding no. Instead, she offered this bit of improbable soothsaying: "Today you are going to catch a red snapper. And so we don't have to take more than one life, I want it to be big enough to feed all twelve of us." Nice thought. Indeed, I had caught a medium-sized snapper just the week previously. Two snapper that size would have fed the camp. However, after many years fishing these waters, I had never seen a snapper large enough to feed twelve people. I stared at her and slowly shook my head. "How," I asked, "do you plan to conjure up such a snapper?"

Then she served up her own personalized substantiation of the rule of thumb that states that any twelve people generate *at least* twelve original themes on the subject of how we relate to what we put in our mouths. She smiled brightly and locked her eyes on mine. "I'm going to pray for it, of course!"

The afternoon was warm and sunny, the tide just about high and slack. I shut the motor off and reached for my tackle box to commence an arcane ritual of selection that only another fisherman could know and love. It took a few barb-filled minutes to sort through the tangle of colored feathers, metallic spoons, and flashy spinners before I selected a five-inch charcoal and white hunk of metal aggressively named the "buzz bomb." The bauble was secured to the line (which is rated, significantly, in pounds test—the greatest weight it can support without breaking) and immediately dropped over the side. I released the drag, which caused the monofilament to whir off the reel for a good half-minute before the lead lure finally hit bottom. My best estimates placed the buzz bomb on a rocky ledge about 150 feet straight down. Next, I reeled in four feet of line to keep the hooks from snagging on the bottom. I began to jerk the tip of the fishing rod sharply upward, which permits the lure to fall erratically, imbuing it with action.

Actually, fishing has a lot in common with talking on the telephone. But instead of sending our voice down the line, this time we send our dance. We imbue the lure with a life, not its own, but rather a reflection of the fisherman's own store of energy. We are puppeteers, and the dancing buzz bomb is a disguise: a marionette decked out to look like a wounded herring.

Within mere seconds I hooked something that arched the rod over double. "I've got a monster fish," I announced deadpan to Sandra, who answered by laughing goodnaturedly while lightly clapping her two index fingers together. I stood up, set the drag, and started to crank the reel. This was a serious fish. Every time it chose to lunge, the heavy tip of the rod bent completely into the water, peeling more line from the reel in the process. I turned the handle once, twice, three, ten times, always careful to allow the fish to match my mechanically compensated prowess with whatever juice it could muster from within its own survival-prone frame. Any less effort would have snapped the line.

But really, I must pause again because I do not wish to cultivate the kind of grandiloquent fish story that fills the pages of so many outdoor[2] magazines. This is no blood sport because, in all humility, it is no sport at all. The doyens of recreation portray fishing as if it were all a game. So the fish exists in a semantic limbo; a caricature of a living creature; devoid of a soul; misinterpreted as a cross between a sentient game ball and the trophy. Yet for my own part, just as I choose not to eat chickens because of the adrenaline pooled in their flesh, so I cannot measure the importance of fishing by the amount of adrenaline it pools in my own.

This does not mean, of course, that anyone denies the excitement implicit in hooking a big fish. But the standardized literature about fishing and hunting dwells too ardously and too indulgently on titillation to the detriment of burden. Likewise, if any transfer of emotion is to be made between author and reader, then let it not be one of thrills, but rather of probity. What sense of responsibility do I feel when I snuff out another life to nourish my own? If I am to be called a fisherman at all, then my mentors in this occupation are not of my own time. They are the native hunters, like the original beluga hunters of the MacKenzie delta, who comprehended the act of killing prey primarily as the ultimate gift of life force from one being to another. That which was once outside, is taken inside. Fishermen of the world, take note.

And let's be honest about it. Although any dance between human and fish certainly creates its own unforeseen dynamic, I would be lying to describe this event as a fair contest. This fish is no competitor. It possesses no just counter to my mechanically enhanced strength or my tactical experience. I am not *playing* this fish. Actually, my so-called opponent has only two possible options: pull until the line breaks, or, contrarily, swim directly at the line to generate enough slack to extricate a poorly set hook. Unfortunately for this particular fish, I am using thick, 25-pound test and I know how to tie my knots. Furthermore, I am a meticulous and seasoned proponent of the first law of fishing: once a fish is hooked, never let the line go slack. At worst, I might lose a fresh fish dinner and maybe a few modest moments of deflated self-esteem. The fish loses, as the Spanish say so well, *todo el mundo*—all the world.

This particular fish may have known everything about surviving sluggishly in a cold, dark, pressurized hole, but knew nothing about aerobic pacing. So the mythic struggle between man and beast ended in a mere five minutes. I cranked the line more vigorously now, easing the large fish out of its midnight universe and ever upward into the heady light of day.

Almost any fish brought to the surface from a depth of a hundred feet or more rapidly loses its ability to swim as the air sac within its abdominal cavity expands in relation to the declining water pressure. The sac may eventually inflate so much that it actually pushes through the fish's mouth like a swollen shiny tongue. The fish loses all ability to navigate and tends to float upward with the slow grace of a helium balloon. By the time it attains the surface, the poor creature is already well on its way to dying. In this particular instance, my victim suddenly ceased all fighting maneuvers about halfway to the surface. The line went limp, and all I needed do was reel it in.

Some believe that the most dramatic moment of the fishing experience occurs at first glimpse of the catch. No doubt because we primates are chiefly visual creatures. On a very human level, it consolidates the undeniable excitement of the first strike with the more utilitarian anticipation of *landing* the watery prey. On a superficial level, intellectual curiosity is also satisfied as we identify the formerly invisible quarry as a member of this or that species. Deeper still, this vision/bonding guides me to participate in the death throes of a fellow living creature who also happens to be a fish. A covenant is established that fulfills a critical obligation—one that must unite all predators to all prey. That which is outside starts its journey inside. Death is no ending because it is, instead, a shape shifting.

It is one thing to reach out and examine the void lump of a plastic-wrapped fish at the local meat counter, and quite another to first catch, then kill and gut the fish yourself. After years of doing just that, I still find myself grappling anew with the responsibility involved in taking the life of another. Yet paradoxically, here is where the deed turns itself inside out. When we avoid any direct responsibility for our own sustenance, we are also glossing over the central violent act of our lives. We relegate this much-needed memorandum about the unity of all life to the secondhand status of a trip to the supermarket. How was your own last night's dinner put to death?

Now, the dark shape rises from the depths nearly upside down and backward, with all of its hefty body following in helpless pursuit of a monstrously distended air sac. The dim shadow waving through the monochrome of the murky water gradually takes on substance and then hue.

Given the buildup, could you ever have doubted that the shape materializing before my eyes would reveal the unmistakable vermilion flush of a red snapper? I let out a gasp while Sandra eases the net into place. Now the creature pops to the surface, bouncing upon the still waters like a red beachball. In one motion, Sandra quickly slips the mesh over its body and attempts to lift the red, spiny alien over the side. But it is simply too large, so Gabriel, who has been mostly quiet throughout this process, steps in to offer a hand. The two of them heave upward and deposit the huge body onto the floor of the boat, where it lands with a dull thud. Ironically, the hook immediately falls out of the fish's mouth.

The yelloweye rockfish (*Sebastes ruberrimus*), misleadingly known hereabouts as the red snapper,[3] looks like nothing so much as a refugee from a tropical coral reef. Almost every fish found in these northern waters is either gunmetal gray, mottled brown, or shiny silver. The yelloweye is the exception. It possesses a brilliant, shocking, red-orange, square body tinged with sharp hints of mustard yellow set off by flashes of the purest white. But it is the eyes that stop you cold: utterly enormous flat yellow orbs with jet-black pupils. Its mouth is likewise ungainly, easily capable of swallowing a meal half as large as itself.

The yelloweye is a solitary creature, preferring to live out its life within one small nesting area. There, the female of the species may bear up to three million young at one time. At such an inconceivable rate of reproduction, a fecund yelloweye could just about spawn the equivalent of the entire human population of the United States during a single lifetime. Not to mention the geometric spawning of the next generation spawning the next generation, and the next, ad infinitum. But statistics are a plaything of the human mind, and numbers that unfold into other numbers through the logic of mathematics rarely act according to plan when confronted by the more mutable laws of nature. As it is, nearly none of that monumental spawn ever lives long enough to reach a size larger than a human tongue.

A well-known fish identification book will later inform me that the yelloweye "reaches *up to* thirty-six inches in length." The one lying before my feet is easily three or four inches longer than that. In other words, the miserable bloated creature shivering out of control on the deck of this boat is that rarest of rare creatures, perhaps one in a billion-billion yelloweye to achieve record size. I will also learn much later that the largest representatives of the species may live up to a hundred years. This fish may be just about as old as Sandra, Gabriel, and me put together. Wherever the numbers choose to fall, here is the largest snapper any of us has ever laid eyes upon.

Usually I display an unabashed sense of accomplishment at the moment of landing such a large fish. This time we stare at each other dumbfounded and embarrassed. My own spirits plummet, as if I have somehow committed a terrible, albeit inadvertent, crime. How dare any of us presume that such a magnificent being shall have died for the totally inappropriate purpose of being served up in a sauce of garlic and lemon juice? Had I the choice, I would no more have willed such an outlandish fish onto my hook than I would go into the forest and cut down a 300-foot redwood tree. Take it back! Please! I don't want it! And although I would later find no trace of spawn hidden within its lower abdomen, I intuited strongly that here before me lay a female of the species—matriarch of the yelloweye race, Grendel of the ocean bottom.

What I did next may prove itself a just measure of how much this catch had affected my peace of mind. Years previously, I had read that Eskimo hunters spit fresh water into the mouths of the animals they were about to kill. This, so the soul of the departed would not suffer thirst during its long sojourn up to heaven. Some Eskimo stories go so far as to justify the killing of seals and beluga whales as a favor granted to a desperate animal who gladly offers its body in trade for that fatal taste of fresh water. Now, I sat back against the gunwales and stared at the shivering fish for a full minute. I vocally begged its forgiveness: "I am sorry. I would throw you back if I could." I finally took a swig from a jar of iced tea, moved aside that pink-veined bulb of an air sac with my thumbs, and spat fresh liquid down the throat of the yelloweye. I sighed deeply and spoke one last time, "I just wish there was some way we could throw it back."

The three of us continued to watch the quivering animal for what seemed like a very long time. Slowly, I returned to the reality of the situation and picked up a wooden paddle. Like so many things about fishing, the coup de grace serves two quite unrelated functions. First, there is the act of pure mercy—

animal liberation at its most swift and brutal. Second, the immediacy of the kill insures that the flesh retains its freshness. I crouched down beside the fish and turned its plated, bony face toward my own, noticing for the first time that its yellow eyes had bulged half out of their sockets from the catastrophic change in water pressure. Whack!!! I struck once. Then again—bump!!! on the hard ridge between those golfball-sized eyes. The animal's vivid coloration instantly changed to a dull orange. The creature gave up its disguise. Novelist and fisherman, David James Duncan has described this moment as a kind of dance:

> It's strange to kill your dance partners. But that's what we did. We did it because the world is strange—because this is a world where no matter who you are or where you live or what you eat or whether you choose or don't choose to understand and be grateful, it is sacrifice—sweet bleeding sacrifice—that sustains you. So we killed two trout, but knew no sacrificial prayers, and so simply knelt by the river, commended them on how well they'd fought, whispered, "Swim little soul. Go be a bird, or a singing mouse, or a whale," then broke their bodies to sustain our own.[4]

Swim away little soul. Go be a bird, or a singing mouse, or a whale. Without any further ado, Gabriel yanked the outboard motor to life and headed us back up the coast. As I sat in the inflatable boat with visions of proud fishermen posed beside their outsized trophy fish swimming through my consciousness, I recalled one especially notable childhood memento.

On August 4, 1953, Alfred C. Glassell, Jr. caught a 1,560-pound, 14-foot 6-inch black marlin off the coast of Peru. Five years after that event, when I was eleven, *Field and Stream* magazine published an article about various world record fish replete with glorious photos. I tacked a black and white photograph of Alfred posed beside his marlin up onto my bedroom wall, where it remained for over a year. Mostly, I was impressed by the sheer disparity in size between the two beings. Alfred stood no taller than the marlin's formidable bill, which was identical in proportion to Alfred's tree trunk of a fishing rod. I now recall transforming the man's sweet victory scene into an object of preadolescent veneration. I examined the fetish daily in the hope that Alfred's own fantastic luck might somehow rub off on me as I fished locally for perch and trout.

Now I stare down at my own behemoth snapper and wonder what in heaven's name Alfred had done with such a fish? How many people did it feed? 500? 1,000? Actually, I have to doubt that Alfred's prize ever encountered such a utilitarian and democratic end. Trophy fishing was never meant to express utility or democracy. It is instead about men who would be gods, or at least aristocrats. Here is the modern myth about nature as a playing field, put out there for us to enjoy and conquer. To the victor goes the spoils: a larger-than-life trophy capable of demonstrating that man too, if but for a moment, can also be larger than life.

Alfred's trophy was almost certainly offered up to the taxidermist where flesh was parted from skin like a banana from its peel. Actually, the metaphor of the banana does not serve at all, because only a small proportion, if any, of the meat of a trophy fish is ever eaten. The rest is simply discarded. It is the skin, the peel, that is valuable. This is stretched around a form and treated with life-killing chemicals. Finally, the newly constructed configuration of a fish is painted and varnished in an attempt to synthesize the vibrancy that was once a spectacular sea creature. Perhaps the relic hangs, even today, upon the stuccoed wall of some Peruvian resort. There it continues to serve any trophy's primary function: at once taunting, challenging, and inspiring the imagination of each succeeding generation of trophy fishermen. So, in an imperfect emulation of a real fish, the trophy of a marlin is able to reproduce its own kind—spawning more trophies, cloning itself, sustaining the useless killing of ever greater numbers of marlin. And in the thirty-five years since that fish first felt the novel sensation of gravity as it lay dying upon the stern of Alfred's boat, no one else has ever caught a marlin of that size.

The preserving of large animals for human edification is certainly nothing unique to our culture. There are caves scattered high in the Swiss Alps that, very long ago, served as Neanderthal ceremonial sites. Some sections within a cave were utilized as workshops for the fashioning of tools associated with the bear hunt, while others served as sanctuaries for the worship of the bears that were killed. These latter grottos contain rock slab cabinets within which, even to this day, one can see row after neat row of cave bear skulls arranged in distinctively ritualized patterns. The discoverer of one of these caves, Emil Bächler, has commented on the special status of these grottos:

> What these finds reveal to us is a picture of the completely pious treatment of the largest, handsomest bones of spoils of the hunt, establishing the third section of the cave as a sanctuary, shut off by a tabu. In any case, they have nothing to do with the usual hoarding of bones of the hunt.[5]

These paleolithic cave chapels[6] are especially significant because they probably offer us the earliest known examples of human religion, that which has become popularized as the cult of the cave bear. As in so many totemic relationships, the people and the bear were one and the same. Just as these people may have invented the ceremony of burying their own dead, so they also journeyed high into the mountains to pay a song and dance homage to the sculpturally composed remnants of what was once a living animal. Now, 40,000 years later, we venture inside that same cave and cannot help but stand in awe before the colossal skulls of a long-extinct species of bear. Yet the only thing that lives on is our own lively speculation over the mystical purpose of an animal mortuary preserved for the ages through the ingenuity of protohuman handiwork. I, for one, also wonder if the exuberance of the Neanderthals' cult contributed to the eventual demise of the cave bear. Or for that matter, a deeper lesson in evolution—what if the extinction of the cave bear contributed to the parallel extinction of the Neanderthal race?

Should we venture to the resting place of the stuffed marlin, we would be similarly awed by the sight of that modern monster from the unknown. We might likewise speculate whether or not trophy fishing endangers the marlin population as the primitive cult may have wiped out cave bears. However, as there are rudimentary similarities between the two cults, so there are also vast differences. The contemporary trophy fisherman has no deep beliefs binding him to his prey. That is to say, a trophy is no totem. Alfred's fishing adventure thrives today as sport and vacation recreation, that which serves to innoculate trophy fishermen with the rush of unbridled nature as a cure for leisure boredom. Likewise, stuffed marlin (or stuffed bears, or elephant feet used as waste baskets, or whale penises used as golf bags) exist as the souvenirs of various individuals' glory days. Acquiring them is a last gasp vestige of the same nineteenth-century gentleman's mentality that believed it was our manifest destiny to eradicate the buffalo and the Sioux. One might argue that the voided Western plains as they exist today are not the reward, but rather the punishment of that particular gory period in our history. The taking of animal trophies represents the last irresponsible gasp of that good old boy belief that nature is nothing if not ours for the taking.

Motoring up the coastline with the outboard whining in my ears, I have to wonder if Alfred had experienced any of the same dismay that I feel as I stare at this red-orange champion fish. Did he stare along the marlin's improbable length and feel unnerved by the nagging suspicion that fishing enthusiasm had mysteriously transformed into fishing greed? Did he ever question the death of a marlin as a life taken in vain?

Actually, I would be pleasantly surprised to learn that Alfred had struggled with any emotions of the sort. Anyone who chose the incredible expense and trouble of finding his way onto a Peruvian marlin charter back in the early 1950s seems an unlikely candidate to release a world record fish back to the ocean before it was ever even weighed, measured, or photographed. No purpose of humble compassion could have a chance to compete with the immediate pressure of quantifying all of those impressive physical attributes for the sake of posterity and the *World Almanac*. And so the dying marlin was apotheosized into the divinity of statistics; the recorded statistics transformed what once was a very vibrant being into a tombstone, a memorial to its vitality. The naturalist who currently resides within my own heart cringes at the seductiveness of that *Field and Stream* photograph from so long ago. It enchanted me so thoroughly as a child that it has taken the kiss of another trophy fish years later to finally break the spell.

Sandra, Gabriel, and I arrived back at camp, where I enacted the ritual of hooking my finger under the fish's lower jaw to bear the heavy carcass along its final physical journey over the slippery rocks to our makeshift wilderness kitchen. As usual, everyone flocked to the viewing. Most of my camp mates seemed happy that I had caught such a prize. A firm, whitemeat fish was a happy addition to a camp satiated with the usual fare of oily-rich salmon.

Unfortunately, no amount of congratulation was able to fully attentuate my own gnawing discomfort. I noticed that Sandra too, despite her rationale that it is better to sacrifice one large fish than four or five smaller ones, appeared slightly confused by the entire event. The two of us, and Gabriel as well, would forever share the humbling sight of a grandmother rockfish, devoid of all its dignity, floating up to the surface like an orange beach ball. We were forever touched by a life, and by a death.

As I started to fillet the fish, it suddenly dawned on me that Sandra had not yet taken her customary fishing photos. Over the years, she had snapped many a picture of me in poses worthy of my mentor, Alfred, wielding this or that catch like a sacrificial offering. Here I am off the west coast of Mexico in swim trunks and visor, wielding a forty-pound dorado. Or look at me now, poised on the afterdeck of a sailboat in Baja with a yellowtail in one hand and a sierra mackerel in the other. Or here's one more, me with two buddies in British Columbia, this time wearing handknit sweaters and rubber boots, standing just behind a giant cedar log adorned with the bodies of six salmon.

I tentatively asked Sandra if she might like to take a few pictures. "No," she answered rather tartly, "we don't want to remember this fish as a photograph." So what to do but walk back to the kitchen, only to hear my camp mates offering up four vastly different estimations of the fish's weight: twelve pounds, twenty pounds, twenty-five pounds, thirty pounds. There the matter stood; no accurate weigh-in, no photos, nothing more than a sharp knife and a seasoned ability to quickly separate flesh from backbone. Together, we were all making a mockery of the contemporary human foible that demands a precise assignment of numbers and validating photographs to the very largest of our animal sacrifices.

That night, just before dinner, I spoke to the entire camp about my simmering turmoil. Yes, I would have set the yelloweye free if I'd had the chance. And yet there was certainly no point to turning maudlin over a deed already accomplished. This day had served up one of those rare unexpected revelations about life. Something that had always seemed worthy and even prestigious when judged from a distance now turned out to be shallow, and thus self-defeating when experienced directly. In the spirit of traditional peoples everywhere, I pleaded that each of us pause to consider this dinner as a gift from a special being. Lastly, and perhaps starting to get carried away by my newfound solemnity, I asked how this world might be a different place if our culture honored its food in such a manner.

Across the straits from where I spoke, 250 fishing boats were going about their usual summer business of netting salmon for a hungry North America. One pragmatic member of our group asked if I really expected commercial fishermen to honor each and every fish with a ceremony. After all, on this night alone, as many as 30,000 salmon would be dragged out of the water; and within a mere five miles from where we stood, 300,000 pounds of thrashing fish would be dumped into a hold and crushed ice unceremoniously dumped over them to insure some degree of freshness. By tomorrow morning, most of these 30,000 carcasses would be crated onto cargo planes, destined for markets in Vancouver, Seattle, Toronto, Montreal, San Francisco.

No, I answered, nothing so grandiose as a ceremony for each individual fish. I promote nothing more than a commercial fishery that acknowledges the fact that they cause unnecessary suffering among sentient beings, especially when they allow fish to suffocate in the hold of a boat. If nothing else, why not slow down enough to insure that each fish is killed quickly? Every fisherman knows that a quick kill also preserves the taste of the fish. Other than that matter, I have no argument against the local commercial fishermen.

But enough meandering. I wish to return one last time to that circle of human fish-eaters who have been waiting patiently around the campfire while I finished up this final tangent. They want to sit down and enjoy their dinner before it gets too cold. And so the yelloweyed fish became a dinner. I marinated it for three hours in lemon juice, garlic, and dill, and then barbecued it, covered, over a smoky alder fire, to finally serve it up over a bed of rice, almonds, and carrots. The next morning at breakfast (yelloweye omelets), several people made a point of informing me that in their considered opinion, last night's meal had been the very best fish dinner of the entire month-long expedition.

And three days later I fished again.

Chapter Eight

When Nature Is Larger Than Life

It is said that he who knows well how to live meets no tigers or wild buffalos on his road, and comes out from the battleground untouched by weapons of war. For in him, a buffalo would find no butt for his horns, a tiger nothing to lay his claws upon, and a weapon of war no place to admit its point. How is this? Because there is no room for death in him.

—Lao Tzu[1]

Gosh this is great stuff. Real Nature, real drama.
—Seattle *Times*[2]

In October 1988, I was invited by Greenpeace to join an effort to rescue three gray whales stuck in an ice hole a few miles outside of Barrow, Alaska. Because my consulting firm, Interspecies Communication Inc., (IC) has developed a sound system that permits humans to transmit sound and music directly to whales underwater, it was hoped that I would be able to develop some acoustic method to coax the whales out of their hole and toward the open sea again. Yet despite this obvious connection, it still took three phone calls from the Greenpeace representative in Barrow to coax me away from the balmy fall weather of the Pacific northwest, and up to this Eskimo village where the pre-Halloween thermometer was already hovering around −15 degrees Fahrenheit. Simply put, I was not convinced that the whales ought to be saved.

There was a precedent. Two years earlier, when the Russell Glacier in southern Alaska slid down a mountainside to close off the mouth of a fjord, trapping seals, porpoise, and who knows what other manner of unfortunate beast behind an ice barrier, I had waffled interminably before deciding not to put the resources and experience of IC to work. For one thing, nobody in command seemed to know if the animals were actually in any danger. In more general terms, when efforts to save this or that species come down to saving one of this or two of that, the best of motivations too easily degenerate into a case of human beings tampering with the natural order in order to fulfill their own human agenda. Yet despite my own hollow advice to let the glacier do its thing, the rescuers, like yellow jackets buzzing off to rescue their fallen comrades, decided to fly north anyway, believing as they must that sheer altruism overwhelms any inference of tampering.

Am I callow or just plain stupid to ask what it is about human morality that insists we rally behind any activity that hints of an altruistic outcome? In that case, the incipient saviors of the Russell Glacier savored their essentially archetypal role of good guys possessed of good human know-how utilized in the good cause of aiding the helpless little guy marine mammals. Inevitably, the rescue team also exhibited too much yearning for power and glory, a desire to control and even turn aside a natural process of nature by exerting maximum human ingenuity and minimal wisdom. But why not? Weren't we humans guilty of massacring marine mammals to the point of extinction? By God, didn't we owe it to those icebound porpoises?

The Russell Glacier mission became a media event of the first magnitude. Journalists from every newspaper and broadcast news network within the U.S. as well as from a half-dozen other countries descended on the area like vultures around a poached rhino on the African veldt.

In a typically wry insight, Barbara Tuchman has argued that there could be no history unless there were also historians around to write it.[3] If so, then one must also agree that the task of ordering and reordering history is an act of creation, and that historians dream up history as much as they report it. Yet in my own experience with journalists—who are our historians of the present moment—most disagree violently with this assertion, in fact interpret it as an assault upon their virtue as objective observers. Yet no matter what they, themselves, believe about their own participation in the events they choose to cover, most of the rest of us cannot help but notice that the media creates the news every bit as much as it reports it.

In the case of the Russell Glacier rescue, large-scale media attention meant that the saviors could not easily pack up their bags and go home when they started to suspect that their efforts were hopeless. Not only was the sheer immensity of a cold, wet Alaskan fjord dampening their enthusiasm, the porpoises themselves were stubbornly resisting every opportunity to be corralled. But celebrity engenders its own virtue, as it also certifies validity. The applied force of reading one's own words in half a hundred newspapers and seeing one's own image up there on the tube can induce euphoria. And the impression that the whole world is offering encouragement tends to overwhelm any hunch that it may be time to throw in the towel. At the Russell Glacier, news reporters and news makers ended up working together like a well-oiled team, artificially stimulating what might just as easily have been a natural event bounded by the just laws of entropy.

Unfortunately, the machinery of the news business sometimes clogs when events choose not to develop at the media's own speed. So the rescuers were coerced into providing more and more news morsels, known in the trade as soundbites, until even the project's most ardent supporters noted that the effort had deflated into a parody of a rescue. Perhaps unfairly, that subtle shift in mood was not lost on all the articulate op-ed page columnists whose job it is to scrutinize the tone and implications of the news through their very large magnifying glasses. These men and women tend to pounce whenever they perceive even an atom of newsmaking insincerity. Predictably, they pounced upon the rescue operation of the Russell Glacier, never acknowledging the fact that they themselves are another cog of the very same news generating machine that set the operation spinning in the first place. It was a bad moment that turned into a bad media event. Or vice versa.

For its own part, the glacier acted very glacierlike if not also like a superhero. It receded, rescuing sea mammals, rescuers, and journalists in one fell swoop. Ironically, none of the entrapped seals or porpoises seemed very interested to take advantage of what the humans interpreted as a positive swing of the pendulum. To this day, marine mammals cavort intemperately through the waters of the Russell fjord, seemingly oblivious to the dangers that humans insist swirl about them. In conclusion, if not also paradoxically, there is little point in faulting the rescuers for their sincere act of trying. They caused no lasting harm. One does not leave footprints on a glacier. The rescuers disturbed nothing beside that inscrutable perception of place I choose to call spiritual ecology.

I have described the Russell Glacier event in some detail, because I did decide to take my underwater sound system to join the effort off Barrow. The difference between the two events was primarily one of scale: at Barrow there were exactly three whales trapped inside a four hundred square foot breathing hole that was about five miles from the open ocean. Somehow, chopping a skinny channel through the fourteen-inch sea ice seemed infinitely more plausible and less manic than trying to stop the advance of the Russell Glacier, which was described as approaching the size of Rhode Island. Furthermore, the attitude in Barrow took on the attributes of trying to solve a puzzle— what ingenious measures might Sherlock Holmes have taken in order to extricate the whales?—as opposed to the Russell Glacier disposition of dressing up like Don Quixote to go off and joust against nature. All these factors combined to make me believe that, in this particular circumstance, saving three creatures might even bring out the best in the human species.

Everyone in Barrow agreed that, without assistance, the three gray whales would be dead within another week. Significantly, we all regarded them as *active* participants in this, their rescue, not passive creatures to whom deliverance would be given. Perhaps most critical to my own personal participation, I realized that IC held an important piece of the solution. If a channel could be chopped through the ice (and why couldn't it?), then my transmitted sounds would almost certainly attract the whales to the channel, or perhaps evict them from their death hole. IC has long been sponsoring projects that demonstrate one or the other response, for nearly fifteen years.

The ambience in Barrow was typically altruistic and sincere, to which I would also throw in a mood of local Eskimo puzzlement over how such a common occurrence as marine mammals getting stuck in the local sea ice could have mushroomed into such an extravaganza. One broadcaster commented that the rescue had been snatched up as the ultimate good news foil to the superficial mudslinging of the then current presidential campaign. Somehow, all is not lost in an America that permits three stuck whales to preempt national politics for nearly two weeks.

The location was incredibly majestic. All of us—scientist, army member, environmentalist, journalist, and Eskimo alike—seemed to pause every few minutes to gaze upon a very distant sun illuminating the ice. Just as our various jobs tended to keep us separated, so, more often, the environment bound us together into a single organism sharing a profound unanimity of perception. Carlos Castaneda has written volumes about the larger-than-life visioning of a Don Juan who perceives human beings as eggs of light. After a few hours spent outside in this abominable cold, every one of us bundled up in the prevailing beige or white parka started to look like eggs. And at the center of each of these human eggs burned an astonishing flame called body heat. Why had none of us ever detected such an internal flame before? Ultimately, the reporting about the rescue always seemed on the verge of unfolding as the documentation of a mystical experience in nature translated into terms fit for the mass media.

Given the novel perception of our fellow rescuers, imagine the humbling pause each of us felt to behold the faces of three naked and bruised whales just a few inches away from our own. For two solid weeks the global village never lost eye contact with these three neighborly ambassadors representing the mysterious tribe of great whales. If there is a mind in the waters after all, then here was our best chance yet to scrutinize its drift.

When I first considered the whales' ability to survive, their metabolic virtuosity seemed nothing more than an ocean mammal's version of the body heat just described for my fellow humans. But after a single hour spent in the company of these three grays, what at first seemed a difference in degree was obviously a fundamental difference in kind as well. Hadn't one whale scientist commented that, should these whales be freed from their ice hole, they would not eat any food whatsoever as they spent the next *three or four months* swimming 6,000 miles nonstop to the warm Mexican lagoons? Several of us concluded that leviathan was a master alchemist who had somehow learned to stoke some significant part of his/her golden flame directly out of the brutally leaden atmosphere. How did they do it? Or perhaps a better question: Were the assembled journalists forfeiting a monumental opportunity by focusing all of their reportage on the mere mechanics and human emotions of a rescue operation, to the detriment of the whale's own remarkable breathing patterns? As David Guss has written about this essentially shamanic perception of nature:

> Real power exists, not in the external form of a thing, but in its secret, inner one. . . . To reach that hidden world was the purpose of ritual, while to record that meeting was the purpose of myth.[4]

In this case, the potential for recording a myth in the making encountered two major hurdles. First, the mass media's coverage of the meeting between human and whale never stepped into the mythical overdrive of "real power" because it never sought to record anything but the externalized form of the interspecies coalition. And second, the rest of the people in the world who read and watched those reports secondhand, and who diligently construct their perception of contemporary history from the cumulative flow of all such secondhand reports, never heard any reporter so much as whisper about this real power as graphically exemplified by the whales themselves. I wondered, for example, how differently this potential might have manifested had some enterprising TV network simply turned their cameras on the hole, and then left them there for the week. No cogent commentary, no soundbites, no talking heads. Just whales breathing in your very own living room, for an entire week. But as I say, if

the coverage always seemed just on the verge of turning into
"real power," it never actually did so.

Instead, something crucial felt out of sync. On the one hand,
most of the journalists seemed rapt and articulate students of the
mythical images swirling about them. On the other hand, the
strictures imposed by their media proved glaringly incompetent
to liberate that "secret inner world," even though the vitality of
that worldview must have taken a major conspiracy just to keep
it undercover. I started to wonder if the reporters failed to report
about the "real power" because, in fact, witnessing it also
means that one becomes an integral part of it. In a word, they
were *inside* the myth. Just as importantly, their activities as
journalists turned them into protagonists who were as central to
the unfolding myth as the whales themselves. In a word, the
myth was *inside them* as well. Consequently, they could not find
any way to report about the crucial "hidden world" because
their own skewed sense of objectivity demanded that one's own
transformed perceptions not become the leading character of
one's own story. The reporters became publicly struck dumb by
a format suited only to deal with externalized, objective events.

To generalize this predicament: our own cultural quasi-myth,
that which we call history, ends up possessing very little of the
psychic interconnectedness implicit within traditional myth. By
inference, when the media fails to include the contextual whispers
of contemporary ritual and myth in their reportage, they also fail
to include the much fainter whispers of the seventh generation.
After all, those whispers are right inside us—nowhere else.

David Guss echoes Claude Levi-Strauss when he concludes:

> The natural world wasn't just a static analogy for the
> divisions in the human one, for the mythic mind is ulti-
> mately inspired not so much by the need to make distinc-
> tions as by the desire to resolve them. Its genius therefore
> is not the adoption of the animal world as a conceptual
> model, but through it, the ability to overcome the opposition
> between nature and culture and think of them as a whole.[5]

On just that note, a Yupik Eskimo from Nome once described
to me a situation in which 100 beluga whales shared one small

breathing hole for the duration of an entire winter. The belugas simply took turns breathing. That also meant, of course, that the whales developed complex beats to their synchronized breathing; not unlike the polyrhythms of an existential big band concert stretched out to four months' duration. He said, "We go out on the ice to watch the whales breathe; and we learn how to get along with each other through a long winter."

Such anecdotes inevitably prompted nonstop restaurant talk between journalists and rescuers concerning the big picture about life and death on an ice floe (none of which ever made it into the newspapers). One reporter, for example, listened to my rantings about the missing mythical element, only to answer that, yes, it was all true, "Except that it just ain't the news." He then proceeded to ask how I might expect the human race to alter its course, should we all be forced to share a single breathing hole? "Well," I laughed in reply to this essentially psychedelic question, "it would probably transform a much smaller human population into a virtuoso rhythm section."

Now I stand out on the ice, keeping time with my heavily mittened thumb and index finger, trying to determine if these grays exhibit any humanly discernible rhythm in their breathing patterns. They have been lying at the surface for a full two minutes, breathing easily with cavernous two-second-long exhalations. Then a great big three-second breath signifies a change. They dive beneath the ice, disappearing so completely out of sight and sound, and for such a long period of time, that we rescuers might just as easily forget what on earth has impelled us onto this formless Arctic ice sheet in the first place.

My eyes wander over the theatre of this improbable rescue operation. To the south unfolds a scene out of a war movie: great chopping helicopters unloading whale soldiers, half of whom have long spindly projections that at this distance look like rifles, but that are actually camera tripods. In another direction, to the east, a three-foot-high escarpment of solid ice runs along the shoreline all the way to the horizon. It is as if the last wave of a long past summer had frozen as it curled in upon itself. To the west, a white flatland of sea ice charges unbroken all the way to . . . where? Soviet Siberia? Finland? I blink once, twice, unable to locate even the hint of a landmark. But the TV set that is my own mind decides to shut down, adamantly opposed, as it must be, to burning all the precious calories needed to conjure up a mental Mercator projection of the polar ice cap.

So instead, I clap my bulky gloves together just to make sure my hands are still inside, and turn my body another ninety degrees. To the north, twenty eggs stand clutching chain saws along a series of newly dug channels. Yesterday, one observer informed me that the jolly Inupiat Eskimos sat by and giggled as all the imported white boys—marine biologists, oil company laborers, national guard personnel—took hours and hours to cut out slabs of sea ice and then *lift* the 200-pound sections up onto the adjacent ice surface. After a full day of activity they had cut a second and then finally a third small breathing hole. Finally, early this morning the Inupiat *power* that offers local knowledge about ice staged a quiet coup against what they must have considered to be the incompetent although well-meaning *authority* of the stereotypical chain of command of U.S. government scientists and army officers. Just seven hours into this day, and the constant buzz of the chain saws seems to dwindle farther and farther away as the Inupiat workers push the ice blocks *under* the main body of the ice. It is just four P.M., and yet the Eskimo's freshly cut channel stretches an impressive half-mile from the whale's own breathing hole.

Closer to where I stand, ten more eggs hover over one of yesterday's holes that has been kept unfrozen overnight through the electrically powered bubbling of one of three donated de-icers. These eggs are bent over the hole as if praying to the god of whales, "Please! You've got to teach these animals that they must, absolutely must, learn to surface at one of the new holes." There is the rub. This cetacean act of discovery must occur within the next two hours, because if the whales do not discover the channel before the workers leave the scene at dusk, then the entire half-mile channel will surely freeze overnight. A day's work will have been in vain. But if the whales *do* discover the channel, then the entire interspecies brigade of whales and chain-sawyers can continue their dance tomorrow, eventually cutting a channel all the way out to the open lead,[6] five miles offshore. The optimistic Inupiats have already started to cut out a much larger breathing hole at the end of their new channel, with the understanding that all three of the deicing machines will keep only that single hole open overni . . .

. . . Pssssshhhhooooofwaaaww! The smallest of the three whales surfaces to startle me out of my reverie. The second whale surfaces, then the third. All the nearby rescuers emit a parenthetic groan: "Come on whales! Why won't you try out some other hole?" The ocean around the whales' own fifteen-by-fifteen-foot breathing hole is barely thirty feet deep, no deeper than the body length of the largest of the grays. More conjecture erupts between media and rescuers: You would think they'd feel cramped. You would think they would have an ounce of curiosity to explore all the noise made by the chain saws. For that matter, the whale blow prompts one of the more metaphysically oriented of the rescuers to pop a truly wonderful question: Where do the whales go during their three minutes underwater? One of the scientists starts to laugh. "Go? What is that supposed to mean? Where do you think they go?" I stare at the questioner and realize that humans have been tying their minds up in knots for centuries over the anthropocentric issue of whether or not a tree that falls in the deep forest has actually made a noise if there is no human there to hear it. In this case, maybe they take off their whale disguises and enter some cetacean version of the Twilight Zone. That is certainly one way to explain the inability of these three to locate that damned channel. On the other hand, who can blame the whales for refusing to budge? They depend on this hole as they depend on nothing else in this world.

The smallest of the three whales lies on the surface, its snout battered to the very bone, its face skewed sideways to get a good look at the human beings who also turn their heads sideways to gaze upon the meaning of life as expressed by that scanning eye. A reporter from the Australian broadcast news steps gingerly up to the southern lip of the hole, composes himself as his camera crew records the setting, and then proceeds to describe the drama of the multimillion-dollar rescue mission that has bogged down because of the whales unmitigated lack of curiosity. While the camera eye fixes on him from one direction, the baby whale examines the strange human sounds, shapes, and colors from another. As the reporter continues to speak, a crew from the BBC queues up behind the Australian crew, and too improbably, a crew from NBC queues up behind the British crew. The Australian reporter searches to find entirely too much pathetic irony in the fact that "the local Eskimos, who usually kill (pause) and eat (pause) whales, should be working so hard to save these three individuals." But why is he saying this? I am quite certain that the reporter has already been briefed on the fact that local Eskimos never did hunt the grays. So ten thousand years of Eskimo culture is capsulized for ten million Australian viewers in the slander of a single erroneous statement. To make matters worse, the reporter expresses discontent over his own phrasing, and so asks to repeat these same lines two, three, four more times. For my own part, I smack my mittens together and feel embarrassment watching four Inupiat whaling captains listen to this false exposé. Meanwhile, one of the larger whales has chosen to exhale a mighty breath, spraying shards of ice crystals around the commentator's head. The Aussie finally concludes his perfidious report and steps aside, making room for the British reporter to take his turn.

This commentator unzips his hood, takes off his knit cap, and then displays the top six inches of a blue necktie before focusing upon another favorite side issue of the rescue effort. "Can they justify the expense of more than a million dollars, and 100 volunteers, to save three gray whales while they permit children in the Sudan to die of starvation?" I stare at the man in outright astonishment. In a land where a person's body heat is far more valuable to him than his money, the man's opened parka seems to be squandering the equivalent budget of this entire rescue operation.

We are the species that seeks control over each other as well as over nature. So the reporter's impossible question reprimands the ruling class of the human species, those abstract individuals he chooses to call *they,* for losing control by losing their cumulative heads over three foolhardy animals. This question also assumes, of course, that it is more moral—meaning traditional, human-centered logical-moral—to devote the lion's share of our attention to saving the disadvantaged human underclass. In other words, how could *they* have gone so far as to permit a mere interspecies affair to acquire a life out of all proportion to its monetary value, that which is also known as *myth*?

According to Joseph Campbell, myth awakens the human psyche to the mystical dimension of the universe. It accomplishes this by converting what is an inscrutable mystery into a grounded order through the creation of icons and heroes. This grounded order leads an individual in harmony through the various passages of human life, validating whatever moral system and manner of life customs may be peculiar to the local culture.[7]

A rescue operation mounted in the far north of the planet permits us to tackle the task of grounding the inscrutable forces of the universe in the icon of three stranded gray whales. The representative from the BBC asks the question why *they*, actually meaning he and you and I, are not directing our energy to save the starving children of the Sudan. This question is answered in turn by a statement on the editorial page of the Hartford *Courant:*

> The creatures' plight stirred global sympathy. . . . The caring doesn't compensate for any human shortcomings, but it generates hope that this element of human nature will be seen more often.[8]

This particular myth exists as Campbell defined it: validating the morality implicit within the culture. Just as the media worked so diligently (if not inadvertently) to invent the myth of the gray whale rescue, so that myth now encourages the media to focus some of its archetypal juice upon other sympathetic issues, for example, starving children.

But any conclusion that blurs the edges between causes and effects, not to mention myth and real life, is too easily construed as cold dispassion. So just last night at "the world's most northernmost Mexican restaurant," a dinner companion listened to my proposition about the media dreaming up this event, only to pronounce me a basket case of sarcasm. I reacted by steering the conversation into less mythical territory. But within the next hour, it was revealed that marine mammals get stuck in the ice around Barrow every winter. In fact, even as we rescue gray whales at one hole, there is yet another hole just a few miles farther out that contains an iced-in bowhead whale. But the Eskimos *do* eat bowheads, and so no one is interested in covering that situation.

Ironically, if there were no predictable Arctic larder of frozen critters, the threatened polar bears would have a very difficult time making it through the winter. Did that mean, I asked, that we end up killing polar bears when we save gray whales? Everyone at the table reacted with that mixture of sighs and laughter that means no one has the answer. An hour later, the conversation drifted back once again to the relationship between the news media and the rescue effort. The same dinner companion who had earlier chastised me now explained in some detail how the rescue operation was born after a local reporter had written up the story in the local paper because the whale hole was located so close to town and everyone wanted to witness it firsthand. This led to a story in the Anchorage paper, leading to a syndicated story by UPI, leading to the networks, so on, so forth around the world. As syndicated columnist James Kilpatrick finally described it: "The story had taken on the kind of irresistible momentum that defies objective analysis."[9]

And in Barrow, what had started out as a common life and death drama enacted between living beings and the elements, grew, acquired an identity of its own, grew more, and finally became an event that prompted Ronald Reagan to call and offer the U.S. Army to help save the whales. This precipitated what Joseph Campbell calls the conversion of the inscrutable mystery into a grounded order through the creation of icons and heroes. The mystery tale of three whales fighting for their lives along the lip of the Arctic Ocean was quickly transformed into an accessible news flash about human volunteers making incredible donations of time and money, about ingenious equipment whose only function was to keep an ice hole open, and how an international media event was altering the October ambience of down-town Barrow. We would hear over and over again about these heroes and icons, all of whom represented the oil companies, the U.S. Army, the environmental movement, and the Inupiat whaling captains—all joined together in common cause. Yet if this was the high ground of an unfolding myth, it also was bound to acquire its dark side, as represented by this statement from the *Seattle Times:*

> Standard Oil of Alaska couldn't buy this kind of front page network news positive publicity for four times the [$500,000] amount. Oil companies have battled a land-raper image since the first oil pipeline was proposed. . . . What is warmer or fuzzier for Big Oil than saving three whales?[10]

That, should anyone need reminding, is sarcasm. It is spoken with the voice of someone who never made it out onto the ice, where every one of us got stripped of whatever *job* we may hold in the real world, to become initiated into a mindset where human beings are primarily eggs of heat. Nor is it great news to learn that there is always someone within the infrastructure of big business who schemes up gestures of public relations. So that individual must always find his clone observing the world through the magnifying glass of any major newspaper.

But enough about sarcasm. Let me focus attention not on the faraway non sequitur of starving children, but on the more linear issue of saving *all the whales*. As I sat at the restaurant enjoying a plate of enchiladas, the Japanese were out on the high seas killing endangered whales under a dubious loophole known as "scientific whaling." In a nutshell, scientific whaling means that the Japanese totally disregard the international moratorium against killing whales, and then justify their affront by asserting they need to study a thousand or more whale organs. Back in the early 1970s, the U.S. Congress passed a farsighted law called the Pelly amendment that demanded, among other provisos, that the government impose trade sanctions against any country that disregards international whaling accords. It seemed the height of irony, although not untypical, that the same president who sent the army into Barrow refused to uphold the Pelly amendment. When I arrived in Barrow with that background information well in mind, I found myself politicizing the answer to the reporters' stock question about why I had joined the rescue: "I hope that the focus accorded these three whales brings attention to the whaling policy of the current administration in Washington." It means, in effect, that the U.S. government is breaking its own law as a means to encourage the Japanese to kill more whales.

But that was when I arrived. Now that I have passed through my initiation by spending time out on the ice, the urgency of the Pelly amendment seems like a faraway memory from my early childhood. Out on the ice, you enter another world. All I can think about is moving whales. All I can feel is body heat.

The 2:00 helicopter back to Barrow has carried away almost all of the news reporters. The stories about today's activities have to be written and sent off via modem or satellite to make it into tonight's newspapers or telecast. Viewed from a media perspective, anything that occurs out on the ice after 2:00 P.M. will never have happened for millions and millions of people. Although this fact prompted no more than a chuckle when it was explained to me at Pepe's last night, now that I am actually out on the ice about to commence my own job, I feel strangely liberated.

Actually, there remains a single reporter with a tape recorder who has just spent fifteen minutes interviewing me in some depth. Furthermore, he plans to stay out here until dark, "just to see how the music turns out." He says that he represents the Voice of America, and that this interview will be broadcast tomorrow morning throughout Eastern Europe and the Soviet Union. But my mind cannot quite comprehend what that means, so my eyes try to fill in the gap by staring north, trying one more time to sense some (or all) of the Soviet people who are going to hear that interview. All I can see is the well-coordinated team of Inupiat whaling captains, who continue to slice hole after hole through the ice, neither concerned about nor deterred by the momentary hiatus in noncommunist coverage. Now I turn in a circle just to see this panorama one more time. Off to the southwest, bright rainbows of ice, called sundogs, have precipitated on either side of the sun. All of my wry beliefs about media events seem to slide off my heavy shoulders and sink into oblivion. It is time to go to work.

The engineer who built IC's electronic underwater sound system recommended that I try to keep it above 0 degrees Fahrenheit if at all possible. So the scientists in charge have set up a heated three-by-eight-foot shed on runners at the fourth ice hole to the north, located about 100 yards from the whale's own. This particular hole should be an easy underwater jaunt for even the most battered of whales. Most important, this particular hole is the gateway to the half-mile channel. If the whales decide to join me, then they will also inevitably discover the channel. Everyone involved in this task hopes that the discovery will prompt the whales to zoom down the channel's entire length searching for an outlet to the ocean. At the end of the channel they will find, instead of the ocean, a very large hole kept ice free by all three of the deicing machines. Then, the entire day's worth of channel can be allowed to freeze overnight.

And of course, tomorrow the Eskimos will start the entire process again. By that time, all of us would like to believe that the whales will have gotten the general idea. If not, then I'll play again.

I drop the underwater speaker and the hydrophone into the hole, tie them off to one of the sled runners, and step inside my 35-degree nest where I start connecting the electronic leads into a power amplifier and a tape recorder. I have chosen to commence this acoustic experiment on a positive note, trying to *attract* the whales away from their own certain death trap hole and *to* the source of the sound.

Yesterday, when I told the various scientists in charge that I had spent part of the past fifteen years developing guitar techniques "for attracting or repelling the whales," all the assembled men and women looked at one another as if I had said I was from the Pleiades. I explained that live sound has enjoyed a long history of attracting whales, because the ever playful whales tend to play with the call-and-response medium of improvisational music. Live sounds, even electronically generated live sounds, may even lead to that paradigm-shifting phenomenon known as the interspecies dialogue. In this specific case, if the trapped whales feel that their own rhythmically based grunts have been answered, they may actually search out the source of that sound. One man asked if he could bring his flute along, which got a chuckle. Someone else asked if I had brought any recorded sounds? "Well, yes, now that you ask, my preferred choice for recorded sounds is a cassette of a South African a capella group, Ladysmith Black Mombazo, because their music consists of whispering voices singing in harmony, without any sharp edges."

My ever-diplomatic sponsor from Greenpeace recommended that I first transmit a recording of gray whales made in Baja California and recorded by a very senior scientist from the National Marine Fisheries Service. "Yes," said she, "let's agree to try the gray whale tape first. Maybe *our* grays will be tricked into believing that there are other whales just a few hundred yards away." "Well, no," I answered in my most expert tone of voice. "My experience makes me believe that the whales will probably respond more to a live musician emulating gray whale sounds in real time, than to any dead cassette of grays. No matter who recorded it."

But our difference of opinion offered no grounds for an argument because, in all honesty, everyone agreed that nothing else was working. Had I proclaimed that I would conjure up a 50,000-year-old cetacean ascended master to transport the whales up the channel, the rescue leaders would have felt obligated to try that as well. In fact, here was Greenpeace invoking a guitar-playing interspecies communicator, who had arrived in this nest of commando helicopters, a skycrane right out of *The Empire Strikes Back,* an 185-ton icebreaking barge, a seven-ton icebreaking needle, an eleven-ton Archimedes-screw, wheeled, icebreaking pontoon vehicle, all of which cost a whole lot more and make a whole lot more noise than my little guitar. But, critically, none of those machines had worked at all. By contrast, this self-proclaimed nonexpert matter-of-factly proclaims that no, it shouldn't be too difficult to get the whales out of the hole using South African choral music. So very quickly, two very different views about the human/nature interface achieved a conciliation that pleased everyone: play what you like, *after* you try the gray whale sounds.

Out on the ice, I now completed all the electronic connections to the sound system, donned a set of headphones, handed a second set to my friend from Greenpeace, and tapped on the power to give a listen to the under-ice environment. All was silent except the faraway sounds of the chain saws. In fact, the acoustic ambience under the ice attained a quiet I have never encountered in any other ocean. Next I popped the gray whale cassette into the tape recorder, flipped the play button, to be greeted by the grating cacophony of VERY LOUD STATIC. This was terrible. I turned off the tape recorder and announced that if there were any gray whale sounds on this tape, then no one, either whale or human, was going to hear them through such a dense wall of noise. Without another word, I plugged my soprano guitar into the transmit connector, turned up the volume to achieve maximum clarity, and started to strum a D-modal drone. I do not know what it is about the key of D major, but in my experience, more species seem to utilize its harmony than any other scale. Jazz musician Paul Winter has discovered the very same thing while recording his albums with many different animals.

But after fifteen minutes spent in the key of D, and another fifteen spent in variations thereof, the whales have still not budged. I turn off the system, don all my layers of clothing, step outside, and walk over to the whales who are lollygagging on the surface. The two adults still look fairly healthy. However the baby looks more beat up and listless than ever. "Hey, you guys, please pay attention to what I'm trying to do, will you? You've got to move out of this hole within the next hour or the channel is going to freeze overnight. Try to understand. OK, listen: I'm going to go back and try it again." The whales, for their own part, eyeball this babbling two-legged in their midst. I walk to the very edge of the hole, reach out a heavily mittened hand. One of the two grown whales reaches up to nudge my hand with his/her badly bruised snout.

Back at the shed again, I put Ladysmith Black Mombazo into the box and turn it up. Whispery male harmonies fill up the icy

Arctic water with a song about the struggle of living homeless under a warm South African sun. On and on they warble. But half an hour later, at 5:30 P.M., with just about one more hour of daylight left, the whales still have not budged. I shut down the system, pull in all the loose wires, dress, step outside into a cold wind, trudge a half-mile out to the end of the channel, walk all the way back again, trot laterally away from the rescue operation, watch the sundogs dancing across the sky, and then finally return to the shed, where I flag down the first snowmobile and ask if the Eskimo driver will drag my shed over to the hole where the whales live. This is quickly accomplished. Now, just as quickly, I drop the hydrophone and underwater speaker into the water and hook up all the wires again.

Several of the Inupiat chain-sawyers gather around me as if waiting for an explanation about the wires and the guitar. When I tell them that I plan to play some a capella South African choral music into the hole, they all laugh and then exclaim that the whales really gonna love that rock and roll. I can only remind these good-natured men that at least three times during the past two days they have gone so far as to drape plastic tarps over the breathing hole in an aggressive attempt to force the whales to use an alternate hole. The whales continued to surface right into the plastic, and pushed the tarp upward until the wind took it away. And no, I could not be sure that the sounds would redirect the whales to the channel. Actually, that was not my intent. Rather, I wondered if the whales might make the connection between the sounds I was about to play at this hole, and the sounds I would later play when I returned to my original location. But enough talk. I stepped inside the shed, handed a pair of headphones to the Inupiat leader, and very quietly turned on Ladysmith Black Mombazo. The whales, for their part, immediately dove out of sight.

They resurfaced a minute later at the hole to which I had spent the last hour trying to attract them. Too much! All the rescuers who had assembled around my little shed started to jump up and down in sheer delight. Now I turned off the tape just to see what would happen. The whales evidently took some note of the silence as well. They dove again, only to resurface back at the original hole. "Turn the tape back on!" everyone yelled. On it went. As if on cue, the three whales dove again. But this time they vanished for at least three minutes. Where did they go? Finally a keen-eyed rescuer shouted, "Look!" pointing his finger a good quarter-mile down the length of the channel. Yes, I saw it too, we all saw it—a blow, and then another blow. The whales had discovered the channel! Success! Hooray!!!

We all went waddling across the ice toward the last hole of the channel. By the time I arrived, the whales had already found their new home and had turned about, dashing vigorously back and forth along the entire length of the channel. They seemed as delighted by their own liberation as we obviously were. So, in effect, there was nothing more for me to do but return to the shed, collect up the sound system, and lug it across the ice to the main command hut to wait for a ride back to Barrow.

But then, tragedy. Someone reports that the baby whale has not been sighted for the last ten minutes. Someone else suggests that it is already too dark, and the channel much too long, to be certain of anything so ephemeral as a whale spout. Yes, I had seen the baby return to their original breathing hole *after* the music had been shut off that first time. But look over there, you can see the two adults quite plainly. All eyes search the channel for a sign of a third whale. If it *is* true, and the baby is gone, then it must have happened when the whales dove for so long. Although the baby could have surfaced at any of several holes along its path, it may instead have tried to keep up with the two adults. Already listless, it could have quickly exhausted its very limited store of energy and so drowned.

I returned home late the next day to newspaper headlines tolling the death knell of a baby whale. The reports also noted that the two remaining whales had inexplicably left their death trap of a hole, but made no mention whatsoever of Ladysmith Black Mombazo. The whales seemed to be keeping pace with a now fortified team of chain-sawyers as they all cut their way toward the open sea. Unfortunately, three days into this new marathon, the diggers finally met their match at an immense pressure ridge. The sea ice had cracked, solidified, cracked

again, and finally solidified to an improbable thickness of thirty
feet. But these two whales, like the hero of Lao Tzu's epigram,
did not seem fated to meet any tigers or wild buffalos they could
not overcome. The Soviet military, of all candidates for white
knight status, arrived in the nick of time to break a passage
through the pressure ridge. So, the myth of a gray whale rescue
ended on the upbeat note of U.S./Soviet collaboration. The gray
whales were last seen as they were also last filmed, spouting
beside a Soviet icebreaker and setting a safe passage toward the
Bering Strait.

On a more personal note, I take leave of this story by assuring
you that I felt a good deal sadder and wiser from the entire
affair. I too had been transformed by what Joseph Campbell
calls a safe passage, in harmony, through one of the vital
passages of human life. So the circle of myth completed itself.
Just as we humans had to save the whales, so undoubtedly, the
whales had to save us as well.

Chapter Nine

✿

A Sense of Place

Where I live, on an island in Puget Sound, the earth wears winter clouds like a snake does its skin. Because these clouds are so constantly low in what is a very leaden sky, any clearing seems most aptly described as a shedding—a function of the earth, rather than of the sky relaxing its usual tight grasp. Yet despite the northwest's rainy reputation, two weeks of nonstop cloud cover can never be equated with actual rainfall. During the dry winter of 1987, for example, the clouds arrived as usual in mid November, but we received little more rainfall that winter than did Southern California.

When the clouds finally clear out, it's like winning at Lotto but even better, because it doesn't mean that someone else loses. One evening when we least expect it, the earth eases off a bit in its vaunted control over the atmosphere. The clouds part. Winter seizes its golden opportunity and rushes in through the hole, causing the prevalent 33-degree weather to plummet an automatic five to ten degrees. We wake up in the orange light of seven A.M. to the chatter of juncos and purple finches searching for seeds over the rich carpet of green winter mosses. Their songs disorient. Close your eyes a moment to be transported into a warm June morning bursting with columbines and peonies. Open your eyes again to find yourself back in a February world all crystalline moss and glowing gossamer spider webs. My young daughters run outside to examine the frost heaves as if they were an outright treasure, something far more precious than the less accessible but more common trumpeter swans and bald eagles that fly overhead every day at this time of year.

To this biased observer, all the best natural displays at this time of year occur at ground level, and right here in my own front yard. All the juicy and overblown harbingers of the cultivated human spring—the hyacinth, daffodil, galanthus, crocus, to name but a few—are already well along in their seasonal cycle. These imported cultivars seem especially rowdy celebrants of the end of winter. They peak up through the loam as if seeking some externalized verification of their own earthly existence. Is it time? Is it time? In fact, the accelerated growth of these newcomers predicts the alterations in weather over the next few weeks time better than any human weatherman. Nonetheless, I can still be found out in the garden on bended knees pleading with the bulbs to push their luck a little less exuberantly. Be careful, I warn, it may not be time.

But the cultivars never listen. By the first week in March, all these immigrants—the daffodils, sweet william, tulips, iris, Canterbury bells, radishes, kale, so on—rumble to full attention, expanding, churning, kicking away the topsoil in an athletic thrust to open their flowers in anticipation of a new season. Yet, surprise of surprises, everything flourishes. And in that rarest of climatic events, when the March mercury plunges below 20 degrees, the cultivars seem to bear it, although they grow slightly more passive for a few days, patiently awaiting the inevitable turn back to spring.

It makes me pay special attention to the difference between the exuberance of the cultivated bulbs and the conservatism of the native species. In fact, the far less ostentatious and yet far more tenacious natural flowers of my own neighborhood—the skunk cabbage, shooting star, coral root, stork's bill, chocolate lily, hairy cat's ear, devil's club, Oregon grape (the names just roll off my tongue)—have not shown much of anything, even in mid February. They seem to have accrued a special wisdom of place, garnered through millenia of growing and dying, thrusting and waiting—all of that cumulative and quite mutable experience we know as evolution.

Then, one remarkable day, everything in the garden, wild and tame alike, seems to agree that it has warmed up for good. I learn about their unanimity by paying particular attention to the wild calypso orchid that flourishes in the deep woods. When the little pink flowers start to open, you might as well bet the bank that there is not going to be any more frost.

Now the plants push, flex, ram, impel upward and ever outward. If this verbiage seems too overtly sexual, then visualize the cup of a chocolate lily, or a bed of asparagus thrusting their tips through the steamy black humus on a sunny April afternoon. Is it any wonder that the Turks used the wanton tulip as a sex augury? Red petals offered a declaration of love, yellow signified hopeless love, and a black center caused the heart to burn with unabated passion.[1] Actually, the plants have always put us animals to shame when it comes to matters pertaining to reproduction. Imagine how differently the human mind might have evolved if we all sprouted a riot of bearded irises or fragrant lilies where our genitals now reside.

You may have guessed that I feel connected to these plants in a way that goes far beyond orthodox horticulture. In fact, I consider the plants to be my mentors simply because their straightforward advice about the cycles of the seasons teaches me how to connect with the earth. It also makes me wish that I were a better student, because then I might be able to better teach that same lesson of interconnectedness to the rest of the human race. I would teach everyone how to garden. If spiritual ecology is defined as perceptions and activities that lead one to an interconnectedness with nature, then gardening offers one of its most pragmatic practices.

But I'm not talking about just *any* kind of gardening. Consider, for example, the many gardening books that urge gardeners to take a spade to their late-fruiting tomato plants. Cut the roots in half, shock that sucker, stress the plant to the point that it soon acts out a tomato's version of paranoid schizophrenia. All those little fruits quickly turn from green to red, from hard to soft, from sour to sweet; and far before the plant's natural clock recommends. But all such gardening practices seem akin to mean-spirited agricultural slavery, because they make no mention whatsoever of the connectedness that can exist between garden and gardener, not to mention between humans and their food.

That is a method of gardening equivalent to marlin fishing. It reduces gardening to the adjectives "earlier" and "more," as well as to an ample chemical fertilizer bill. It is typified by the county fairs that turn horticulture into a contest, dispensing awards for the largest zucchini and cauliflower, no matter that such winners might easily be eligible for the award for being the least tasty as well.

In other words, a dedication to "gardening" means many things to many people. I recommend that every novice gardener dedicate a few minutes each day to sitting right smack in the dirt doing nothing but watching the plants grow. Such an exercise indubitably helps us humans learn how to slow down. Now we learn to eat tomatoes when the tomatoes say so. And although I consider patience to be any garden's wisest counsel, it is perhaps the most difficult task for us humans to put into practice. As I wrote in *Dolphin Dreamtime,*

> This relationship is not about observation, but rather about participation. It is the difference between all that is static and all that is dynamic.[2]

Although I stand responsible for instigating this landscaping process in the first place, after five years of living within it I am convinced that the garden has acquired a perception of itself quite apart from its gardener. In that light, consider me as I like to consider myself: one vital component of that self-aware perception, one member of a self-sustaining neighborhood. I provide nutrients in the form of compost, a watershed in the form of catchments, weeding in the form of abundant mulching, and no poisons. For their own part, the flowers provide eye-popping displays of beauty, the vegetables provide fresh food for our table nearly twelve months a year, the herb garden provides emollients, purgatives, teas, and rich flavors, while the trees and berry bushes provide shade as well as a veritable heaven of fruits.

That last should also make it clear that I am the predominant predator of this neighborhood. But predation is a vital component of any peaceable kingdom you can name. Where beings live, there is always going to be sustenance and sacrifice, living and dying, giving and taking. Furthermore, it may only be the *human* being who truly wants to live forever. We fear death as the unfair culmination to a too-precious life. By contrast, if the plants have a religion at all, then it must be akin to the worship of time as practiced by the Maya—a spiritual ecology that lives and dies as the fulfillment of the cycle of the seasons. As the seasons provide one to the next, so we gardeners reciprocate by providing a healthful continuity to the growth and withering of the seasons.

If you happen to be a local mule deer, it is February and not April that is the cruelest month. The deer's known stores of young tree shoots and other browse material have already been nearly exhausted. Everything that grows wild is in-between, and there is not very much to eat. But there is more to this than meets the eye. To understand the eating habits of a deer is also to learn the winter strategy of the low-lying green plants. It took me years before I realized that I had it all wrong when I concluded that the native plants choose to lie low solely because of the dangers of frost. That may be one part of the strategy, but a far greater part lies in the fact that by February the deer are ravenously hungry.

So the plants have schemed up a botanical version of price fixing. They agree to remain underground until all are ready to rise as one. For example, if the wild camass flowers followed the profligate example of the imported tulips—pushing through the earth in February instead of late April—they would be deer-nipped to the quick, and be quite extinct before the fourth month began. But by April the world is exploding into leaf and bud, offering abundant browse to sustain a normal deer population. Naturally, every wild plant that chooses to remain succulent or leafy all winter long, as for example the Oregon grape and the wild rose, also possesses a formidable armor of needle-like thorns. Anything less vicious is fair game for browsers.

Until I started a garden I had never considered the deer to be a predator, simply because I could not consider plants as prey. As a transplanted city-dweller, I imagined the sighting of a mule deer from my own living room window as a major blessing of a rural lifestyle. Were I a nongardener, no doubt it would still be so. However, this ardent planter now gazes upon his front yard with an entirely different set of eyes. For example, I now see that the wild rose has concocted as awesome a defense as any fleet-footed impala on the African plain. Likewise, the deer appears as ruthless as any tyrannosaurus rex. Actually, the earlier lesson of the yellow jackets teaches that, except in cases describing the motives of the human race, the adjective *ruthless* is but a synonym for that other adjective, *hungry*.

It took the local deer exactly two winters to discover this garden full to the brim with daring young bulbs poking four inches or more above ground by early February. I watched one of these early forays, quite transfixed, from behind the blind of my living room window. The small female would have made an effective role model for Eve, gesturing quite tentatively, as if she were unwilling to believe that this vegetative Eden held no hidden devils waiting to lunge at her should she make the wrong move. She stared at a young plum sapling in careful apprehension for nearly a minute, then finally grabbed hold of a branch with her teeth, ripped it loose, and immediately jerked her head up high to survey the scene as she chewed. She gobbled it down and immediately took a single step back before cocking her ears forward.

Something spooked her. It might have been the fact that the yard offers no cover. Or that the smell of wood smoke permeates this knoll at this time of year. The threat of a brightly lit house may have implied the potentially deadly threat of a nearby dog, although we don't have one. Perhaps she finally spied me spying her from behind that otherworld of glass. Or was it some fundamental intuitive distrust of this uncommon winter feast laid out before her senses? Here was a magical kingdom beyond her imagination to grasp. A situation simply too foreign, all full of prune plum cambium and gargantuan raspberry canes. After all, the deer seems a creature whose every sense seeks after mistrust. Inevitably, she dashed into the woods and was gone.

From that point on, I inspected my kingdom every single morning right into June. As far as I could tell, she never returned. Was this predation a one-time occurrence? I should have known better.

The next year saw the start of my long-held dream of growing and harvesting food through all twelve months of the year. The concept of year-round gardening in a climate that hovers around freezing for three months demands careful planning of the beds, a genuine compulsion, and a thorough knowledge of what to plant and when. For one example, cole crops such as broccoli thrive in the lengthening days of early spring, while other coles, like Chinese cabbage and certain cauliflowers, seem to prefer the shortening days of fall.[3] I also kept three small beds in Jerusalem artichoke tubers, potatoes, and parsnips. All three vegetables share the characteristics of surviving underground and looking very white, which somehow seems a proper color for any crop that needs to harmonize with the whiteness of winter. Likewise, all three offer up their bounty during the coldest days in January, and in fact seem to grow sweeter as the days grow colder. My hard work was paying off.

On a blatantly political level, I came to believe that in organic gardening lies the salvation of the world. Herein lies the single most meaningful and accessible step any of us can take to end the hegemony of the centralized technological fix that is so central to our lives and so debilitating to our ecosystem. Even a city-dweller can grow something in a window box. And if not, let every one of us support organically grown produce as the ultimate good cause for the environment.

Gardening has a power that is political as well as democratic.[4] It can be applied constantly, whereas one can only vote or demonstrate occasionally. I learned to sing the praises of the lowly earthworm who neutralizes the soil, builds enriched topsoil from its castings, provides oxygen to the roots of growing plants, and whose clan can recycle as much as thirty tons of soil per acre up to the surface each year.[5] So, also, I learned that *2.7 million pounds* of earthworm-eradicating pesticide is spread on this American land every single day.[6] Consequently, a world of bountiful organic gardens may be the most realistic way to put the pesticide companies out of business permanently. Begin with yourself: simply stop using pesticides, stop buying produce sprayed with them. Furthermore, a home garden needs no transport, no elaborate distribution system. It thus offers a viable self-realized means to contain petroleum overconsumption.

Look at it in terms of the apparently disconnected example of your TV set. The Rocky Mountain Institute informs us that new television sets draw between 1.5 and 8 watts of standby power when the set is nominally "off." The so-called instant on feature has been added to our TVs so that consumers do not have to wait an extra twenty seconds each time they turn the set on. But expanded onto the national level, this means that a 1,000-megawatt power plant (1/750 of the nation's capacity) must be kept running continuously just to power the nation's TV sets when they are "off."[7]

If that massive power consumption can be attributed just to "off" TV sets, try to imagine the commensurate power savings we would achieve by transforming the profligate manner in which we currently distribute food. For one glaring example, almost all of the broccoli consumed on the U.S. east coast is actually grown in California. But broccoli grows splendidly on the east coast, if not through so many varied months of the year. And just as we can start to turn off our TV sets, so we can also start to turn off this profligate 3,000-mile-long distribution system. The lesson: grow your own. Or if you cannot, promote local broccoli by supporting local producers. As strange as it may first seem, local broccoli offers an important energy savings for the seventh generation.

Or consider the transformation that would occur if the culture made a concerted effort to ease off its heavy meat diet. Twenty vegetarians can be fed on the same amount of land needed to feed one human meat-eater. In fact, 90 percent of all the vegetable protein grown in this country is lost because we choose to recycle it through livestock.[8] Or consider milk. Although the American Dairy Council assures us that cow's milk is nature's most perfect food, in fact it is the most perfect food for no one beside a baby cow, which has four stomachs, doubles its weight in forty-seven days, and is destined to weigh 300 pounds within a year.[9] When I learned that my own baby daughter, who seemed overly prone to runny noses, was probably lacking lactase—the enzyme necessary to digest milk—we changed over to organic soy milk and the runny noses quickly ceased.

There have been at least three major results of my taking up food gardening. First, the better I got at providing freshly grown food for my family, the less willing I became to feed them on supermarket produce. I rejected store-bought produce almost too boisterously, and in the process turned myself into a perceived harbinger of doom. I warned my less fortunate friends that those Mexico-grown tomatoes were also a repository for carcinogenic pesticides. And while some of them either joined the local organic co-op or immediately took up gardening for themselves, others found my language akin to the rantings of the preacher in Hawthorne's *Scarlet Letter*. It took a while before I learned to temper my comments.

Second, I found my family growing more healthy. This occurred not only because freshly grown produce contains more vitamins and minerals and fewer fats and chemicals, but also because of what author/farmer Wendell Berry describes so well:

> At a time when the national economy is largely based on buying and selling substitutes for common bodily energies and functions, a garden restores the body to its usefulness—a victory, I think, for our species. It may take a bit of effort to realize that among modern achievements, perhaps the most characteristic is the obsolescence of the human body—but it is true. Jogging and other forms of artificial exercise do not restore the usefulness of the body, but are simply ways of assenting to its uselessness; the body is a diverting pet, like one's chihuahua, and must be taken out for air and exercise. A garden gives the body the dignity of working in its own support. It is a way of rejoining the human race.[10]

Third, and quite unexpectedly, our society's collective fear of total technological collapse suddenly took on an entirely new meaning for me. On the positive side, this is expressed best, and once again, by the formidable pen of Wendell Berry:

> The problems of what to do with radioactive wastes and with decommissioned nuclear plants, for example, have

not yet been solved; and we can confidently predict that the "solutions," when they come, will cause yet other serious problems that will come as "surprises" to the officials and experts. In that way, big technology works perpetually against itself. That is the limit of unlimited economic growth. A garden on the other hand, is a solution that leads to other solutions. It is a part of the limitless pattern of good health and good sense.[11]

There is another side to this, which I feel bound to confess as well. One day it dawned on me that I had a hidden agenda to my gardening passion. I was one of the sober ants diligently working in *preparation* for an utter breakdown of society. Should the petroleum industry collapse, should the trucks, ships, and planes that deliver food to market be exploded out of commission, should any or all of us be called upon to fend for ourselves, then my own family would still be able to set a healthy and sustaining table in perpetuity. I found myself accepting this disturbing state of affairs and, in fact, even arrogantly thumbing my nose at it, as if daring it to come. So, for example, I rejected the use of hybrid seed in favor of open-pollinated types, a measure that makes good sense as a means to add one more degree of independence from a food distribution system that I could no longer trust.

But I also found myself relishing an insidious escapist fantasy. For example, I went ahead and expanded my bed of Jerusalem artichokes only because this marginal crop shows almost nothing above ground from late fall until mid spring. In other words, the tubers grow deep enough to escape the initial onslaught of, you guessed it, nuclear fallout. Should national destruction come, then I would be prepared for the worst. Go ahead, let roving gangs of future food pirates do their worst. They would never find my little larder of Jerusalem artichokes.

There I stood, prepared for the worst, no matter in what shape it might come. However, I was not prepared at all for a real attack as represented by the February onslaught of that delicate female mule deer. I am sure she quickly realized that no dog lived on the premises. Furthermore, no human had yet challenged her with guns, arrows, slingshots, rocks, or any of the other projectiles favored in combating a deer's incursion. And in the course of the year she devised a browsing strategy based on the on/off status of my house lights. Like raiders throughout history, she attacked as we slept.

The second year's raids began in late February. The three deer (she had upped the ante by giving birth to two speckled fawns) destroyed four beds of chard, kale, lettuce, cauliflower, and cabbage in a single night. When I inspected the damage the next morning, for the first time in my life I was moved to consider the implications of owning and, worse, shooting a shotgun. Luckily, this Rambo-fantasy solution soon passed.

Over the next several weeks I spent well over a hundred dollars building a seven foot tall fence around my vegetable patch. I went so far as to string chicken wire along the ground to keep out the local rabbits and rats just in case they got any ideas as well. I then went ahead and replanted two entire beds of radishes, kale, and broccoli. But a hailstorm, a week-long freeze at 20 degrees, and winds in excess of fifty miles an hour soon leveled all my young starts. I had replanted too late. No winter garden that year, but later crops were safe.

Although I solved the problem of protecting the vegetables, I still had a long way to go to safeguard the many smaller beds that abound in my eccentrically landscaped property. *My* property? Is that what it was? Had I become so vain as not to recognize the irony implicit in that contrived term "property"? Here was a legal human term used to describe a skin-deep layer of earth measured and plotted on a map by a pencil-wielding human surveyor. All of this territorial graphing generated for the primary purpose of adding my so called "claim" (that which somebody else might call his town, his nation, his planet) to the local tax register.

That deer and her kin had obviously never read the register. The pronoun *my* as it applies to the noun *property* remains possessive only as long as it applies to human beings crediting the land of other human beings. Instead, this very nonhuman deer preferred to *noster*. That meant, in effect, that she recognized no single-species right to ownership. Unfortunately, that point of view also designated her as a trespasser in terms of my concept of explicit property lines.

On a deeper level, we now encounter one important reason for the extinction of species in a world overpopulated by human beings. In this case, the deer continued to ravish just about everything not set behind that seven-foot fence: tulips, sweet william, lettuce, brussels sprouts, spinach. . . . It made me wish that I could find some way to make all deer extinct within the boundaries of my own piece of land.

Then I noticed a pattern to her predation. One night she bounded up onto the rocky knoll I call home and banqueted her way through an unfenced bed of yellow and red Juan tulips rimmed with sweet william and primroses. Someone in her entourage obviously enjoyed the repast because they all returned the very next night to continue browsing through another tulip and sweet william bed. What was it about these specific plants? I had to find out.

The next morning I picked one of the erect tulip leaves and turned it over in my hand. It was a substantial thing, pea green in color and even more succulent than the kale, considered to be the prize green of any winter garden. Feeling a bit like Alice trying to decide whether or not the mushroom would make her larger or smaller, I went ahead and bit into the leaf. It was sweet and savory at the same time, perhaps a bit stringy, but essentially as tasty as anything I grew for winter salad greens. Next came primrose leaf. This seemed utterly tasteless even though it physically resembled a miniature romaine. I was less sure about trying the sweet william. The cherry-red, lance-shaped leaves looked like nothing else common to the human diet. Just one bite proved to me that it was as bitter as it looked.

Except for a few staggered commando raids, the deer stayed away from my garden for the rest of the year.

I came to expect her arrival sometime during that next winter. Not to be disappointed, at ten one clear evening, I opened the door to let the cat out, only to come face to face with my garden's February persecutor. She stood in the moonlight quite alone, not more than twenty feet away, staring at me through huge doey eyes from the perimeter of the primrose bed. We watched each other for what seemed a full minute. What was it about this beautiful animal that made me so unwilling to share a few meager greens during the coldest time of the year? As I pondered this essential question of control, the deer grew accustomed to my presence. Did she sense my own hesitation? Possibly so, because she began to test it by munching through the last of *my* sweet william. Something snapped. I bolted from the porch like a banshee, determined to jump that deer if I could only catch her. Catch her? Before I had even gotten to the top step of my front porch she was a hundred yards down the hill and gracefully loping over the four-foot-high brush into the forest.

I stood there in the cold night air and, for the first time in this adversarial relationship, felt a glimmer of genuine admiration for the sheer exuberance of the beast. The night was warmer than usual, a hopeful sign that spring was indeed nearby. I had a hunch that as soon as the normal forest growth rejuvenated itself, I would see my adversary only infrequently until next February. So I sat down on the top step to consider the options. First, I could selectively choose to plant only those flower species unappealing to the taste buds of a deer. Daffodils, delphiniums, iris, poppies, are just a few of the plants that no deer in my yard has ever chomped upon. Second, I could entirely disregard the deer's predation, planting whatever struck my fancy, and actively permitting the animal to decide which plants would survive to blossom and which would be deer fodder. Third, I could scare the deer away from my gardens permanently. A resolute dog would accomplish that in no time. Or perhaps I, myself, could become the resolute party, standing by my front door with matches in one hand and a cherry bomb in the other, waiting diligently for the deer to appear. At which point I would light the firecracker and loft it like a grenade to land at the feet of my herbivorous challenger. Or fourth, I could take a hint from any of several traditional cultures as well as the more starry-eyed of my friends, and attempt to "talk" to the deer. I could reason with her, ask her politely to please refrain from eating my cultivated beds, explaining in plain language how much pleasure those blossoms always bring to my family and friends. Why not strike a bargain, offer to plant a special bed of tulips in exchange for her leaving the rest to me?

I decided to get a dog.

And so commenced a campaign to promote the idea of a canine family member with both wife and daughters. Next, I started looking at my neighbors' dogs in an entirely new way, weighing which pedigree best served a household with two young children. One day I got as far as putting on my jacket, ready to make a trip to the local pound. But at that point, car keys in hand, I finally relented. Reward a dog for barking at man and beast? A dog whose sole purpose would be to protect tulips from a doe during the few months of the year when the woods offered little for her to eat? What about the other months?

Good question, if one that not enough of my neighbors ever seem to ask themselves. Stories circulate around town about individual dogs who have been trained to keep deer out of gardens. They skulk off at midnight to form packs, reverting to their feral ancestry, hamstringing already half-starved deer before finally tearing them to pieces. It seems a classic case of our pets doing the dirty work, being the villains in a savage metaphor about how *we humans* exploit and devour nature: the big bad human masquerading as the big bad dog posing as the big bad wolf.

Actually there is an ongoing controversy about the *right* of local farmers to shoot and kill these roving dogs, which have never been trained to tell the difference between a wild fawn and a ranch lamb. Hey mister, that dead dog was somebody else's property . . . which leads inevitably to the evolutionary non sequitur of what is worth more under the law, a lamb killed by a dog, or a dog killed by a farmer? The dead deer, of course, has no standing whatsoever. To be quite honest about it, there are even a few of my own neighbors who seem to believe that any deer accrues more value dead than alive. Some of them go so far as to declare, by deed if not by self-incriminating words, that certain animals like deer and mallard ducks necessarily exist as a function of that strange term *game*. Game is the target of a shooting sport, which is only a game. The deer is the player not equipped with the loaded gun; and often the game is played whether the season has opened or not.

So I concluded that a dog was no longer an option. Instead, to appease what was fast becoming the death throes of my own anxiety, I went out and bought a single firecracker. For the next four nights I rose from my chair at half-hour intervals just to whip open the front door with matches in one hand and an appropriately named *jade garden salute* in the other. When my wife asked what on earth I was doing, I replied, ha ha, that I wanted to give the deer a good scare.

But clutching that explosive, destructive rocket in my hand, I also felt secret discomfort. I had essentially excluded the deer from my own definition of neighborhood. Social philosopher Andrew Schmookler has written about the narcissism of such aggression as primarily

> . . . a sign of distress in the system of relationship, both the sense of self and the sense of connection have been impaired. The sense of self has been impaired because the world from which a secure sense of self must be derived is too hostile a place. And for the same reason—the failure of others to meet one's needs with sufficient dependability— the relationship to others is also impaired.[12]

Whether nuclear bombs, dogs, or jade garden salutes, violent solutions are less fundamentally a manifestation of our power than of our anxiety. In this case, a desire on my own part to recreate the peaceful alternative lifestyle regurgitates itself as an undeniable statement about interspecies war. Kill for peace.

The deer reacted accordingly. She vanished altogether. Nor was there any sign that she had surreptitiously sneaked into the yard during the wee hours. At first, with my sense of credulity stretched to the breaking point, I had to wonder if I had inadvertently, and quite unconsciously, tapped into the original option number four: that of discussing the issue mind to mind. I wondered if my own stubborn fury might be interpreted as an example of what the psychics call focused attention. Yet somehow that made no sense because, everything so far seemed like a classic case of *mis*communication. Lastly, I would be lying not to admit that my own linear education made this supposition as difficult for me to swallow as a bowl full of sweet william leaves.

With the current situation beyond my grasp to comprehend, I relented by spending the next evening immersed in a videotape of *Platoon*. The deer returned. She ambled through a distasteful daffodil bed before commencing her task of granting my sweet williams a crew cut fit for a training camp recruit. Is it possible that she somehow knew I was too busy watching *Platoon* and so would not reach for the jade garden salute? Who can rightly say what she knew and didn't know?

Whether the deer actually possessed the tactical stealth of a Scarlet Pimpernel, or whether instead she was simply a magician able to conjure up an illusion of control, no matter. Actually, this reminded me of the MacKenzie delta—trying to make rational sense out of the mirage of two discrete horizons. And whether or not communication actually took place, the effect upon my vision of neighborhood could not be denied. I must have "talked" to her, albeit unconsciously, because she had obviously gotten some message. Whatever it was that actually occurred, its discovery signified that choice number three, that of watchdogs and fireworks, was no longer an option.

On that note, let me bring this entire affair back to ground level again. After all, the special parameter of this description is not so much that the deer was stealthy, intelligent, or even possibly telepathic, but that the relationship had evolved to include *neighborliness*. For over three years my own single-species, selfish point of view had prevented me from giving the deer its due as a key member of the same ecosystem within which I had built my home. Now something changed. Now, hurting the deer started to take on some of the attributes of a baseball fan's shouting to kill the umpire. But when you kill the umpire you kill the game, or in this case, kill the deer. And you destroy the neighborhood.

When we work too hard to build our world outside the loop of nature, we lose sight of a fundamental ability to see the loop for what it is: the central glorious fact of our existence. Likewise, the flourishing relationship between gardener and deer truly offered a key that opened up a deeper entry into that natural system to which I had long sought admission as a planter of flowers, trees, and vegetables. The role of the little doe had changed from devious thief to arbiter of ecology.

Lest anyone still doubt it, reality is foxy stuff; it intervenes in several contradictory forms at the same moment. In this case, the deer returned and returned and returned. Like the toniest New York cafe, my yard had been discovered. So it seemed one thing to revel in the deer's attention as a precious gift from a gifted being, and quite another thing to find some way to nurture a garden of unfenced flowers within the very same ecosystem utilized by a hungry herbivore and her spanking new fawn. It's true, she had given birth again.

I noticed that the deer never touched certain plants. For example, she avoided the entire ranunculus family, including such ornamentals as the anemone, delphinium, peony, and columbine, to name a few of the better known species. Neither would she eat rhododendrons, marigolds, poppies, lilies, tomatoes, potatoes—in fact, a veritable country garden full of flowers and vegetables. This observation provided a glimpse of a more farsighted strategy for replanting my ravaged beds. For instance, because the potato plant served as a forbidden fruit (the leaves made me feel queasy when I tried one), I planted the potatoes *outside* the garden fence. And I wondered what would happen if I surrounded my young and still quite vulnerable plum trees with the nearly pharmaceutical aroma of a bed of self-seeding poppies and wormwood.

In fact, what I had stumbled upon was the first tentative stages of what is properly known as a *permaculture* garden. This is a method of horticulture that favors the permanent approach, with a minimum of artificial primping by a human overseer. For example, we eliminate the use of all poisons, artificial fertilizers, and violence as a means of inducing plants to do our bidding. We eschew the horrendous commercial practice of first annihilating every living thing that grows over, on, and under a plot of earth, then laying on a coating of chemical fertilizer that imbalances the soil, before planting just one variety of one crop, which is only kept alive by spraying some pesticide that taints everything that feeds off the land for years to come. Permaculture avoids all that.

Permaculture insists that we stop planting hybrids because these infertile athletes of the flower world are not actually self-perpetuating. Instead, we favor annual flowers that will reseed themselves, and perennials that do not need special pampering just to grow at all. Nor do we exhaust huge amounts of time, energy, and money to excavate a garden plot out of solid rock or deep forest, but rather mold the garden to fit the contours of the land. That also means that we learn about mini-environments and, for example, place the geums and the squash where the sun can hit them full on, while we locate the bleeding hearts and the gooseberries where they will get some shade. The garden grows itself. In sum, permaculture is a gardening method fit to feed the seventh generation.

In my case, I discovered how to garden in my own neighborhood by first learning how to participate with that deer as a neighbor. With a little luck, my own great-great-great-great-great grandchildren will still be gardening alongside the progeny of that little doe.

Just as I went ahead and moved the potato bed outside the fenced vegetable plot, so I also moved most of the remaining tulips inside the fence. I retained one bed of black tulips where the deer might easily locate them. Last January, with apples overflowing my family's winter larder, I actually went so far as to lay an entire bushel of half-turned banana apples beside one of the deer's favored paths. I snickered to think she might also get a bit inebriated from eating too many of them. She found them within forty-eight hours and ate every last one of them, which led me to believe that this surreptitious deer might have been browsing the knoll more often than the evidence suggested.

One naturalist neighbor offered a counterpoint to this purported benevolence, opposing the gift as my own inadvertent attempt to tame the deer, to turn her into a dependent. I wasn't so sure. To lay a gift at the feet of a wild animal once a year seemed more an act of coevolution than of coercing subservience. I preferred to treat my act as a contemporary counterpart of the practices of the Huichols of Mexico, who honored the deer as a harbinger of abundance. Or of the ancient Chinese who honored the deer as a teacher of communication within the supernatural realms. Or lastly, the conduct of the many shamanic peoples who recognized the deer as a possessor of grace and compassion,[13] a creature who merited a yearly gift-giving. In fact, these had all coevolved in our own relationship.

Perhaps coincidentally, it is now mid February as I tell this tale about the deer in my life. It has been a brutal month after an otherwise mild winter. The area was hit with a storm just two weeks ago that brought zero temperatures and 90-mile-an-hour winds—perhaps the first such "storm of the century" to actually deserve that designation. As usual, the tulips, the daffodils, the iris all had a few inches of greenery thrusting above ground when the storm struck. Now two weeks later, the edges of their leaves are obviously frostbitten, but nonetheless they have started to grow again. Actually, I was more surprised to learn that about half of the semi-native foxglove had succumbed to the cold. And my winter garden? Until the storm hit it had seemed a miracle that provided parsnips, Jerusalem artichokes, kale, cabbage, beets, and even some romaine lettuce as late as the end of January.

But winter gardening must remain the ultimate challenge for at least one more year. Almost every vegetable within my seven-foot-high fence succumbed to the cold. Only the spring leeks and parsnips seem to have made it. And as always, the Jerusalem artichokes growing outside the fence have produced more tubers than any of us could possibly eat. This year, despite doom and self-sufficiency fantasies, I plan to cut that bed in half.

I sit at the word processor this morning in an attempt to put the cap on this chapter. By noon I had saved the file, left the computer humming, and walked into the kitchen to fix some lunch. A woodpecker, a jewel of a creature saddled with the zany name of red-breasted sapsucker, contentedly knocked its head back and forth against a Douglas fir just outside the kitchen window. I watched this strange variation on the universal theme

of working for a living, only to have some movement at the
opposite end of the yard steal my attention. Two deer stood
browsing across the northwest slope of the knoll. These were
newcomers and, at least at this distance, appeared larger than
the little doe. I guessed that they might be her twins, now grown
and already possessed of the knowledge needed to ravish my
February garden on their own behalf. I also noted just how
unperturbed the deer seemed to be in the face of that raucous
drumroll knocked out by the woodpecker. By contrast, when I
started to wash the dishes just to keep busy as I watched, I
dropped a serving spoon into the sink. The clatter brought the
two deer to full attention, despite the muffling barrier of a
double-pane window, six inches of fiberglass insulation, and
fifty yards distance.

Half an hour later the deer still browsed, although they also
seemed to be spending an inordinate amount of time licking
each other's faces. They wandered up onto the top of the hill,
seeming to shrink to normal size as they approached my own
eye-level vantage point. To be honest about it, I can no
longer be certain that this "new" female is not actually my
old friend seen for the very first time by the bright light of
noon.

Deer are said to *browse;* they do not forage, or even graze.
They take a few steps this way and that, drop their heads, and
almost blindly bite whatever looks promising directly in front of
them. Then they quickly lift their heads, scan the lay of the
land, cock their ears, eventually take a few more steps, drop
their heads again, and grab hold of another bite. It seems not
that much different from browsing in a library. The deer are
munching on some grass, madrone leaves, and even the first
tender growth from a patch of *my* Canterbury bells. They step
right up to my plum tree, take a whiff of the bar of Irish Spring
soap hung up as deer repellent on one of the branches, and
quickly move back to the Canterbury bells.

I have not yet made so much as a twitch. Next, they stop to
fully savor two or three licks from the inside of each other's
huge ears. Is it love or is it grooming? Or perhaps it is just salt
that they crave.

Now the male spots me through the window. Yes, he is looking right at me. I freeze. He moves sideways to me, and cocks his ears stiffly. I keep staring directly into his eyes. The female keeps licking his ears. The male widens his eyes, and then freezes as if uncertain what to do next. He bolts. She bolts. Clomp, clomp, clomp, they bounce across the rocky moss of the knoll, and down the hill. Gone. The woodpecker keeps on knocking. Knock-knock-knock. . . .

Chapter Ten

Blurring the Edges Between Myth and Reality

One question I have so far overlooked in this discussion about connecting with nature is a difficult one: How can a book such as this deign to ask any of us to embrace the whole of nature when so many of its parts frighten us out of our skin?

I share the property upon which I built my own home with huge colonies of red and black thrashing ants who construct large dome-shaped mounds as the aboveground manifestation of what must be giant underground cities. Somehow, it seems best to describe the impact of these cities upon my own peace of mind by first comparing them to yellow jackets, which have already been portrayed. Yellow jackets, no matter how ominous they may first appear, are easy to monitor. Even my elder daughter who got stung so regularly last summer, has already mastered the art of wasp coexistence. Next year will come the summer of our discontent for her sweet-smelling younger sister.

Wasps are one thing, ants another. It is all a matter of scale. The ants build a nest containing at least several hundred thousand occupants. These occupants cover a territory a hundred yards on any side. At any time my home is surrounded by twenty or thirty of these nests. And each and every ant within offers its own tiny bite whenever provoked.

I step too close to a nest and dredge up a fantasy of myself as the hero of one of those male adventure magazines. My family has gone away for the weekend. I am out in the woods, splitting firewood when an overhanging branch breaks loose, falls on my head and knocks me unconscious. I wake up to find my clothes torn, my face scratched, my right arm broken, and my left leg pinned underneath the fallen branch. With an expression of terror on my face right out of Edvard Munch, I am frozen forever as the cover subject of this month's *Saga* magazine, my right leg disappearing through the dome of an ant colony that, at this low angle, looks as big as Mt. Rainier. My lower body is covered by well over 1,000 ants and they are all traveling north toward my eyes.

Of course this vision is a dream, an invention of my imagination. It is, however, pertinent to our understanding of spiritual ecology simply because most of our fears about nature start out as dreams and imagination.

I would have to be either very drunk or very, very, curious ever to get close enough to a nest to risk falling in. Meanwhile, these ants are exemplary at minding their own business. Furthermore, they are among the most useful critters in the entire interspecies neighborhood. Scavengers by nature, they keep the yard gloriously free of most other insect pests. Unfortunately, life, or should I say, fear, is never quite so straightforward. Coexistence with a large mound of ants is not a matter of simple familiarity as it is with yellow jackets. This has never been an issue about what they do or how they live. It is the sheer number of beings who are doing it. Whatever it is that they actually do.

I have taken to spending time sitting on a rock just outside their personal space, some fifteen feet from the mound, for no other reason than to exorcise the demons from my own collective unconscious. On any normal day the entire mound lies before me totally covered with living ants, pulsing and glistening in the sunlight like a sepia satin blanket. They keep themselves busy remolding and cleaning the mound, dredging debris from their underground chambered city, adding sticks and fir needles and even the exoskeletons of other insects onto the outside surface of this heaped-up monument to their own ingenuity. So they are organized like the world's most efficient construction company, building a structure that compares to their own body proportions as the Great Pyramid compares to our own.

A mound that was four inches tall and six inches wide last week is now a foot tall and two feet wide. Imagine building a Cheops pyramid in four or five weeks. The very substantial individual sticks, as large, by comparison, as the building blocks of that pharaoh's pyramid, are carried in the jaws of a single ant from as far away as 100 yards—equal to about sixteen miles in human scale. South African naturalist Eugene Marais, who spent a decade in the 1920s studying termites and ants, has described a termite colony in the desert that sunk a well shaft sixty-five feet (equivalent to three and a half human miles) straight down into the earth. It was the only way they could get a drink of water.

Once in a while—for example, when a colony builds too close to my daughters' swing set—I feel forced to don the hat of interspecies landlord and evict the ants before some little girl falls into a nest. To rid yourself of a small nest, stick a shovel into it, mess it up a bit, and by the next day it may be gone. When I tried it, the workers picked up their disarrayed rice-sized eggs and immediately started to relocate en masse to a new site farther down the hill and increasingly away from my own house. At least that is what I think they were doing. Just as I plainly recognize and react to their house, so they seem to recognize mine: one builder reacting to the handiwork of another. And within a week's time, the colony is the same size as before.

If I persist in maintaining that I have smashed their *house,* I have done absolutely nothing to impact their *home*. This latter entity is not so much personified by a structure or even a place, as it is by the living presence of their goddess queen. She is queen ant, mother of a city, Gaea incarnate. Unmitigated violence has succeeded in delivering a concise message to the queen. I request her to direct her daughters (ant workers are female) to relocate their house a little bit farther away from my own. She is more than accommodating, and so the job is soon accomplished.

Because in essence the queen *is* the colony, the workers register in my mind more as cells rather than as independent beings. This sense of the seeming mindlessness of the individual ant brews within me its own bizarre sense of morality. When I uproot a small colony, what at first appears to be a violent and bloody holocaust seems to register in the *no-mind* of the workers as little more than the next extemporaneous job on the daily agenda. What is house building, anyway, if not an endless procedure of placing one stick on top of another? From the point of view of a worker ant, what does it matter that a few of their number die, or that the nest is disrupted. After all, the queen lives.

A large mound tells a different story. Just a year after I laid out my vegetable garden, a small ant's nest started to grow itself a few feet away from one of the raised beds. I could have messed it up with a stick, which would have prompted the ants to move their nest-in-the-making farther down the hill. As it was, I did nothing, believing that the nest in March was about as big as it was going to get. But the ants kept building. One day in June I finally noticed that they had worn down a highway twenty-five feet long, one inch deep, straight as an arrow across two of the planted beds. All day long they marched back and forth, hundreds, thousands of ants, a veritable population explosion of little beings going about their appointed rounds. They seemed to waver off the highway only when a bit of food or a prospective twig showed itself.

One day I watched silently as twenty of them attacked and then sucked dry a slug that, itself, was feeding on my choicest romaine. Another day, a neighbor who came to visit quickly pointed out that I had ants climbing all over the buds of an unopened peony. I was about to run for the hose to spray them off when he explained that the peony bud is covered with a kind of protective cuticle. Unless some diligent ants happened to be about to gnaw through that sweet binder, the peony might not be able to open on its own.

Was this an example of ant/peony symbiosis? The man chuckled and suggested that I be glad the ants didn't send me a bill for their services. For their part, the peonies opened in all their glory about a week later.

Actually, of all the vegetables in the garden, the ants never bothered much beside the artichokes. But even this ostensible predation ended up being infinitely more complex than a simple case of insects chewing up vegetables. The ants cared not a whit for the taste of these cultivated representatives of the thistle family. Rather, the artichokes had become infested with aphids. The ants were milking these tiny insects like human farmers milk dairy cattle, and licking up the aphids' own sweet droppings. A stiff soaking from the hose knocked off the aphids, which the ants duly carried back to their nest.

Then one day I noticed that three new hills had sprung up, seemingly overnight, in spots just outside the perimeter of my garden. They had me surrounded. Yet I didn't act. Meanwhile this insect river in flood continued to tromp indented trails through the moss, up the cedar boards of the raised garden beds, across the rich loam, spending every waking moment scouring the garden clean of any litter they might find along their random wanderings. When something choice showed itself—a small stick, a fir needle, a dead larva—a signal was somehow transmitted across vast distances. Within minutes, however many ants were needed to do that particular job were there getting it done. No more, no less. In most cases, the job at hand usually consisted of freighting some treasure across a prodigious expanse of garden and back to the nest.

Another neighbor came to visit and commented how fastidiously manicured my garden always looked. Ants, I answered. The ants do it. And it's true, there seems no end to the things to be said in favor of ants. I'd like them too, if there just weren't so many of them.

Then came the last straw. An ant pinched my eldest daughter as she lay sleeping, causing her to start screaming at two in the morning. It was time to act. I decided to evict the ants with gasoline.

But I have already told this story. Just as I stood before the yellow jackets with a swatter, and stood before the deer with a firecracker, so I now stand before an ant colony holding a five-gallon gas can. Swatting the yellow jackets led to a change of heart, and not bombing the deer involved a change of heart.

And now? I incinerated that ant colony three times over a twenty-four-hour period—and it led to a change of heart.

But a change of heart that refers to ant dreams invokes a very different moral, and therefore makes this particular version of my fundamental tale well worth recounting. In the cases of the yellow jackets and the deer, the control I so desperately sought to retain was overwhelmed by a more powerful perception of a mutual coexistence within nature. Living in harmony offered me a more life-enhancing proposition than persisting with the stereotypical onus of human control.

The ants told a different tale because, to be honest about it, I have never attained that friendly perception of neighborliness. And if I lost the burden of attempting to control them, it was not because I finally saw the light of harmony. Rather, I recognized that the ants, as represented by the hidden persona of an underground queen, were always going to be in control. I could no more eliminate *her* from *my* property, than I could eliminate the dirt itself. In fact, the harmony I finally achieved went much deeper than either yellow jackets or deer. In this case, the queen put one nonnegotiable demand on the table. She demanded that I surrender to her my own deepest nightmares about ants. If I agreed to do so, coexistence would soon follow.

As with the image of a yellow jacket field hospital, do I stand guilty of dreaming up an anthropomorphic scenario that exists no place in nature beside my own mind, imparting too much amateur psychology into this relationship between myself and social insects? Do I need to recognize that there is a distinct difference between myth making and reality? In fact, I answer my own question by declaring that spiritual ecology asks all of us to start blurring the edges.

Eugene Marais spent ten years observing termites and ants. He concluded that colonies are best understood as a composite being possessed of both a group purpose and a group mind. We actually misconstrue a whole organism when we perceive individual workers as if they might be independent little insects living out their lives in a tight social context. Consider them instead to be mere building blocks, like brain cells that carry out the functions of brain without also being privy to the functions of mind. They are the ultimate slaves, internally programmed to do the bidding of their queen and nothing else.

For her own part, the queen's control over her workers seems based upon some communicative mechanism far beyond our ability to explain, although some might liken it to telepathy. For example, when Marais enclosed a termite queen within a tiny steel-plated prison, the colony continued to flourish. But if he killed the queen, even inside that same prison, the whole community soon ceased to work. If another termitary grew close by, the workers soon drifted into the new colony where they apparently "swore allegiance" to the new queen, because there was no sign of fighting. However, if these same disinherited termites were immediately brought to a nest a hundred yards away, a fight quickly led to the deaths of all the intruders. As Marais explains it:

> The mysterious power which streams from the queen functions only within a limited distance. Every termite is under its power. If the two termitaries are situated close to each other, the power of each queen operates in both nests. It is through this psychological power of the queen that the termites of one nest are capable of recognizing their fellow citizens and discovering strange intruders.[1]

When Marais waited a few days before attempting to transfer the befuddled workers to a more distant nest, he found that they were no longer attacked. Whatever power the old queen might have possessed over her minions had evidently evaporated. The now *empty* workers, like bits of computer memory, were available to be filled up with the program of a new hostess. But by what power does the queen hold the community together? Marais comments:

> We will assume that it is something analogous to scent. Personally I do not think it is scent but something much more subtle. But if we think of it as scent it will simplify matters for we are actually dealing with something far and away beyond human sense.[2]

If it were humans being discussed here, we might call this communication channel a psychic phenomenon. Yet although this "something far and away beyond human sense" seems better established today than in Marais's time, it is still no better accepted.

Psychic phenomena have a place but no home within our culture. On the one hand, much of the scientific establishment seems forever bogged down trying to quantify that which is most ephemeral and emotionally based, denying its existence altogether until such time as it can be squeezed into some all-encompassing definition. Too often, the phenomenon's main value aboveground seems to lie in its own debunking. On the other hand, the fringes of the New Age movement tend to view that which is most transparent and subconscious as nothing less than that which is most opaque. The concept of psychic phenomena resounds through that particular subculture as a solved mystery, and connotes just about anything and everything that eludes scientific substantiation.

As usual, the truth exists somewhere in between. In fact, a profound lesson emerges when we are able to transcend both sides of the controversy, and in effect learn to blur the edges between scientific substantiation and personal myth making. A simple acceptance of just the *possibility* of psychic phenomena probably offers quite a bit more opportunity for enhancing personal growth than either denouncing the subject outright, or actively promoting the potential as if it were a path toward an elitest supermind. The *process* of attunement, not the outward results (or the scientific debate about those results) is what is most pertinent to spiritual ecology. It is much more important that we take the time to attune inward, than to verbalize that inwardness, outward. Actually, the inscrutable process that earlier I call *tuning osmosis* is finally defined here as a kind of listening meditation. Because tuning osmosis connects us to the long-term processes implicit within nature, it also offers the very best method for attending to the songs of the seventh generation.

While most people may have a hard time associating psychic phenomena as the fundamental mechanism governing ant colo-

nies, the psychic connective process seems much more acceptable (if not just as controversial) when associated with other
nonhuman species. For example, perhaps, nowhere is the issue
of psychic phenomena more controversial than at the point of
contact between human beings and the dolphins. Stories about a
direct human-cetacean mindlink have always existed as a quiet
undertone at the various scientific and environmental confer-
ences I have attended—the stuff of backroom discussions where
personal anecdotes garner far more attention than quantified
data. Yet, unfortunately, this intuitive subject matter rarely makes
it to the central podium, from where it most needs to be heard.
First, psychic experience remains too risky an area for many
professionals to even acknowledge as a valid realm for study.
Second, no one in attendance seems to possess either the language or the certitude to know what to say about it. This occurs
because the contemporary science of biology is so utterly based
in objectified information-gathering that it has forgotten how to
blur the edges.

But the rumors (potential kernels of myth that they are)
persist, and for good reason. The immediate sense of connection
that some people say they perceive in the company of certain
animal species (not only dolphins) serves to awaken the future
primitive in all of us: This is where we all were when we
were less civilized, and this is where we shall all be when
we are more civilized. The resultant meditational interface
between human and nature offers a genuine bridge between
the current scientific-objective and the ancient shamanic-
mythic view. The process promotes a *personal* interconnectedness with nature as a primary path leading to *cultural*
interconnectedness; without also negating all the circuitry that
already drives our thoroughly modern twentieth-century brains.
My own first book, *Animal Dreaming*, dealt with this issue
in some detail.[3]

In *Gödel, Escher, and Bach*, computer scientist Douglas
Hofstadter clarifies the quasi-metaphysical findings of Marais
even further, and so describes many eerie similarities between a
functioning ant colony and the self-aware human brain. For

example, ant workers are eminently programmed to follow trails and so bring back nourishment that animates the whole. This talent finds its analogue in the firing of neurons, which are trails that animate the true function of brains. Furthermore, even though an ant colony is comprised of ants, its power and function can no more be apprehended as a collection of ants than the power of the brain can be apprehended as a collection of brain cells. As Hofstadter and Marais both tell us, when you kill the queen the workers are soon as helpless as Humpty Dumpty in putting themselves back together again.[4] Just as our minds cannot sense the firing of individual brain cells when we think our thoughts, so the colony cannot sense the movements of individual ants off fulfilling their programmed functions. When the colony loses control over its ants, the ants also lose their colony.

Yet despite this mutual inability to sense the *lower level of meaning,* human brains and ant colonies both remain mysteriously unified and coordinated through some as yet unexplained teleological mechanism. We call the sum total of all these functions "consciousness" when it refers to brains. Although there is no official term to describe the same process as it refers to ant colonies, could we do any better if we also called the ant colony a conscious entity? Conscious, although a nonhuman consciousness very alien to ourselves.

Which may explain why I find myself prey to the most uncomfortable of fantasies whenever I step inside the ten-foot radius of an ant colony's self-aware, personal space. Is this a case of the simple heebie-jeebies, or has my intensive relationship to the colony made me supersensitive to the hypnotic brainwave spell cast by a telepathic queen?

One part of my mind fears that it is about to be taken over, my own braincase filled up with ant thoughts every bit as uncomfortable as ant bodies. I sense that the colony has tacked up a psychic signal inside the billboard of own mind: Beware you fool—inner sanctum; trespass at your own risk. This risk is double-edged because the danger I face also seems a real-time confrontation with my own worst fantasies. What if a sudden stiff gust of wind should pick me up bodily and drop me onto the mound? What irony. Even as I dream a nightmare of ants as the incarnation of mindless terror, so that same nightmare prompts me to void my observed realization of essentially helpful ants. The queen's nonnegotiable demand reasserts itself.

I am not unlike a sleepwalker, bound to perpetrate a waking nightmare holocaust upon ants who, despite aggravating outward appearances, are trying to go about their business of living outside my dream. Unfortunately, they are never going to succeed as long as I live next door. In that light, regard Tweedle-dum's commentary to a bewildered Alice who wishes to wake up a sleeping Red King because he happens to be dreaming about her:

> "It's no use *your* talking about waking him," said Tweedledum, "when you're only one of the things in his dream. You know very well you're not real." "I *am* real!" said Alice, and began to cry.[5]

I play both Tweedledum *and* Red King to the ant's Alice.

Carl Jung wrote that we cannot know ourselves fully until we start to live the "symbolic life," an individual existence guided as much by our dreams and subconscious psyche as by ego and career responsibilities.[6] When we fail to heed the messages issuing from within our dreams, many of us end up guiding our lives by one or another small part of our own best self. We fall prey to a sickness and are no longer conscious enough to perceive the convoluted signs of low self-esteem, addictive behavior, neurosis.

Expanding Jung's inward realm ever outward so that it encompasses more than the single individual, we encounter what can only be called the "symbolic culture." Here is an existence guided by the collective unconscious, perhaps best explained as an ant colony awareness translated into an energy field fit to supervise the unified human condition. For example, one way that traditional people have always expressed their own symbolic culture is through an ongoing retelling of the animal myth-dreams that concern their own deepest connections within the larger field of nature. They have blurred the edges between objective reality and myth making in what we call *totemism*. Totemism has never been satisfactorily explained as only a primitive religion, or *animism,* because it is, instead, a set of timeless rules guiding individual and group identity within the interpenetrating web of symbolic culture.

When the symbolic culture fails to heed these dream messages, it falls prey to the same sense of incompleteness that besets the symbolic life. Thus, for example, the message of totemism identifies a human society interacting with other species-groups as teachers and students within a neighborly world. We learn how to structure both our lives and our culture not merely by observing nature, but by participating with nature.

But look around you. Few if any contemporary human institutions ever participate with other species of animals as peers. They have consequently fallen into an exploitive hierarchical approach initiated by either a precise reading of the Bible, a misreading of Darwin[7] or both. Unlike the many traditional peoples who guided their lives by totem interconnectedness, we do not permit our own natural connectedness to be guided by anything but one small objective component of ourselves. The symbolic culture, guided by dreams, has been left unheeded, in effect leaving us blinded to destroy a *neighborhood* we no longer acknowledge.

Just as the individual who voids the symbolic life finds him/herself falling prey to low self-esteem, addictive behavior, and neurosis, so the culture that disregards its group dreams falls prey to an alienation that, at least at the present moment, manifests as gluttony, selfishness, and possibly self-destructiveness.

Yet if we *could* perceive the connectedness right from the center of all our various institutions—were, in fact, no longer blind to it—we simply could not continue to operate as we do. However, this change in perception need not exist as something unbearably mystical and therefore quite beyond our current grasp of reality.

Well, then, how do we get connected?

It is the wrong question. For example, my own junior high school science teacher got it right when she taught that we are now breathing in atoms that once made up the body of a dinosaur, a Buddha, our own great grandmother, a queen ant, and the sun. The seventh generation breathes you and me. In other words, we *are* already connected. We have simply forgotten how to perceive the truth of the situation.

Therefore, a better question might be: How do we *perceive* that connectedness as a way of life? Practice totemism? On some level, yes, of course; we must start to respond to the other creatures as both mentors and students.

I, for one, also promote the Zen *sudden school* for changing perceptions. A teacher of Zen gives his students a kind of quasi-riddle, known as a *koan,* which the student is obligated to answer. "What is the sound of one hand clapping?" is a well-known koan. However, as you can see from this example, koans are not the same thing as *questions* whose answers about the sound of clapping are found in books about acoustic engineering or through the observation of enthusiastic audiences. Rather, to answer the koan means to change one's deepest perceptions about reality. We blur the edges. And when the answer comes, it is both *sudden* and *complete*. There is no turning back to the old perceptions.

This "how-to" book you are reading is full of koans for that very same reason: they change perceptions. I happen to believe the Zen masters when they tell me that perceptions can be quickly transformed when we know how to ask the right koans. So I have already offered you several: How do we listen for the songs of the seventh generation? How do we dance through the streets of our cities with long-dead native Americans? How does a sea turtle relate to the Gettysburg Address? What do the animals look like when they take off their costumes? What is a yellow jacket field hospital like?

Or this difficult one: Imagine that nature herself is a queen ant, dreaming each of us as dreamers who dream her up disguised in the cosmic garb of the physical universe. Actually, it sounds very much like Alice's Red King turned into a red ant queen. Now the koan: What does that make of you and me and ants and nature? Hindu mythology provides one "answer" to this particular koan which makes splendid use of just about all the cogent elements of this ant-generated worldview.

As the story goes, Indra, god-king of the *waking world,* is furiously exploiting all the resources of the world in a vain attempt to build a huge palace as a monument to his own glory. The other creatures cannot long endure this folly. Finally, they lodge a complaint with the sleeping god Vishnu. It is Vishnu who holds the ultimate responsibility for every single event of this waking world, simply because he is actually dreaming the whole thing. Now, in an effort to mollify Indra's growing number of plaintiffs, Vishnu dreams up an army of ants to parade through the half-finished palace of the god-king. And of course, when Indra sees this nightmarish invasion he angrily summons Vishnu's lieutenant, demanding an immediate explanation.

The lieutenant explains, "As you know, the waking world we perceive is nothing but Vishnu's dream. However, even Vishnu has to wake up once in a while, which he does about every three hundred thousand years. He flickers his eyes for a few minutes and then falls back into a deep sleep again. At that moment, all the events and inhabitants of the waking world are simply dreamed up all over again."

Now the lieutenant peers directly into Indra's eyes. "And of course, that is why Vishnu thought that living ants might be a far better monument to your splendor than even the most magnificent of palaces. You see, each individual ant is the reincarnation of an Indra from a unique dream of Vishnu."

Indra stares at the ants busily going about their work, and then turns very pensive. "There must be millions and millions of them," he cries in despair. "Yes," replies the lieutenant. "You see, the deeds you accomplish in this lifetime are the things that affect your future incarnation. Ants, for example, are the most skilled builders of palaces. In your own case, the better you get at building a palace as a monument to yourself, the better chance you have for getting incarnated as an ant in your next life."

The lieutenant shakes his head and watches the ants cover every surface within the palace. "As you can plainly see, the ant colony has grown very large. Literally millions upon millions of former Indras listened to this very same injunction, and then forged ahead to build magnificent handiworks. Naturally, they achieved their reward. And of course, unless you decide to stop building this palace, you too will be rewarded by turning into an ant. Somebody else will have to play the part of Indra, god-king of the waking world.''

By the time the lieutenant takes his leave, with the ants following him, Indra has stopped all work on the palace. So the world is saved.[8]

On that note, permit me to quietly clunk the gasoline can next to the rock while I jog back into my own house to find a pack of matches, jog over to the hose nozzle to turn on the water as a safety precaution, jog over to the woodpile to find a good stout pole, and finally jog back down to the ant colony, hose, matches, and pole in hand. I jab the pole deep into the mound, stir up the insides until the ant eggs bubble up to the surface like the viscera of a rotten carcass full of maggots, pour a half-pint of gasoline onto the perfect dome of their domicile, step back, and throw in a lit match. Ten thousand ants are incinerated in a blazing instant.

When the blue fire has subsided, I sink the stick in a second time, dredging up thousands upon thousands of quarter-inch long eggs that, this time, remind me of nothing so much as the leavings of an office paper-punch. Meanwhile, all those ants who had been out gathering building material and food start to arrive back at the holocaust site. Without so much as a pause to survey the situation, they immediately set upon the task of gathering up the eggs to carry them back inside the steaming mess that was once a nest. Reading my Marais correctly, that observation of functioning workers also signifies that the queen is still quite alive and presiding over the whole operation. Is she guiding my hand as well? An hour later I return to the nest, drop in another half-pint, stand back, light a match, and watch the remains ignite. Another 10,000 brain cells vanish in an instant. And one last time the next morning.

A week later, the newly constructed nest was fast approaching the size of the original, but a substantial twenty feet farther down the hill. We had communicated in the only way I knew how, and so achieved a compromise. Mostly, I was very glad that my pyromanic lust seemed to be over. I watched the mound pulsate with the bodies of black and red ants piled up on top of one another until they were a foot high and two feet wide. In fact, I could barely see the mound at all through the opaque mass of tightly intertwining ant bodies. A hundred thousand organically bound beings, tending to the needs of their young, setting up ingenious transportation and communication links to food sites, building a splendid palace as a monument to their own collective self. Leading to still another crazy koan: How could it ever be otherwise?

Their queen ant's willingness to cooperate, whether conscious or unconscious, has also helped me to overcome whatever fear I may have ever felt toward them. In other words, the waking world of ants has finally overwhelmed my own private dream world of no ants. I have learned the same dream lesson of spiritual ecology as channeled from Vishnu to Indra and finally, to me. The queen's nonnegotiable demand has been met in full. Now, perhaps, I am ready to accept her as a next door neighbor.

Two years have gone by since that act of incineration. The colony has remained in that same place well away from the house. The workers continue to surge across the area with a sound that doesn't seem to emanate from anywhere in particular. Likewise, the colony itself continues to palpitate with an aura of consciousness, like some strange alien pod from another galaxy. And every March the colony sends out emissaries searching for new sites upon which to build suburbs, just to take some of the pressure off their overpopulated city. And so, every March they invade my house anew. For two weeks my family endures a restrained invasion of fifty or so ant scouts parading across the living room floor and once in a while falling off the dining room ceiling into somebody's soup. After two weeks these domestic explorations subside just as mysteriously as they began.

Every so often, out in the environs of *our* front yard, I discover one of their suburbs under construction too close to the house. I push a stick into it. The ants always comply by moving farther down the hill. At least that's my version of it. For all I know, the queen is dreaming it quite a bit differently.

Chapter Eleven

⚘

Connecting with the Seventh Generation

Art critic John Berger reminds us that whereas animals were once central to our very perception of the world, now in the late twentieth century they have been reduced to the margins of our lives.[1] They live on in our imagination via secondhand models of nature, including TV documentaries, children's toys, and the kinetic sculpture we find at zoos. At those places where humans daily confront the natural environment, whether urban or rural, real animals seem forever in retreat. And when we do not see them, do not relate to them, we soon forget the experience of living in a world in which they are part and parcel. That real world is, of course, nature; ours is a nature devoid of *the experience of nature.*

We know more than we experience. For example, as I write, an earthquake in Soviet Armenia has become the subject of all reports arriving from the outside world. I have never been to Armenia, may never go there. And while political pundits argue brilliantly about a global village that generates profound connections between current events, any small amount of self-reflection makes me painfully aware that my own head has become a passive repository for too much useless information. Although we do well to acknowledge the koan about a butterfly flapping its wings (or an earthquake rumbling) in Central Asia eventually affecting weather patterns (or taxes) in our own hometown, we must also consider the way a secondhand perception of the world effectively filters the relationship we hold to our own experiences. In terms of the themes of this book, filtering the world through a secondhand connectedness makes it impossible for us to hear the songs of the seventh generation.

Our schools encourage an object-oriented relationship to the psyche, rewarding an ability to hold information while discouraging dreaming. Twenty-five years out of high school, and in good secondhand fashion I can still rattle off most of the kings and queens of England in chronological order. Yet about my own ancestors I know nothing beyond three generations ago. I can even remember an earthquake in Iran that took 10,000 lives just before the start of my sophomore year. But what year was that?

I remember learning how to dissect a frog that same year. But my biology teacher certainly never mentioned the fact that many traditional peoples who existed closer to nature than either she or I, believed that the frog lying there before my shaky blade was a good neighbor dressed up in a frog disguise. Twenty-five years after that event, and I remember nothing at all about body parts, and everything about the trauma that followed because I was not able to sublimate[2] my own gut feelings of connectedness to that being.

Who knows what is right, especially when what we think is right so often appears outside the context of the ecosystem? That implies, of course, that the health of the ecosystem is probably the best standard against which we measure our health as a society. And although such a conclusion is certainly a major tenet of most environmental writing and action, look around you—it is almost nowhere in force. Instead, there are many who would have us believe, certainly by their deeds if not by their words, that a healthy environment is a quite secondary matter to the consumption-oriented process of their own lives. The more utilitarian minded often respond, also by their deeds if not by their words, that such a primary allegiance to natural processes is both naive and unrealistic because it imposes too many restrictions upon social, cultural, and industrial progress. The words of novelist and critic Brigid Brophy spring to mind:

> Whenever people say "we mustn't be sentimental" you can take it they are about to do something cruel. And if

they add, "we must be realistic," they mean they are going to make money out of it.[3]

The feeling hits me hardest when I drive up Vancouver Island. The 150-mile stretch of highway from Victoria to Campbell River winds through some of the most beautiful vistas to be seen anywhere in North America. The road rolls and flows northward, with exquisite views of snow-peaked mountains far off to the west as well as across the Strait of Georgia to the east.

Campbell River, situated just about midway up the island, signals the change that is about to occur. A pleasant enough town, definitely growing, it has made something of a name for itself as a salmon fisherman's mecca. But unfortunately for those real estate developers who dream about upwardly mobile vacation revenues, Campbell River possesses one terrible antitourist flaw. Anyone walking on the streets must also learn to contend with an acrid, septic tank odor that permeates every inch of the town. It issues from the giant stacks of a mammoth pulp mill. This mill is Campbell River's preeminent employer. It is also a precursor of all that is to come as one continues driving.

The highway north should be one of the most incredible sightseeing paths in North America. Not more than ten years old, it cuts through a steep and craggy mountain range where one would expect the trees to grow large, the water to run pristine, and the vistas to sweep off to the horizon in wild splendor. Unfortunately, this is no longer the case. About twenty miles north of Campbell River begins the most egregious disregard for nature that I have witnessed anywhere in North America. For the next 130 miles the road follows what seems to be a nearly contiguous series of giant clear-cuts. On and on they go, out to the horizon—forests that once covered entire mountain ranges sheared off at the roots, yanked from the earth, bulldozed down the slopes, and finally left eroding and devastated.

During the 1980s, the MacMillan-Bloedel lumber company started a multiyear project to log the expansive Tsitika River basin—what used to be the last virgin watershed forest on the entire east coast of Vancouver Island. Home to moose, mountain lion, bear, steelhead salmon. No matter. No matter that the

Tsitika delta is the central gathering spot of the largest pod of orcas on the west coast of North America. The lumber company likes to think (and promote) that they made a concession to the whales—200 meters up from the shore would be left uncut and designated whale refuge. But to be precise, this political concession was not actually made to the whales, but rather to the whale-watching businesses, who begged that the Tsitika must retain at least a veneer of its lost grandeur if anyone hoped to make a living in the tourist trade. Thus, in the spirit of British Columbia's high-profile and highly fallacious ad campaign of SUPERNATURAL BC, a small rim of trees, a kind of stage-set facade of what a real watershed looks like, was left standing to mask the devastation beyond. Everything else, an entire river basin, was dragged from the earth with heavy machinery.

Those in power argue that it should make no difference whatsoever to whom the concession was made, as long as it was actually done. However, there remains that crucial distinction between the secondhand contentment found in a theatrical facade and the firsthand connection that could be found in a protected and respected watershed. As it is, no such sense of firsthand connectedness exists between British Columbia's government and its ecosystem. This is best demonstrated by realizing that when there is no human industry demanding to be factored into the equation, no protection of the biota is ever forthcoming. I reach this harsh conclusion because wilderness has no value in the eyes of a government, any government, so long as the laws and priorities of that government are focused only upon the human use of territory. Almost all measures of conservation spring from that same human center.

I drive up the island feeling quite bewildered by the motivations of the people responsible for this extermination of forest. Someone else who is a human being with identically sensitive eyes, ears, brain; someone else who possesses a western education mostly indistinguishable from my own—one day that person peered over a map of northern Vancouver Island, drew some boundary lines, and then mobilized his employees to go out and devastate the mountains. Hundreds of square miles of *first-growth forest* destroyed, because, according to the logging companies themselves, reforested trees simply do not grow fast enough to sustain the demons of our culture.

I am evidently not alone in feeling that the destruction seems too much like the act of a crazed person. As environmentalist Gar Smith has written in terms of the quite similar devastation wreaked by the Exxon Valdez oil spill in Prince William Sound, Alaska:

> As the damages mount with each new outrage, oil company officials are beginning to sound like problem drinkers who continue making promises they can't keep. How many more times are we going to allow these companies to throw up on our living room rug before we draw the line? Oil-hauling, like alcoholism, is a form of addictive behavior that is inevitably destructive. When [will we be] ready to renounce the pleasures of petroleum?[4]

Actually, these hypothetical men (once again, why am I so sure they aren't women?) possess both a clear voice and a clear conscience about their own handiwork. Forestry managers talk about providing jobs, balancing world trade, the growing need for paper products, selective cutting, and even a rigorous tree-planting program to provide for the seventh generation. And look, over there by the side of the highway: Every few miles a neatly printed sign announces when this particular stretch of forest was harvested, when it was replanted, and when it was selectively thinned of those trees neglected on the first pass "for maximum yield." By mile thirty, one starts to play a game with the signs. You enter an area where the trees are eight feet high and venture a guess that the section was replanted in 1973. Or the trees are forty feet tall, so you guess correctly that this stretch was replanted in 1949. The signs provide all the answers.

The signs were conceived, no doubt, as a public relations gesture to inculcate the motorist with a sense of the wisdom utilized in clear-cutting this or that watershed. They try to assure us: don't worry about the destruction, we have it all under control. Unfortunately, by mile sixty a very different message begins to wash down the heavily eroded slopes. For one thing, there has been no meaningful respite from the woodsman's saw for over thirty miles now—off to either side of the road all the way out to the horizon. More telling still, and despite the fact that some of these dates reach back fifty years, there has not yet been a single sign announcing that a complete cycle of cut, replant, and second cut has transpired. In other words, every single tree cut from this part of Vancouver Island was old growth. This realization implies that the guiding principle of sustained growth has to be a ruse because, obviously, the *growth* of the trees, themselves, cannot keep up with the *demand* for wood products. Thus we have reached a point in our coevolution with furs, cedar, hemlock, and spruce where 90 percent of true old-growth forests have been cut out of the heart of what is sometimes referred to as the greatest unbroken temperate forest on the face of the earth. The rest of the old growth is being cut as I write.

Nor has any sign yet announced: "This area was intentionally left uncut as a representative sample of the old-growth forest." No significant area has been left intact as a kind of *city of refuge* for all the forest creatures who must, instead, disappear forever from this part of "Supernatural" British Columbia. Rather, I have just passed a sign conveying the shocking sentiment that this unrepresentative old-growth area I am now driving through is actually designated an *overmature* forest. But don't worry, declares the sign, we have it under control. It has been assigned its proper place in the queue and will be clear-cut within the next year.

Every tree will be cut down. Then the area will be sprayed with a death-rain of noxious herbicides to assure that even the ground upon which the forest once stood will be void of any sign of uncontrolled life. So, all the noncommercial bushes, as well as the slower growing cedars, are kept from sprouting. Even the smallest ground squirrel is either poisoned outright or left no place to hide if it does manage to survive.

I finally take a right-hand turn off the main road and head down toward the water. This 100-mile-long advertisement promoting the current state of forestry management compels me to make one more pronouncement: Logging of old-growth forest destroys not only trees but the entire web of life dependent on it. The temperate rain forests of the Pacific Northwest are being destroyed with little sign of letup. At the end of the product-consumption chain you and I may be using those trees, but we remain the victims of deplorably shortsighted forestry practices. Our own economic stewards of the forest have failed us miserably.

This is an important point, because it emphatically tempers the logger's confusing message that he is working for us. Just as we also believe in freedom and democracy, so an American (and Canadian) citizenry may rightly deplore and even unseat its government's aggression in Viet Nam or Nicaragua. Or just as we all eat apples, so we may also overturn apple growing policies that destroy both the land as well as our own health. Which leads to still another prophecy: Every single day, more and more people are going to recognize that their own personal commitment to consumer activism is the most powerful statement they can make to alter the current destructive relationship that exists between culture and nature.

This signifies that the changes needed will never be complete until we recognize that the logging equation includes Americans, Canadians, and Japanese consuming all that Vancouver Island wood in our own homes, businesses, and schools. My own house is framed in Douglas fir, sheathed in plywood, paneled in knotty pine, and floored with oak. How can I deny it? Many obviously do. Gar Smith reflects on this denial in his analogy between alcoholism and oil spills:

> When this sort of denial is encountered in the families of an alcoholic, doctors refer to the phenomenon as "co-dependency." If the Exxon obscenity—and the innumerable environmental insults that proceeded it—are to mean anything, we must begin to question our complicity in the disease.[5]

For example, *Time* magazine dispassionately informs its own readership that its issue devoted to the Earth as "Man of the Year for 1988," used upward of 16,000 trees just to get into print. Or they say that the Sunday issue of *The New York Times* utilizes seventy acres of trees. A year of Sunday *Times* utilizes 3,640 acres. Two thousand years of the Sunday *Times* would use 11,375 square miles, just under the 12,000 square miles of the immense whole of Vancouver Island. Mind you, this is one weekly issue of one newspaper. In that light, does it seem overly aggressive to ask why more of us do not stop reading the Sunday *New York Times, Time* magazine, or any of the many other publications whose major function is to alleviate a moment's boredom while filling our heads with secondhand information? The time spent reading magazines could be better spent taking a walk outdoors.

And on that very note, began my own personal commitment to the forests of the seventh generation. I decided to make a difference by switching all my business and literary needs to recycled paper. I soon discovered that paper generated from the remains of yesterday's papers costs less to produce than the energy-intensive paper extracted from forest flesh. But it costs *more* to buy recycled paper because, ostensibly, there is less of a demand for it. Finally, one supplier admitted to me that the high price is also the result of the paper companies, themselves, insuring a low demand.

How do we increase the supply? Perhaps by asking a major publisher to publish its books on recycled paper. Good idea. And if you find a logo on the back cover stating that this book has been published on recycled paper, you know that I succeeded in convincing my own publisher to that effect. Here is my own immediate commitment to the seventh generation. If you do not find that note, realize that one story has been left untold.

To generalize: A revolution is starting to simmer all around us. It is the connection between the self-destructive alcoholic and his codependents moved onto the field of the environment. It is the same old story told by power companies spending more money on oil exploration in the Arctic than on cheap, decentralized solar energy alternatives. The same old story told by any industry or bureaucracy that possesses too much outdated momentum. All of them remain part of the problem as long as they cling to their destructive practices, no matter how much the cost to the environment. In my own case, I learned that the paper manufacturers have little interest in promoting or developing recycled products until such time as they have exhausted the known reservoir of forests to be clear-cut. The seventh generation is not yet capable of making itself heard over the din of the chainsaws. Likewise, any significant act such as paying the extra cost for recycled paper is going to still the saws, save the trees, and permit those songs to be heard again.

The environmental crisis begins and ends inside each of us. We alter the equation when we alter our own relationship to the planet. We get connected when we act connected.

So I offer a few humble advertisements for the seventh generation. For example, our political leaders still promote nuclear reactors that, at best, provide power for thirty years, and poisonous waste for 250,000. Meanwhile, groups like the Rocky Mountain Institute offer convincing evidence that we co-dependents would eliminate the presumed need for more nuclear power plants by simply curtailing our own personal, and exorbitant, consumption of electricity. They prescribe that we immediately switch over to more efficient light bulbs, which are already available, although, once again, not promoted.

Or save the dolphins: stop eating tuna fish. Either that, or accept the political sentiments expressed by such as Ronald Reagan, who vetoed the Law of the Sea Pact because, as he once told his cabinet, "I kind of thought that when you go out on the high seas you can do what you want."[6] Or another: We stop future oil exploration in borderline areas like the Arctic National Wildlife Refuge by using public transportation and by making sure the next car we buy gets five miles per gallon more than the present one. We walk more often and nurture our own health. The Worldwatch Institute recommends that all countries of the world institute a 50 mpg efficiency standard for new automobiles, to be reached by the year 2000.[7]

Or still another: vegetarian advocate John Robbins argues that the simple act of not eating fast-food hamburgers (often made from beef raised in Central America) might save more rain forest than if we donated the cost of the hamburgers to any organization you can name. As already noted, as much as 85 percent of all topsoil loss *in the U.S.* can be directly attributed to livestock raising.[8] Rid all red meat from your diet and you help save everything nourished by topsoil including, well, just about everything that lives. Ironically, as the effects of this commitment to diet spin outward, you also combat a veritable host of inward maladies including colon cancer and heart disease, both directly attributed to a heavy meat diet.

This book offers many such advertisements about personalizing the relationship to our world. I have arrived at this underlying theme by the only manner possible: getting both very personal and very subjective, and finally offering up my own firsthand perceptions to prove the point. It is all very unscientific, which is one reason I exhausted so many early words to undermine the outdated belief about objectivity as truth telling—it is not. If you end up agreeing with my basic assertion that the environmental crisis is a crisis in perception, and that the remedy lies in an ecology of the spirit, then you do so because you trust me with all my warts exposed. I am you. We are them. The strange verb *noster* pops up once again, this time as the intrinsic structure of this book.

Somehow I tend to doubt there are very many readers who believe that my own handle on my own perceptions is quite as typical or normal as I have depicted it to be. After all, anyone who spends extended periods each year immersed in musical communication with dolphins and whales has probably acquired an atypical slant on things. True. But although my perceptions may not be of the everyday, they remain classic Everyman (and Everywoman).

Consider the Cree Indian belief that stories are animate beings who ordinarily inhabit a kind of oral Limbo. They sit around and tell each other to each other, waiting on call, as it were, for that special circumstance in need of illumination. "My" story about the neighborly deer, for example, was not so much created by me as I coaxed it out of hibernation. And the gift must keep moving, meaning that the story has now grabbed hold of you as well. It will dwell inside of you for a bit, perhaps change its wardrobe of a word here, a phrase there, as it acclimates to its new surroundings, and then either drift back to story limbo, or be passed on in those new clothes when you tell it to somebody else. The Cree believe that a three-way symbiotic relationship unfolds between storyteller, story, and listener. Ultimately, if people nourish a story properly, it tells them useful things about life.[9]

As I tell my various stories about deer and yelloweye rockfish, so they start to live inside of you and, in a sense, become your story as well. Once again we are confronted with a worldview that insists upon blurring the edges between myth and reality, between subject and object, between you and me. The medium is the message and vice versa. Actually, this traditional view also reads suspiciously like a Cree version of postdoctoral physics. As quantum mechanics continues to push up against the bulwarks of human comprehension, it confronts the physicists, themselves, with a nasty incompatability between nonparticipatory objectivity, and the quite *participatory* maps presented by the mathematics involved. The best known example of this dichotomy is Heisenberg's uncertainty principle, which states that an observer may either measure the momentum or the position of a sub-atomic particle-wave, but not both. Put another way, the physicist dresses the particle as either a particle of matter or a wave of motion depending upon the way the physicist decides to tell its story.

One of the most recent and controversial ideas offered to neutralize this quantum schizophrenia is called the *anthropic principle*. It boils down to this reflective statement: Humanity's observation of the universe has actually molded what we perceive as the laws of physics.[10] In other words, we dreamed up the laws. The story about the universe (that which we call physics) gets the opportunity to dwell inside the physicists for a while, changes its furniture to match the wallpaper of human comprehension, and finally ends up telling us useful things about life. The universe, itself, is now understood as a symbiotic relationship between story, storyteller, and listener. The inside is outside and vice versa.

When we become fully aware of the stories that make up our lives, we also find ourselves being much more careful about the kind of information we want to let through the portal of our eyes and ears. However, if we do not take the trouble to animate the information ourselves, someone else is sure to do it for us. This makes room for another child of our own disconnectedness: the hard-sell, multibillion-dollar advertising industry, a tool capable of drilling through even the thickest human skull, and founded upon the anti-Cree premise that we have no inherent responsibility to or for our own story. This leads to a veritable cornucopia of inscrutable advertising koans. What does it mean, for example, when Quaker State motor oil assures us that the *Q* stands for quality? Or when a double-page magazine spread of Monument Valley in winter is accompanied by the words: Marlboro Country?

The seventh generation silently scrutinizes our growing inability to penetrate the armor of this disconnectedness and shudders. Yet, they seem quite incapable of doing much of anything in their own behalf. They remain seated along the temporal sidelines, holding their collective breath, and wait in anticipation of how our future is going to transmute into their present. They fall down on their unborn knees before us, pleading with us to undertake the monumental task of transforming not just one issue of one newspaper, but an entire culture. Who hears them? Who listens to their point of view?

The Australian aborigines certainly do. Richard Murphy describes the 40,000-year continuity of aboriginal culture, whose *very primitive* lifestyle has made almost no negative impact upon its shared environment in all that time. After spending an extended period working in the outback, Murphy returned once again to contemporary culture only to be faced with this uneasy conclusion:

> One of my lingering reentry questions has been: "Can we call a human system, whether it be a civilization or a culture, successful if it creates the potential to bring about its own demise and incurs in its decline greater hardship and misery than existed before its development?" History shows that civilizations are not enduring human systems.

From an evolutionary point of view, the fact that Aborigines still exist demonstrates that their culture and survival strategies have some redeeming qualities.[11]

Perhaps the aborigines have, indeed, found that magical mouthpiece for speaking directly to the seventh generation. The key element of their spirituality is known as the *dreamtime*, which has been described as a conscious perception of past, present, and future unfolding all at the same time, an *everywhen*.

Although we must incorporate the surrealistic spiritual wisdom of the aborigines into any general recipe for survival, we cannot hope to ask anyone to also give up their steel tools, their underwear, and their laser printers. Murray Bookchin, for one, chides what he considers to be an *ecolala* sentiment of finding solutions that demand a regression to the primitive lifestyle. It is a "holism [that] evaporates into a mystical sigh." Instead, he offers the practical advice:

Indeed, there is a level at which our consciousness must be neither poetry nor science, but a transcendence of both into a new realm of theory and practice, an artfulness that combines fancy with reason, imagination with logic, vision with technique. . . . Poetry and imagination must be integrated with science and technology, for we have evolved beyond an innocence that can be nourished exclusively by myths and dreams.[12]

Bookchin's statement also forces the same unforgiving question to bubble up to the surface again: What contemporary institutions connect with the seventh generation? Well, the environmental movement certainly does that, whether it be the establishment-oriented Sierra Club fomenting legal battles to preserve redwood trees, or Greenpeace generating media events about whale consciousness, or Earthfirst! driving spikes into old-growth trees—making them dangerous to push through a buzz saw, and in effect canceling the clear-cut of an ancient forest.

Our artists seem to have become as disaffected as the rest of us, yet they could be trying harder to reconnect than they are.

After all, the aboriginal idea that culture is one vast poetic construct suspended in space and time, and incorporating all aspects of life within it, may still be radical to the sciences and the social sciences, but not to the arts.[13]

We need a new aesthetic of natural interconnectedness that is able to swallow up every one of us. Yet any aesthetic that actually succeeds at connecting humans to nature is going to be resisted because its driving metaphor is *participation* by every faction, nation, and species. Thus, it must also be compelling, engaging, incredibly unifying, and gentle all at the same time—it must *noster*. I am you. They are us.

As noster biology may be defined as the *study* of interconnecting to nature, *nosterart* may be understood as the *art* of interconnecting to nature. It is an art that depicts a nature we exist inside of, and that is simultaneously inside of us. *Nosterart* functions as a promotional message, an advertisement as it were, for the seventh generation.

Nosterart is a close relative to environmental art, earth art, and the European biopoesis. Conceptual artist Christo's Running Fence, which wound its way across twenty-four miles of California pastureland, was Nosterart. It balanced natural landscape with cultural landscape, a fence that ran right through fences, preventing the eye from stopping at the usual property lines. And while the fence exposed the natural landscape under the cultural overlay, it also exposed the prejudices, foibles, humor, and humorlessness of the California social structure. Art confronted the mystique of private ownership, rational science, and governmental authority as they relate to a sense of place, and made the entire superstructure seem berzerk.[14] And when the event of the fence had run its course, the object of the fence was taken apart. All the post holes were filled in, while all the material of the fence was cut into squares, framed and finally sold as objets d'art. In this case, the profits paid for the event. Beside the photos, nothing else remained.

Unlike most contemporary art, nosterart can also be construed as an art devoid of artists or art-as-product as we usually conceive of it. Because of that, some art critics might justifiably note that it is really no art at all. For example, when the Rocky

Mountain Institute prompts a worldwide dance that culminates in people climbing up ladders to change the wattage of their light bulbs, that dance is nosterart. No matter that the choreographers of the light bulb dance, Amory and Hunter Lovins, never conceived of themselves as artists. Nosterart encourages participation by children, nonartists, in fact anyone wishing to noster the connection to nature so others may hear it. In such a manner nosterart also borrows from that same old primitive tradition of the artist as no-artist.

So-called primitive art was essentially any technique utilized by traditional peoples to both preserve and animate the unity that exists between humans and nature. For example, the 40,000-year-old Australian aborigines possess a nosterart known as *songlines:* a physical trail of chants that are sung only at specific locations and that serve to animate the natural features. Even today, these songlines are used as a kind of acoustic running fence or geographical music score, a map for the ears that explains both the relations as well as the responsibilities that exist between humans, animals, and landforms. Sing the correct song, and you may even locate water in a desert you have never visited before. Significantly, the aborigines do not have a concept of ownership like our own. Because land, spirit, and self are inseparable; the Earth can no more be sold than can one's soul. So the songlines serve as a kind of nonpossessive aesthetic relationship to place.

Continuing our metaphor of boundaries, contrast the songlines with this contemporary description of the U.S.-Canadian border:

> While climbing recently in the Pasayten wilderness in north-central Washington, Cascadia, we spotted something so out of place it stopped us in our tracks. Standing on a peak on the U.S.-Canadian border, we gazed at the strange sight of a narrow, cleared swath running straight up and down 8,000 foot peaks. . . . In order to mark legal jurisdiction over their respective territories, the U.S. and Canada not only clear-cut the longest unguarded border in the world, but poisoned the ground itself![15]

I start to free associate and am reminded of the old Yippy battlecry: "U.S.A. out of North America." Or listen once again to John Lennon asking us to imagine a world without countries. This is a bioregional worldview, where boundaries between peoples are defined by the natural dividing lines of watershed and landform. Although there are many who believe it to be a naive understatement to conclude that it is going to prove difficult to redefine our territories in nonnationalistic terms, there is also a growing minority of bioregionalists who actively promote this restructuring of property and territory. Nosterart is always going to push up against the edges of the possible. The crisis in perception demands such metaphors if we are ever going to perceive with new eyes and ears.

Or consider another example: a child's uncontrived version of nosterart. I conjure up a picture of my daughter Claire at two years of age. Continually surrounded by a roost of stuffed and plastic animals, this menagerie acquired, for her, the solid attributes of extended family. Her Dakin stuffed lion seemed to live inside her imagination with more attributes of totem lion-ness than any live lion that you or I, or any adult, might experience within a zoo environment. I would watch in awe as this two-year-old spent hours, days, and weeks coddling and discussing the state of the world with her lion. But what am I saying? This was no lion; it was a thing stuffed full of the worst kind of anthropomorphic fantasy. Fortunately for Claire, most such petty annoyances to the adult psyche never registered within the growing mind of a two-year-old. Actually, I sometimes wondered how Claire's relationship to her own lion was different than, say, the Neanderthal relationship to their own stuffed cave bears.

Once, during our annual late-summer interspecies communication sojourn with the orcas of western Canada, Claire brought along her entire menagerie of stuffed cetaceans, including three orcas. This in an environment where she got to interact with live orcas three or four times each day. One morning, as her mother sat in front of the campfire suckling Claire's newborn sister, Sasha, Claire pulled up her own jersey to place the smallest of the fluffy orcas up against her own nipple in a gesture to emulate mama. The symbolic implications of this human mother/ child who interacted with nature-as-family through the pretend issue of a polyester toy/baby/orca had all of the philosophers among us reaching for our notebooks.

I reached for mine, started to describe the incident, and then found myself strangely incapable of fusing the connections afforded by varied elements into any sort of meaningful statement. Yet somehow, that image also transformed my own connection to the real whales—although I cannot actually say how this was achieved. Nosterart, like any other art, achieves its purpose not by reason, but by feeling and connecting. Once again we are faced with Bookchin's declaration of a new realm of theory and practice, an artfulness that combines fancy with reason, imagination with logic, vision with technique. Such metaphors construct literary space heaters that insinuate themselves directly into myriad hearts and minds.

Examples, and even counterexamples, abound. Consider Buckminster Fuller's "Spaceship Earth." Here was a conscious attempt to create a metaphor[16] of Earth as vehicle or toy or perhaps both. Fuller, a clever builder of devices if there ever was one, coined the image in an attempt to bring the invocation of a vehicular earth with limited seating directly into the consciousness of the culture. But the term never meant much as nosterart. A spaceship is a machine that needs a pilot, probably a pilot with opposable thumbs as well. By contrast, the image of Gaea, Earth as mother and goddess, alive and nurturing, resilient, generative, and self-sufficient, has been well established for millennia.

Or yet another example. There is hardly an animal or plant on Earth that has not had contact with human technology, or has not been indirectly exposed to the impact of technology on the environment. A gut feeling suggests that the all-pervasive extent of this exposure is an insult to the integrity of natural systems. Thus people who live in, and even appreciate the thrills of, a metropolitan lifestyle, may find themselves in a particular dilemma when it comes to relating to nature. Some may secretly feel that they have to deny the urban situation they live in. But this is impossible because that is where they support their material existence. By contrast, some others may feel they have to deny being in touch with nature. But this is also impossible, because in many cases that is what supports their souls. A point of incompatability emerges. As always, it seems important to acknowledge the unavoidable confusion.

Whatever the name of the boundary we come up against, its perception might just as easily stimulate transcendence. The European artist Mickey Remann has pointed out that urban people who want to renew relations with nonhuman animate neighbors are challenged to devise a viable means to send out contemporary feelers to touch them, and new antennae to listen to them.[17]

For three years in a row, Mickey was granted the opportunity to interact musically with free, wild orca whales every night for hours on end from a boat moored in a small bay along the wilderness coast of British Columbia. He writes of feeling three things:

1. This is fantastic.
2. I want to tell everybody.
3. Nobody will believe me.

What to do? Trying to import anybody's hometown out into the wilderness seemed less than appropriate, so I decided to try it the other way around, to bring into the city the real taste of free music and free whales.[18]

Our culture usually manifests this very strong desire to bring the natural sensibility into an urban context by imposing the ultimate disconnectedness between animal and audience. For example, we construct concrete pools and then plop dolphins down into them. These animals are then taught to perform ingenious tricks in payment for the basic essentials of food and companionship.

Remann turned this concept right on its head. Thus was born the Underwater Concert, a phenomenon originated in a large swimming pool complex in Frankfurt, Germany, and since staged in half a dozen other sites all over Europe by several other promoters. In the Frankfurt performance, underwater speakers were placed at both ends of the pool. Then musicians from every possible background were invited to improvise along with orca songs recorded in the wild at the Tsitika River delta in British Columbia. The human musicians were soon playing together in, under, and above the water. Likewise, sculptures were hung in, under, and above the water. And instead of importing whales from off Vancouver Island, this time it was the human audience who plopped themselves right into the concrete pool. The audience swam. And far beyond Remann's wildest expectations, the first underwater concert sold out two shows and attracted television coverage from all over Europe as well as from Japan. As Remann has since commented:

> Between the lines there was a yearning to bridge a gap upon culture and psyche, a hidden promise that was touched upon by the connotations of an underwater concert. Because the yearning had been neglected for so long, it couldn't even be sure of itself; but now that it was brought out into the open, it became a magnet for mystery and excitement, projected fantasy and skeptical disapproval . . . oceanic dreamtime and "don't miss the special event" hype.[19]

It seems important to add that none of the extensive media reviews forgot to tell how it all started: that in the beginning there was the whale and the wilderness, and an attempt to create a shared space with members of a musical race of beings so vastly different than our own. As one young man commented after the concert, "I was already familiar with whale songs played over record and tape. But to experience them underwater was like listening to them for the first time."

And in a world that nosters, it is important to remember that not only human beings perform nosterart.

Just as this book started out by promising to teach you how to listen to the seventh generation, so it concludes with one final nosterart tip about learning how to listen. Most species of songbirds spend their winters in the rain forests of the planet. In fact, the drastic decline in population of these emissaries is the single critical indicator of rain forest destruction that directly touches those of us who live in North America and Europe. Furthermore, these orioles and tanagers (among other species) are going to continue to decline until the rain forests are replenished to their former grandeur. Their increasing silence makes a statement and then asks a question: "There are fewer of us now. Who will permit us to return?"

Do you ever hear the songbirds where you live? If not, make the effort to get to a place where you can hear them. Their buoyant song takes you right into the heart of the burned-over rain forest in a way that slide shows, films, or books never can. Listen closely to the song. You may even start to hear the gasp and lunge of a human culture bumbling its way toward the panacea of its own future. Bring the song into yourself. Now you may start to hear some very faint voices whispering inside the overtones. These are the songs of attunement as sung by the dying Amazonian Indians who learned some of their own songs directly from the birds, and knew in their hearts and traditions that they were one and the same with the rain forest. For example, the Jivaro used to sing that when you harm the web of the Earth you set in motion a kind of masochistic masturbation. Destroy nature and you commit suicide.

You don't hear it? It makes me wonder if you are *thinking about* it, rather than *listening* to it. You say you do hear it? If so, then don't bother describing it to anyone else. Traditional people were the very first to warn that words never really do suffice.

Instead, take the songs inside yourself and try to *sing* them to somebody else. Don't worry too much about melodic accuracy. Improvise, change the notes at will. But work hard to retain the mood. And don't forget to include both the statement as well as the question articulated within the increasing silence: "There are fewer of us now. Who will permit us to return?"

If enough of us attune to these rain forest melodies, sing them from enough rooftops, share them with enough other people, perhaps we can sing the songbirds back to their former status. Perhaps that same song can motivate us to free the laboratory rats, save the turtles, hoot the orcas back to their prehistoric proportions. Attune to it, day by day, year by year. The connected spirit of nature starts to enter your body through a kind of *tuning osmosis*. We get connected when we act connected. Good medicine. Thank you.

Notes

Prelude

1. Compiled by TC McLuhan, from *Touch the Earth*, Touchstone Books, 1971; p. 6.
2. Andrew Bard Schmookler, *Out of Weakness*, Bantam Books, 1988; p. 172.
3. From *Seeing Castaneda*, edited by Daniel Noel, G.P. Putnam's Sons, 1976; quoted from Morris Berman, *The Reenchantment of the World*, Bantam, 1984; p. 84.
4. Chief Seattle, on the occasion of surrendering his land; upon which the city of Seattle now stands. From *Touch the Earth*, op. cit., p. 30.
5. TC McLuhan, op. cit.

Chapter One

1. From the Great Law of the Haudenosaunee, the six-nation Iroquois confederacy.
2. Roderick Frazier Nash, *The Rights of Nature*, Univ. Wisconsin Press, 1989; p. 147.
3. Erich Fromm, *The Heart of Man*, Harper and Row, 1980; p. 41.
4. Mathew Fox, "My Final Statement Before Being Silenced by the Vatican," *Earth Island Journal*, Winter 1988–89; p. 50.
5. Religious, in this case means longevity.
6. From the cover letter to a grant request, sent to this author "The Guardian Site Proposal—A corporation for permanent above-ground storage of nuclear waste," Joanna Macy, December 1988.

Chapter Two

1. Bryan Jay Bashin, "Bug Bomb Fallout," *Harrowsmith* magazine, May/June 1989.
2. *The Reader's Digest Almanac,* 1985; p. 183. The Mac-Kenzie is listed as 2,635 miles long, the Mississippi 2,348, the Missouri 2,315, and the Mississippi/Missouri/Red Rock 3,710.
3. Associated Press, as reported to the Cetacean Society International Newsletter, Wethersfield CT, February 25, 1985.
4. The Franklin expedition searched for the Northwest Passage in the two ships *Terror* and *Erebus.* During the winter of 1846–47, the ships got stuck in the ice of Victoria Strait (1500 miles due east of our own location) and all hands were lost. For an account of this and other Arctic explorations, read: Barry Lopez, *Arctic Dreams,* Bantam, 1987; p. 361.
5. Ibid., p. 200.
6. J.G. Frazer, *The Golden Bough,* Macmillan, London, 1963; p. 291.
7. W.J. Hunt, *Domestic Whaling in the MacKenzie Estuary, Northwest Territories,* Can. Fish. Mar. Serv. Tech. Report 769, 1979.
8. Mark A. Fraker, *Status and Harvest of the MacKenzie Stock of White Whales (Delphinapterus leucas),* Rep. Int. Whal. Comm. 30, 1980.
9. Hugh Brody, *Living Arctic,* Douglas and McIntyre, Vancouver, 1987.
10. Frederick Turner, *Beyond Geography,* Rutgers Univ. Press, 1986.
11. Hugh Brody, op. cit.
12. Aldous Huxley, *The Art of Seeing,* Montana Books, Seattle, 1975.
13. David Guss, *The Language of the Birds,* North Point Press, Berkeley, 1985; p. ix.

Chapter Three

1. Gregory Bateson, *Steps to an Ecology of the Mind,* Ballantine, 1975.
2. Stephen Nachmanovitch, "Old Men Ought to be Explorers," *CoEvolution Quarterly,* published by Point Foundation, Fall, 1982.
3. Jorge Luis Borges, *Labyrinths,* New Directions, 1962; p. 56.
4. Semantics are important, so I shall always employ the many variations on the term "human," instead of the more common "man" or "mankind." The use of a masculine term to denote our entire species seems inappropriate in a world crying out for the feminine perspective. Likewise, the use of a term of gender to denote what is actually a term of species seems one more example, albeit subtle, of our need to gloss over the crucial fact that we are one animal species among many. Last, I admit to a personal shudder and groan whenever I hear the self-aggrandizing and very official term *homo sapiens* (meaning, "wise man"), employed to describe the 5 billion members of my own bipedal species. I must opt, instead, for a Taoist perspective: "Exterminate the sage, *discard the wise man,* and the people will benefit a hundredfold."
5. Buckminster Fuller's *I Seem To Be A Verb* offers one discussion about this concept.
6. Lawrence LeShan and Henry Margenau, *Einstein's Space and Van Gogh's Sky,* Collier, 1982; p. 174.
7. Ibid.
8. Paul Shepard, *Animal's Voice,* April 1988.
9. Which, not coincidentally, Webster's defines as the life principle.
10. Marie Louise Von Franz, *Interpretation of Fairytales,* Spring Publications, Dallas, 1987. Because fairy tales are a manifestation of our subconscious, and because the subconscious is such a crucial part of our whole being, that entire skewed description of so-called reality that is sometimes manifested in the form of fairy tales, sometimes as myth,

sometimes as dreams, must be considered when describing reality as it exists for the whole human mind.

11. Gary Comstock, writing in *Between the Species Journal* (Schweitzer Center, Summer 1988), defines it this way: A reductio is a philosophical attempt to prove an opponent wrong by showing that his/her position leads to an absurdity. Suppose someone wanted to argue that animals have rights, and that it is our obligation to prevent animal suffering. To perform a reductio, you would, for example, argue that this view requires us to lock up wolves that maul sheep, to punish cats that eat mice. . . . The problem is that reductios are often aimed at nothing more than straw men. Criticism is directed at a reduced, easier-to-attack version of your opponent's position. In this case you score against a position that no one really holds.

Chapter Four

1. Hölldobler and Wilson, "The Multiple Recruitment System of the African Weaver Ant," *Behav. Ecol. Sociobiol.* 3:19–60 (1978), quoted in Donald R. Griffin, *Animal Thinking,* Harvard Univ. Press, 1984; p. 171.

2. Griffin, *Animal Thinking,* p. 172.

3. K. von Frisch, *The Dance Language and Orientation of Bees,* Harvard Univ. Press, 1967. Of course, the speculated disciplines in parentheses are entirely my own.

4. Griffin, op. cit., p. 177.

5. Jim Nollman, *Animal Dreaming,* Bantam, 1987; p. 164.

6. Lawrence LeShan and Henry Margenau, *Einstein's Space and Van Gogh's Sky,* Collier, 1982; p. 5.

7. From a speech delivered at the Summit for Animals Conference, March 12, 1989.

8. Steven Nachmanovitch, "Old Men Ought to Be Explorers," *CoEvolution Quarterly,* Fall, 1982; p. 34.

9. J.G. Frazer, *The Golden Bough,* Macmillan, London, 1963; p. 289.

10. David Bohm and F. David Peat, *Science, Order, and Creativity,* Bantam, 1987; p. 11. These two well-known physicists describe the inaccuracies inherent in a science that tries to freeze its methodology. Science should, instead, promote a generous, playful spirit in answering questions.

Chapter Five

1. A. Rus Hoelzel, *The Journal of the San Juan Islands,* July 16, 1986.
2. Richard Osborn, research director, the Whale Museum, Friday Harbor, Washington; personal communication to the author.
3. C.M. Scammon, *The Marine Mammals of Northwestern Coast of North America,* Putnam's, New York, 1874. The attacks were usually by females protecting their young who had been harpooned.
4. Paul Spong, director, Orcalab; personal communication to the author.
5. The International Whaling Commission, in an attempt to clearly delineate what is proving to be a major rift in the way that whales should or should not be studied, sponsored an entire conference on the subject, entitled WhaleAlive, in Boston, in 1983.
6. Paul Spong, personal communication to the author.
7. R.D. Laing, *Knots,* Pantheon, 1970.
8. Quoted in the *Newsletter of the Pacifica Foundation,* Spring 1989.
9. *Disorder* offers still another example of a word that describes a natural process that is almost always perceived in its negative connotation. Disorder is somehow bad, and perceived as part of the problem. Taming disorder has long been one function of science.

Chapter Six

1. Meaning that although there is a legal statute upon the books, no one seriously attempts to enforce it.

2. That guilty verdict also implies, of course, that the dolphins themselves were accessories to the crime since it was they who stole themselves away from their "owners" by swimming to safety. For more about Iki Island, read Jim Nollman, *Animal Dreaming,* Bantam, 1987.

3. One of the very few books of economic theory that includes a responsibility for natural systems as its basic premise, Hazel Henderson's *Creating Alternative Futures* (Berkley, New York, 1978), is aptly subtitled "The End of Economics."

4. Theodore Roszak, quoted in Roderick Frazier Nash, *The Rights of Nature,* Univ. Wisconsin Press, 1989; p. 13.

5. Any of the works of Murray Bookchin or Jeremy Rifkin elaborate this basic assumption. For that matter, even *Silent Spring* by Rachel Carson implies much the same thing.

6. The word "incidental," as it applies to the relationship between nature and business, may say it all. For one example, American tuna fishermen describe the millions of dolphins killed while fishing for tuna, as "an incidental take" of dolphins.

7. It seems significant to add that to find a strong example of this paradox, I simply picked up the first newspaper I could find: reported from *Seattle Sunday Times,* March 5, 1989, "Chemical Dilemma," by Mike Merritt.

8. Ibid.

9. Noel Perrin, in *Harrowsmith,* March/April 1989; p. 12.

10. The Colville people, like most native Americans, did not discriminate between human persons and animal persons. Were we also able to worm that singular semantic neighborliness into our language, one can only wonder how our overall sense of place within nature would alter.

11. Ella B. Clark, *Indian Legends of the Pacific Northwest,* Univ. of Cal. Press, 1953; p. 91.

12. Gary Snyder, *Turtle Island,* in Roderick Frazier Nash, op. cit.

13. Owen Byrd, op. cit., "Green Capitalism," *Earth Island Journal*, Earth Island Institute, SF, Fall 1988; p. 47.

14. An interpretation, by biologist Lyall Watson, of a behavior attributed to Japanese Macacque monkeys. As Watson describes it, after one inventive monkey discovered the good idea of washing sweet potatoes before eating them, the other monkeys living on the same island soon began to follow her example. When a "critical mass" of potato-washing monkeys on the one island was reached, monkeys on other nearby islands also started washing their potatoes although there had been no direct contact between islands. By inference, Ken Keyes has suggested that the hundredth monkey syndrome serves as a viable model for eliciting change across human cultures. Watson's interpretation of the monkey's behavior has since been discredited. More recently, the work of botanist Rupert Sheldrake suggests that any idea or behavior can, indeed, pick up momentum and so resonate its way through species and cultures via a vehicle he calls the morphogenetic field.

Chapter Seven

1. Lao Tzu, *The Tao Te Ching,* trans. by D.C. Lau, Penguin, U.K. 1963.

2. Nor do I intend to call this locale "the outdoors," which always seems to measure wilderness in terms of its relationship to one's living room.

3. Which is actually a more southerly species.

4. James David Duncan, *The Rivery Why,* Bantam, 1984; p. 282.

5. Emil Bächler, "Das Alpine Paläolithikum der Shweitz im Wildkirschli, Drachenloch und Wildenmannlisloch," quoted in Joseph Campbell, *The Way of the Animal Powers,* Harper and Row, 1983; pp. 54–57.

6. One of them is even called *Wildkirchli,* the wilderness church.

Chapter Eight

1. *Tao Te Ching*, trans. by John C. Wu, St. John's Univ. Press, 1961; p. 71.
2. The *Seattle Times*, October 20, 1988; editorial about the gray whale rescue.
3. Barbara Tuchman, *The March of Folly*, Knopf, 1984; p. 26.
4. David Guss, *The Language of the Birds*, North Point Press, Berkeley CA, 1985; p. xi.
5. Ibid. p. xiii.
6. A lead is a natural open channel in the sea ice; formed by a combination of ocean upwellings, currents, and tides, all of which serve to keep the water circulating at a temperature above the freezing point of salt water.
7. Joseph Campbell, *The Way of the Animal Powers*, Harper and Row, 1983; p.9.
8. The *Hartford Courant*, October 29, 1988.
9. James Kilpatrick, Universal Press Syndicate, 1988.
10. The *Seattle Times*, op. cit.; editorial.

Chapter Nine

1. Laura C. Martin, *Garden Flower Folklore*, Globe Pequot Press, 1987.
2. Jim Nollman, *Dolphin Dreamtime* (previously titled, *Animal Dreaming*), Bantam, 1987.
3. Binda Colebrook, *Winter Gardening*, Maritime, Everson WA, 1984; p. 96.
4. Wendell Berry, "The Reactor and the Garden," *The Cultivator*, Little Letterpress, Brooks ME, vol. 14, no. 3.
5. Jerry Klieger, "In Celebration of Worms," *The Whole Earth Catalog*, Point Foundation, Sausalito, CA, 1970.
6. Tom Parker, *In One Day*, Houghton Mifflin, Boston, 1984.
7. Rocky Mountain Institute *Newsletter*, Snowmass CO, February 1989; p. 8.

8. John Robbins, *Diet for a New America*, Earthsave Foundation, Felton CA.

9. Ibid.

10. Wendell Berry, op. cit.

11. Ibid.

12. Andrew Bard Schmookler, *Out of Weakness*, Bantam, 1988; p.137.

13. Joan Halifax, *Shaman the Wounded Healer*, Crossroads Publishing, 1982; p. 82.

Chapter Ten

1. Eugene Marais, *The Soul of the White Ant*, Penguin, UK, 1973; p. 122.

2. Ibid.

3. Jim Nollman, *Dolphin Dreamtime*, Bantam, 1987.

4. Douglas Hofstadter, *Gödel, Escher, and Bach*, Vintage Books, Random House, 1980; p. 332.

5. Lewis Carroll, *Through the Looking Glass*, Random House, 1946; p. 63.

6. Maria Von Franz, *The Interpretation of Fairy Tales*, Spring Publications, Dallas, 1970; p. 70.

7. The concept about humans being "more highly evolved" because of large brains or prehensile thumbs is a purely human, anthropocentric invention. Who is to say that paramecia, or even genes, are not more evolved by virtue of their ability to survive while larger creatures become extinct.

8. This is my own elaboration of a Hindu myth as retold by Joseph Campbell, *The Power of Myth*, Doubleday, 1988.

Chapter Eleven

1. John Berger, *About Looking*, Pantheon, 1980.

2. The sublimation that gets you a passing grade.

3. Brigid Brophy, quoted in John Robbins, *Diet for a New America*, Earthsave Foundation, Felton CA; p. 73.

4. Gar Smith, *Earth Island Journal,* Spring 1989, inside cover.

5. Ibid.

6. Quoted in Anne W. Simon, *Neptune's Revenge,* Bantam, 1985; p. 104.

7. Speech by Lester Brown on National Public Radio.

8. John Robbins, op. cit.

9. Howard Norman, *The Wishing Bone Cycle,* Ross-Erikson, Santa Barbara, 1982, cited in David Guss.

10. Michael Talbot, *Beyond the Quantum,* Bantam, 1988; p. 184.

11. Richard C. Murphy, *The Calypso Log,* A journal of the Cousteau Society, vol. 16, no. 1, February 1989; p. 10.

12. Murray Bookchin, *CoEvolution Quarterly,* Bioregions Issue, Winter 1981; p.16.

13. David Guss, *The Language of the Birds,* North Point Press, Berkeley CA, 1985; p. xiii.

14. Peter Warshall, "Christo's Running Fence," *CoEvolution Quarterly,* Winter 1976/77; p. 71.

15. David McCloskey, "On Bioregional Boundaries," *The Planet Drum Review,* Winter 1988–89; p. 5.

16. R. Buckminster Fuller, *Operating Manual for Spaceship Earth,* Simon & Schuster, 1970. I am quite aware that spaceship earth is not properly a metaphor, but is, instead, a simile. And although it may cause certain English teachers to grade me with a C-, I prefer to consider the simile as a form of metaphor.

17. Mickey Remann, *The Interspecies Newsletter,* Winter 1986–87.

18. Ibid.

19. Ibid.

The author is president of Interspecies Communication Inc., an organization dedicated to promoting new relationships between humans and nature. Information about this ongoing work may be gotten by subscribing to the IC Newsletter. For more information, write Interspecies Communication, 273 Hidden Meadow, Friday Harbor, WA 98250, asking for a sample newsletter.

About the Author

As a pioneer in the field of interspecies communications, Jim Nollman is well-known in scientific and artistic communities. He is the founder of Interspecies Communication Inc., the first organization dedicated to promoting dialogue between humans and wild animals, and author of DOLPHIN DREAMTIME. DOLPHIN DREAMTIME has been excerpted in *Omni* magazine, and Jim Nollman has also published in *Orion, New Age, Guitar Player,* and *CoEvolution Quarterly,* among others. He has been awarded grants by Greenpeace, World Wildlife Fund, *Sunflower Foundation,* Threshold Foundation, International Whaling Commission, and the Human/Dolphin Foundation. He is still involved in communicating with several species including Beluga whales and ants. He lives in Washington state with his wife and two daughters.

Index

223